D0472017

OVER 1000 FANTASTIC FACTS

First published in 2010 by Miles Kelly Publishing Ltd
Harding's Barn, Bardfield End Green, Thaxted, Essex, CM6 3PX, UK

Copyright © Miles Kelly Publishing Ltd 2010

This edition printed in 2015

4 6 8 10 9 7 5 3

Publishing Director Belinda Gallagher
Creative Director Jo Cowan
Cover Designer Simon Lee
Project Manager Amanda Askew
Production Elizabeth Collins, Caroline Kelly
Indexer Jane Parker
Reprographics Anthony Cambray, Jennifer Cozens, Ian Paulyn
Assets Lorraine King

All rights reserved. No part of this publication may be reproduced,
stored in a retrieval system, or transmitted by any means, electronic,
mechanical, photocopying, recording or otherwise, without the
prior permission of the copyright holder.

ISBN 978-1-84810-291-0

Printed in China

British Library Cataloguing-in-Publication Data
A catalogue record for this book is available from the British Library

Made with paper from a sustainable forest

www.mileskelly.net
info@mileskelly.net

OVER 1000 FANTASTIC FACTS

Miles
Kelly

Contents

EARTH & SPACE

SCIENCE

PREHISTORIC LIFE

THE ANIMAL WORLD

HISTORY

EARTH & SPACE

1 **Space is all round the Earth, high above the air.** Here on the Earth's surface we are surrounded by air. If you go upwards, up a mountain or in an aircraft, the air grows thinner until there is none at all. This is where space begins. Space itself is mostly empty but there are many exciting things out there such as planets, stars and galaxies. People who travel in space are called astronauts.

▶ In space, astronauts wear spacesuits to go outside the space shuttle as it circles the Earth. Much farther away are planets, stars and galaxies.

Astronaut

Space Shuttle

Earth

Moon

Our life–giving star

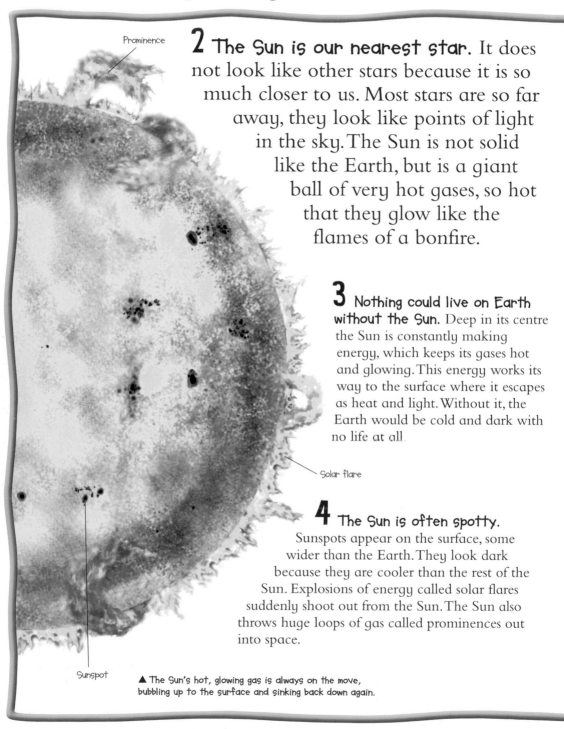

Prominence

2 **The Sun is our nearest star.** It does not look like other stars because it is so much closer to us. Most stars are so far away, they look like points of light in the sky. The Sun is not solid like the Earth, but is a giant ball of very hot gases, so hot that they glow like the flames of a bonfire.

3 **Nothing could live on Earth without the Sun.** Deep in its centre the Sun is constantly making energy, which keeps its gases hot and glowing. This energy works its way to the surface where it escapes as heat and light. Without it, the Earth would be cold and dark with no life at all.

Solar flare

4 **The Sun is often spotty.** Sunspots appear on the surface, some wider than the Earth. They look dark because they are cooler than the rest of the Sun. Explosions of energy called solar flares suddenly shoot out from the Sun. The Sun also throws huge loops of gas called prominences out into space.

Sunspot

▲ The Sun's hot, glowing gas is always on the move, bubbling up to the surface and sinking back down again.

5 When the Moon hides the Sun there is an eclipse. Every so often, the Sun, Moon and Earth line up in space so that the Moon comes directly between the Earth and the Sun. This stops the sunlight from reaching a small area on Earth. This area grows dark and cold, as if night has come early.

▶ When there is an eclipse, we can see the corona (glowing gas) around the Sun.

Sun

WARNING
Never look directly at the Sun especially through a telescope or binoculars. It is so bright it will harm your eyes or even make you blind.

Moon

Shadow of eclipse

Earth

I DON'T BELIEVE IT!

The surface of the Sun is nearly 60 times hotter than boiling water. It is so hot it would melt a spacecraft flying near it.

▲ When the Moon casts a shadow on the Earth, there is an eclipse of the Sun.

13

A family of planets

6 **The Sun is surrounded by a family of circling planets called the Solar System.** This family is held together by an invisible force called gravity, which pulls things towards each other. It is the same force that pulls us down to the ground and stops us from floating away. The Sun's gravity pulls on the planets and keeps them circling around it.

7 **The Earth is one of eight planets in the Sun's family.** They all circle the Sun at different distances from it. The four planets nearest to the Sun are all balls of rock. The next four planets are much bigger and are made of gas and liquid. The tiny dwarf planet at the edge of the Solar System, Pluto, is a solid, icy ball.

8 **Moons circle the planets, travelling with them round the Sun.** Earth has one Moon. It circles the Earth while the Earth circles round the Sun. Mars has two tiny moons but Mercury and Venus have none at all. There are large families of moons, like miniature solar systems, round all the large gas planets.

Saturn

Uranus

Neptune

Pluto,
dwarf planet

Sun

Mercury

Moon

Jupiter

Venus

Earth

Mars

▲ The eight planets are all different. Mercury, nearest the Sun, is small and hot. Then Venus, Earth and Mars are rocky and cooler. Beyond them Jupiter, Saturn, Uranus and Neptune are large and cold. Dwarf planet Pluto is tiny and icy.

9 There are millions of smaller members in the Sun's family. Some are tiny specks of dust speeding through space between the planets. Larger chunks of rock, many as large as mountains, are called asteroids. Comets come from the edge of the Solar System, skimming past the Sun before they disappear again.

I DON'T BELIEVE IT!

If the Sun was the size of a large beach ball, the Earth would be as small as a pea, and the Moon would look like a pinhead.

15

The Earth's neighbours

10 **Venus and Mars are the nearest planets to the Earth.** Venus is closer to the Sun than the Earth while Mars is farther away. Each takes a different amount of time to circle the Sun and we call this its year. A year on Venus is 225 days, on Earth 365 days and on Mars 687 days.

▲ All we can see of Venus from space are the tops of its clouds. They take just four days to race right around the planet.

11 **Venus is the hottest planet.** It is hotter than Mercury, although Mercury is closer to the Sun and gets more of the Sun's heat. Heat builds up on Venus because it is completely covered by clouds, which trap the heat, like the glass in a greenhouse.

12 **Venus has poisonous clouds with drops of acid that would burn your skin.** They are not like clouds on Earth, which are made of droplets of water. These thick clouds do not let much sunshine reach the surface of Venus.

▼ Under its clouds, Venus has hundreds of volcanoes, large and small, all over its surface. We do not know if any of them are still erupting.

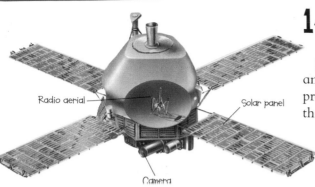

Radio aerial

Solar panel

Camera

14 Winds on Mars whip up huge dust storms that can cover the whole planet. Mars is very dry, like a desert, and covered in red dust. When a space probe called *Mariner 9* arrived there in 1971, the whole planet was hidden by dust clouds.

◄ *Mariner 9* was the first space probe to circle another planet. It sent back more than 7000 pictures of Mars showing giant volcanoes, valleys, ice caps and dried-up river beds.

13 Mars has the largest volcano in the Solar System. It is called Olympus Mons and is three times as high as Mount Everest, the tallest mountain on Earth. Olympus Mons is an old volcano and it has not erupted for millions of years.

PLANET-SPOTTING

See if you can spot Venus in the night sky. It is often the first bright 'star' to appear in the evening, just above where the Sun has set. It is sometimes called the 'evening star'.

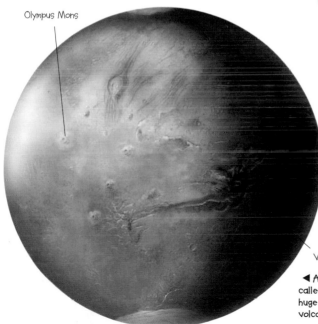

Olympus Mons

Valles Marineris

15 There are plans to send astronauts to Mars but the journey would take six months or more. The astronauts would have to take with them everything they need for the journey there and back and for their stay on Mars.

◄ An enormous valley seems to cut Mars in half. It is called Valles Marineris. To the left is a row of three huge volcanoes and beyond them you can see the largest volcano, Olympus Mons.

The smallest of all

16 Tiny Pluto is so far away, it was not discovered until 1930. In 2006, Pluto was classed as a dwarf planet. It is less than half the width of the next smallest planet, Mercury. In fact Pluto is smaller than our Moon.

▲ Pluto is too far away to see any detail on its surface, but it might look like this.

17 Dwarf planet Pluto is the farthest planet from the Sun. If you were to stand on its surface, the Sun would not look much brighter than the other stars. It gets very little heat from the Sun and its surface is completely covered with solid ice.

18 Space probes have not yet visited Pluto. So astronomers will have to wait for close-up pictures and detailed information that a probe could send back. Even if one was sent to Pluto it would take at least eight years to travel there.

19 No one knew Pluto had a moon until 1978. An astronomer noticed what looked like a bulge on the side of the planet. It turned out to be a moon and was named Charon. Charon is about half the width of Pluto.

▼ If you were on Pluto, its moon Charon would look much larger than our Moon does, because Charon is very close to Pluto.

20 Mercury looks like our Moon.
It is a round, cratered ball of rock.
Although a little larger than the
Moon, like the Moon it has no air.

▼ Mercury's many craters show how often it was
hit by space rocks. One was so large that it
shattered rocks on the other side of the planet.

MAKE CRATERS

You will need:
flour   baking tray
a marble or a stone

Spread some flour about 2 centimetres
deep in a baking tray and smooth over
the surface. Drop a marble or a small,
round stone onto the flour and
see the saucer-shaped crater
that it makes.

21 The sunny side of Mercury is boiling
hot but the night side is freezing cold.
Being the nearest planet to the Sun, the
sunny side can get twice as hot as an oven.
But Mercury spins round slowly so the night
side has time to cool down, and there is no
air to trap the heat. The night side becomes
more than twice as cold as the coldest place
on Earth – Antarctica.

▼ The Sun looks huge as it rises
on Mercury. This is because it
is so close to the planet.

The biggest of all

22 Jupiter is the biggest planet, more massive than all the other planets in the Solar System put together. It is 11 times as wide as the Earth although it is still much smaller than the Sun. Saturn, the next largest planet, is more than nine times as wide as the Earth.

Jupiter

23 Jupiter and Saturn are gas giants. They have no solid surface for a spacecraft to land on. All that you can see are the tops of their clouds. Beneath the clouds, the planets are made mostly of gas (like air) and liquid (water is a liquid).

24 The Great Red Spot on Jupiter is a 300-year-old storm. It was first noticed about 300 years ago and is at least twice as wide as the Earth. It rises above the rest of the clouds and swirls around like storm clouds on Earth.

▼ Jupiter's fast winds blow the clouds into coloured bands around the planet.

Great Red Spot is the biggest and oldest storm

Jupiter's Moon Io has many volcanoes

► Although Saturn's rings are very wide, they stretch out in a very thin layer round the planet.

25 The shining rings round Saturn are made of millions of chunks of ice. These circle round the planet like tiny moons and shine by reflecting sunlight from their surfaces. Some are as small as ice cubes, while others can be as large as a car.

26 Jupiter and Saturn spin round so fast that they bulge out in the middle. This can happen because they are not made of solid rock. As they spin, their clouds are stretched out into light and dark bands around them.

I DON'T BELIEVE IT!
Saturn is the lightest planet in the Solar System. If there was a large enough sea, it would float like a cork.

27 Jupiter's moon Io looks a bit like a pizza. It has many active volcanoes that throw out huge plumes of material, making red blotches and dark marks on its orange-yellow surface.

So far away

28 Uranus and Neptune are gas giants like Jupiter and Saturn. They are the next two planets beyond Saturn but much smaller, being less than half as wide. They sldo don't have a hard surface. Their cloud tops make Uranus and Neptune both look blue. They are very cold, being so far from the Sun.

▲ There is very little to see on Uranus, just a few wisps of cloud above the greenish haze.

29 Uranus seems to 'roll' around the Sun. Unlike most of the other planets, which spin upright like a top, Uranus spins on its side. It may have been knocked over when something crashed into it millions of years ago.

30 Uranus has more moons than any other planet. So far, 21 have been discovered, although one is so newly discovered it has not got a name yet. Most of them are very small but there are five larger ones.

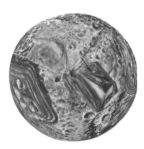

◄ Miranda is one of Uranus' moons. It looks as though it has been split apart and put back together again.

31 **Neptune had a storm that disappeared.** When the *Voyager 2* space probe flew past Neptune in 1989, it spotted a huge storm like a dark version of the Great Red Spot on Jupiter. When the Hubble Space Telescope looked at Neptune in 1994, the storm had gone.

32 **Neptune has bright-blue clouds that make the whole planet look blue.** Above these clouds are smaller, white streaks. These are icy clouds that race around the planet. One of the white clouds seen by the *Voyager 2* space probe was called 'Scooter' because it scooted round the planet so fast.

33 **Neptune is sometimes farther from the Sun than Pluto.** All the planets travel around the Sun along orbits (paths) that look like circles, but Pluto's path is more squashed. This sometimes brings it closer to the Sun than Neptune.

▼ In the past, astronomers thought there might be another planet, called Planet X, outside Neptune and Pluto.

Orbit of Neptune

Orbit of Pluto

Orbit of Planet X

◄ Like all the gas giant planets, Neptune has rings. However, they are much darker and thinner than Saturn's rings.

QUIZ

1. How many moons does Uranus have?

2. Which is the biggest planet in our Solar System?

3. Which planet seems to 'roll' around the Sun?

4. What colour are Neptune's clouds?

Answers:
1. 21 2. Jupiter
3. Uranus 4. Blue

Comets, asteroids and meteors

34 **There are probably billions of tiny comets at the edge of the Solar System.** They circle the Sun far beyond Pluto. Sometimes one is disturbed and moves inwards towards the Sun, looping around it before going back to where it came from. Some comets come back to the Sun regularly, such as Halley's comet that returns every 76 years.

▶ The solid part of a comet is hidden inside a huge, glowing cloud that stretches into a long tail.

35 A comet is often called a dirty snowball because it is made of dust and ice mixed together. Heat from the Sun melts some of the ice. This makes dust and gas stream away from the comet, forming a huge tail that glows in the sunlight.

36 Comet tails always point away from the Sun. Although it looks bright, a comet's tail is extremely thin so it is blown outwards, away from the Sun. When the comet moves away from the Sun, its tail goes in front of it.

37 Asteroids are chunks of rock that failed to stick together to make a planet. Most of them circle the Sun between Mars and Jupiter where there would be room for another planet. There are millions of asteroids, some the size of a car, and others as big as mountains.

▶ Asteroids travel in a ring round the Sun. This ring is called the Asteroid belt and can be found between Mars and Jupiter.

38 Meteors are sometimes called shooting stars. They are not really stars, just streaks of light that flash across the night sky. Meteors are made when pebbles racing through space at high speed hit the top of the air above the Earth. The pebble gets so hot it burns up. We see it as a glowing streak for a few seconds.

▼ At certain times of year there are meteor showers when you can see more shooting stars than usual.

QUIZ

1. Which way does a comet tail always point?

2. What is another name for a meteor?

3. Where is the Asteroid belt?

Answers:
1. Away from the Sun
2. Shooting star
3. Between Mars and Jupiter

A star is born

39 Stars are born in clouds of dust and gas in space called nebulae. Astronomers can see these clouds as shining patches in the night sky, or dark patches against the distant stars. These clouds shrink as gravity pulls the dust and gas together. At the centre, the gas gets hotter and hotter until a new star is born.

▶ Stars are born and die all over the Universe and by looking at stars in different stages of their life, astronomers have learned about the stages of their existence.

1. Clumps of gas in this nebula start to shrink into the tight, round balls that will become stars.

2. The gas spirals round as it is pulled inwards. Any left over gas and dust may form planets around the new star.

3. Deep in its centre, the new star starts making energy, but it is still hidden by the cloud of dust and gas.

40 Stars begin their lives when they start making energy. When the dust and gas pull tightly together, the star gets very hot. Finally it gets so hot in the middle that it can start making energy. The energy makes the star shine, giving out heat and light like the Sun.

4. The dust and gas are blown away and we can see the star shining. Maybe it has a family of planets like the Sun.

41 Young stars often stay together in clusters. When they start to shine, they light up the nebula, making it glow with bright colours. Then the starlight blows away the remains of the cloud and we can see a group of new stars, called a star cluster.

▶ This cluster of young stars, with many stars of different colours and sizes, will gradually drift apart, breaking up the cluster.

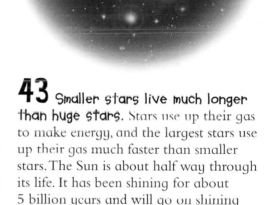

QUIZ

1. What is a nebula?
2. How long has the Sun been shining?
3. What colour are large, hot stars?
4. What is a group of new young stars called?

Answers:
1. A cloud of dust and gas in space 2. About 5 billion years 3. Bluish-white 4. Star cluster

43 Smaller stars live much longer than huge stars. Stars use up their gas to make energy, and the largest stars use up their gas much faster than smaller stars. The Sun is about half way through its life. It has been shining for about 5 billion years and will go on shining for another 5 billion years.

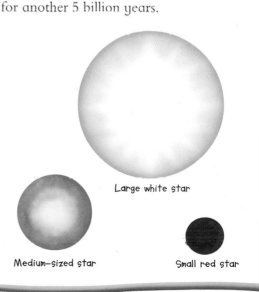

Large white star

Medium-sized star

Small red star

42 Large stars are very hot and white, smaller stars are cooler and redder. A large star can make energy faster and get much hotter than a smaller star. This gives them a very bright, bluish-white colour. Smaller stars are cooler. This makes them look red and shine less brightly. Ordinary in-between stars such as our Sun look yellow.

Billions of galaxies

44 The Sun is part of a huge family of stars called the Milky Way Galaxy. There are billions of other stars in our Galaxy, as many as the grains of sand on a beach. We call it the Milky Way because it looks like a very faint band of light in the night sky, as though someone has spilt some milk across space.

▶ Seen from outside, our Galaxy would look like this. The Sun is towards the edge, in one of the spiral arms.

45 Curling arms give some galaxies their spiral shape. The Milky Way has arms made of bright stars and glowing clouds of gas that curl round into a spiral shape. Some galaxies, called elliptical galaxies, have a round shape like a squashed ball. Other galaxies have no particular shape.

I DON'T BELIEVE IT!

If you could fit the Milky Way onto these two pages, the Sun would be so tiny, you could not see it.

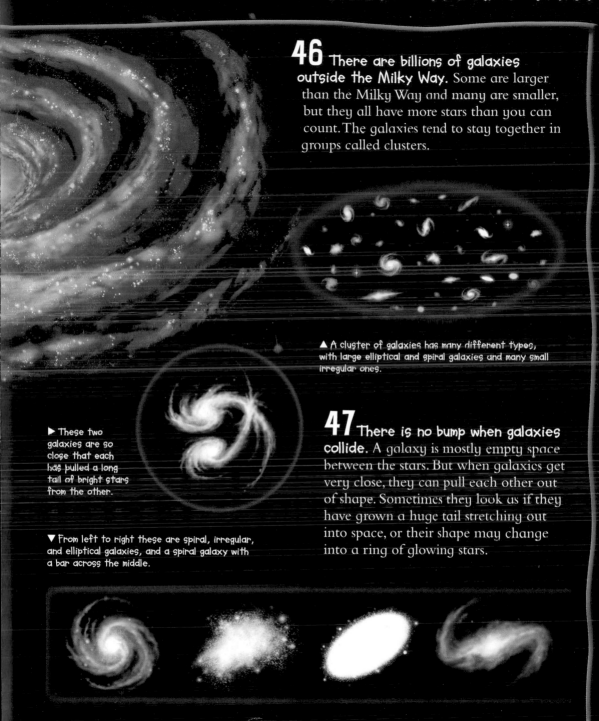

46 There are billions of galaxies outside the Milky Way. Some are larger than the Milky Way and many are smaller, but they all have more stars than you can count. The galaxies tend to stay together in groups called clusters.

▲ A cluster of galaxies has many different types, with large elliptical and spiral galaxies and many small irregular ones.

▶ These two galaxies are so close that each has pulled a long tail of bright stars from the other.

▼ From left to right these are spiral, irregular, and elliptical galaxies, and a spiral galaxy with a bar across the middle.

47 There is no bump when galaxies collide. A galaxy is mostly empty space between the stars. But when galaxies get very close, they can pull each other out of shape. Sometimes they look as if they have grown a huge tail stretching out into space, or their shape may change into a ring of glowing stars.

Looking into space

48 People have imagined they can see the outlines of people and animals in the star patterns in the sky. These patterns are called constellations. Hundreds of years ago, astronomers named the constellations to help them find their way around the skies.

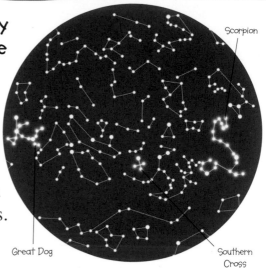

Scorpion

Great Dog

Southern Cross

▲ If you live south of the Equator, these are the constellations you can see at night.

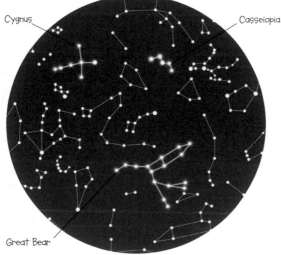

Cygnus

Casseiopia

Great Bear

▲ From the north of the Equator, you can see a different set of constellations in the night sky.

49 Astronomers use huge telescopes to see much more than we can see with just our eyes. Telescopes make things look bigger and nearer. They also show faint, glowing clouds of gas, and distant stars and galaxies.

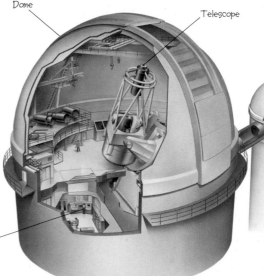

Dome

Telescope

Control room

▲ A huge dome protects this large telescope. It opens to let the telescope point at the sky, and both the dome and telescope can turn to look at any part of the sky.

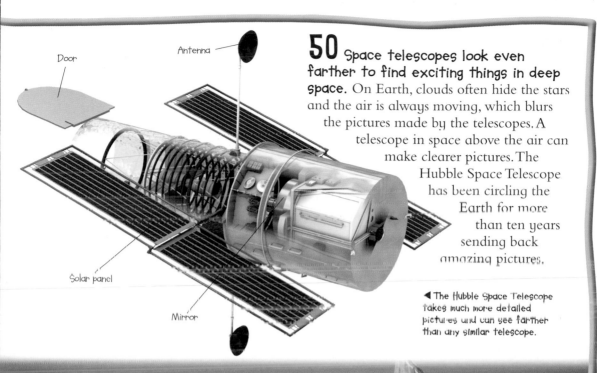

Door

Antenna

Solar panel

Mirror

50 Space telescopes look even farther to find exciting things in deep space. On Earth, clouds often hide the stars and the air is always moving, which blurs the pictures made by the telescopes. A telescope in space above the air can make clearer pictures. The Hubble Space Telescope has been circling the Earth for more than ten years sending back amazing pictures.

◀ The Hubble Space Telescope takes much more detailed pictures and can see farther than any similar telescope.

51 Astronomers also look At radio signals from space. They use telescopes that look like huge satellite TV dishes. These make pictures using the radio signals that come from space. The pictures do not always look like those from ordinary telescopes, but they can spot exciting things that most ordinary telescopes cannot see, such as jets of gas from black holes.

▼ Radio telescopes often have rows of dishes like these to collect radio signals from space. Altogether, they act like one much larger dish to make more detailed pictures. The dishes can move to look in any direction.

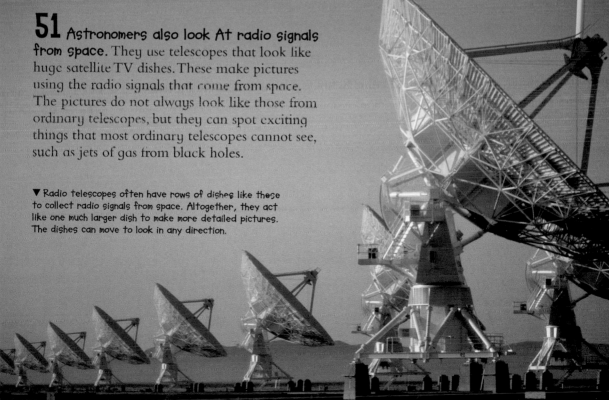

Flying in space

52 **Powerful rockets can fly into space.** There is no air in space, so wings are of no use. Rockets are pushed upwards by their powerful engines. Also, without air there is no drag to slow the rocket. Once started by a boost from its motor, the rocket keeps going, only needing extra boosts to change direction or speed.

2. Booster rockets fall away

1. Rocket engine's fire

▲ The Shuttle's rocket engines and boosters give it enough speed to reach space.

◀ The Ariane 5 rocket launches satellites into space. A new rocket is built for each launch.

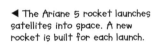

Liquid oxygen tank

Liquid hydrogen tank

53 Rocket engines are similar to jet engines. Inside the engine the fuel burns, making hot gases rush out through a nozzle at the back, and the rocket shoots forwards. However a rocket carries its own oxygen gas to burn the fuel. A jet engine uses oxygen from the air. This means a jet engine only works in air, but a rocket engine works in air and space.

▲ The solid fuel in the Shuttle's booster rockets burns very rapidly for maximum thrust.

3. Fuel tank separates

54 **The Space Shuttle takes off as a rocket.** It has three rocket engines, but it also uses two huge booster rockets. These only fire for two minutes before dropping back to Earth. The engines use fuel from a separate tank that also falls away when the Shuttle reaches space. The booster rockets land in the sea and are used again, but the tank burns up as it drops into the atmosphere.

4. Return to Earth

5. Touch down

55 **The Shuttle lands on a runway like a huge glider.** When the Shuttle returns to Earth it does not use its rocket engines. It swoops gently downwards and uses its wings and tail to slow and guide it towards its long runway. It touches down much faster than an airliner and uses a parachute to help it slow down and stop.

Exhaust nozzle

▶ Orion does not need wings like the Shuttle because it will not land on a runway.

Solid fuel booster

QUIZ

1. How many booster rockets does the Shuttle need to reach space?

2. Will a jet engine work in space?

3. Does a rocket need wings to fly in space?

Answers:
1. Two 2. No 3. No

56 **A new spacecraft called Orion will replace the Shuttle.** It will be launched by a rocket called Ares, which is similar to the Shuttle's boosters. Four to six astronauts will travel in the cone-shaped capsule. They will be able to go to the International Space Station, or the Moon – or even the planet Mars. When they return to Earth they will float down using parachutes and land in the sea.

Robot explorers

57 Robot spacecraft called probes have explored all the planets. Probes travel in space to take close-up pictures and measurements. They send the information back to scientists on Earth. Some probes circle planets taking pictures. For a really close-up look, a probe can land on the surface.

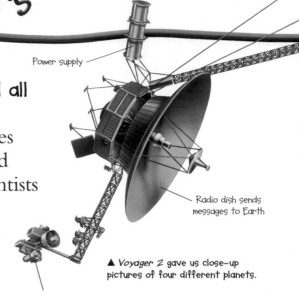

Power supply

Radio dish sends messages to Earth

Cameras

▲ *Voyager 2* gave us close-up pictures of four different planets.

58 In 1976, two *Viking* spacecraft landed on Mars to look for life. They scooped up some dust and tested it to see if any tiny creatures lived on Mars. They did not find any signs of life and their pictures showed only a dry, red, dusty desert.

59 Two *Voyager* probes left Earth in 1977 to visit the gas giant planets. They reached Jupiter in 1979, flying past and on to Saturn. *Voyager 2* went on to visit Uranus and then Neptune in 1989. It sent back thousands of pictures of each planct as it flew past.

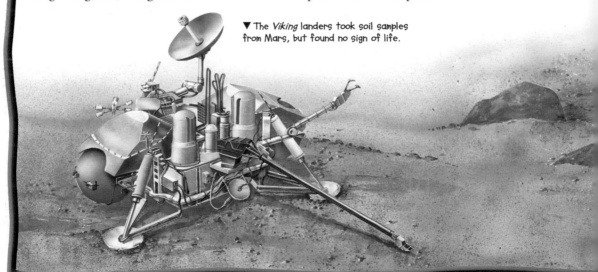

▼ The *Viking* landers took soil samples from Mars, but found no sign of life.

▲ When *Galileo* has finished sending back pictures of Jupiter and its moons, it will plunge into Jupiter's swirling clouds.

60 *Galileo* has circled Jupiter for more than six years. It arrived in 1995 and dropped a small probe into Jupiter's clouds. Galileo sent back pictures of the planet and its largest moons. It was discovered that two of them may have water hidden under ice thicker than the Arctic ice on Earth.

▼ *Sojourner* spent three months on Mars. The small rover was about the size of a microwave oven.

QUIZ

1. When did the *Voyager* probes fly past Jupiter?
2. Which probe sent pictures of Jupiter's clouds?
3. Which probes tested the dust on Mars for signs of life?
4. What was the name of the *Mars Pathfinder* rover?

Answers:
1. 1979 2. *Galileo*
3. *Viking* 4. *Sojourner*

61 *Mars Pathfinder* carried a small rover called *Sojourner* to Mars in 1997. It landed on the surface and opened up to let *Sojourner* out. This rover was like a remote control car, but with six wheels. It tested the soil and rocks to find out what they were made of as it slowly drove around the landing site.

Where did Earth come from?

62 The Earth came from a cloud in space.
Scientists think the Earth formed from a huge
cloud of gas and dust around 4500 million
years ago. A star near the cloud exploded,
making the cloud spin. As the cloud spun
round, gases gathered at its centre and
formed the Sun. Dust whizzed round the
Sun and stuck together to form lumps
of rock. In time the rocks crashed into
each other to make the planets. The
Earth is one of these planets.

5. The Earth was made up
of one large piece of land,
now split into seven chunks
known as continents

1. Cloud starts to spin

▶ Clouds of gas and dust are made
by the remains of old stars that
have exploded or simply stopped
shining. It is here that
new stars and their
planets form.

4. Volcanoes erupt,
releasing gases,
helping to form the
first atmosphere

3. The Earth begins to cool
and a hard shell forms

2. Dust gathers into lumps of
rock which form a small planet

**63 At first the Earth was very
hot.** As the rocks crashed together they
warmed each other up. Later, as the
Earth formed, the rocks inside it
melted. The new Earth was a ball of
liquid rock with a thin, solid shell.

64 Huge numbers of large rocks called meteorites crashed into the Earth. They made round hollows on the surface. These hollows are called craters. The Moon was hit with rocks at the same time. Look at the Moon with binoculars – you can see the craters that were made long ago.

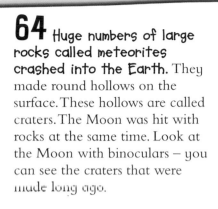

▶ The Moon was also hit by rocks in space, and they made huge craters, and mountain ranges up to 5000 metres high.

65 The oceans and seas formed as the Earth cooled down. Volcanoes erupted, letting out steam, gases and rocks from inside the Earth. As the Earth cooled, the steam changed to water droplets and made clouds. As the Earth cooled further, rain fell from the clouds. It rained for millions of years to make the seas and oceans.

▼ Erupting volcanoes and fierce storms helped form the atmosphere and oceans. They provided energy that was needed for life on Earth to begin.

I DON'T BELIEVE IT!
Millions of rocks crash into Earth as it speeds through space. Some larger ones may reach the ground as meteorites.

Night and day

66 **The Earth is like a huge spinning top.** It continues to spin because it was formed from a spinning cloud of gas and dust. It does not spin straight up like a top but leans a little to one side. The Earth takes 24 hours to spin around once. We call this period of time a day.

Mid–day

Evening

67 **The Earth's spinning makes day and night.** Each part of the Earth spins towards the Sun, and then away from it every day. When a part of the Earth is facing the Sun it is day-time there. When that part is facing away from the Sun it is night-time.

◀ If you were in space and looked at the Earth from the side, it would appear to move from left to right. If you looked down on Earth from the North Pole, it would seem to be moving anticlockwise.

68 **The Earth spins around its Poles.** The Earth spins around two points on its surface. They are at opposite ends of the Earth. One is on top of the Earth. It is called the North Pole. The other is at the bottom of the Earth. It is called the South Pole. The North and South Poles are so cold, they are covered by ice and snow.

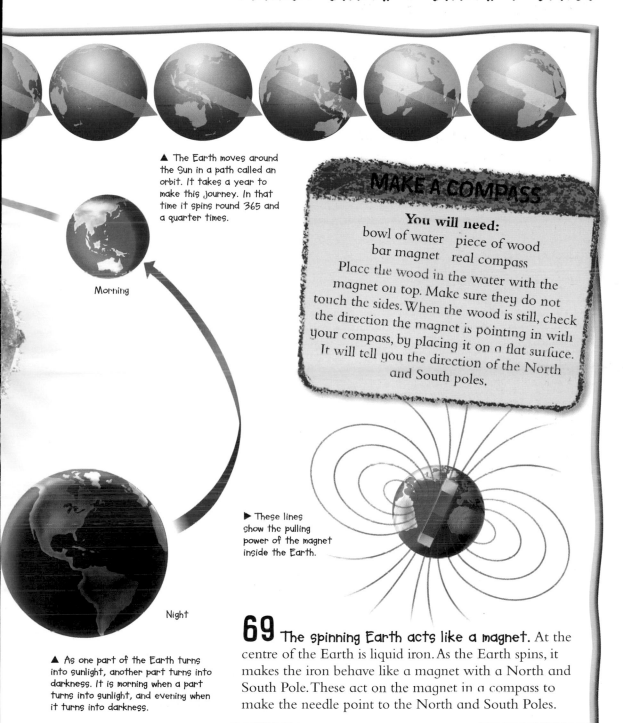

▲ The Earth moves around the Sun in a path called an orbit. It takes a year to make this journey. In that time it spins round 365 and a quarter times.

Morning

MAKE A COMPASS

You will need:
bowl of water   piece of wood
bar magnet   real compass

Place the wood in the water with the magnet on top. Make sure they do not touch the sides. When the wood is still, check the direction the magnet is pointing in with your compass, by placing it on a flat surface. It will tell you the direction of the North and South poles.

▶ These lines show the pulling power of the magnet inside the Earth.

Night

▲ As one part of the Earth turns into sunlight, another part turns into darkness. It is morning when a part turns into sunlight, and evening when it turns into darkness.

69 **The spinning Earth acts like a magnet.** At the centre of the Earth is liquid iron. As the Earth spins, it makes the iron behave like a magnet with a North and South Pole. These act on the magnet in a compass to make the needle point to the North and South Poles.

The four seasons

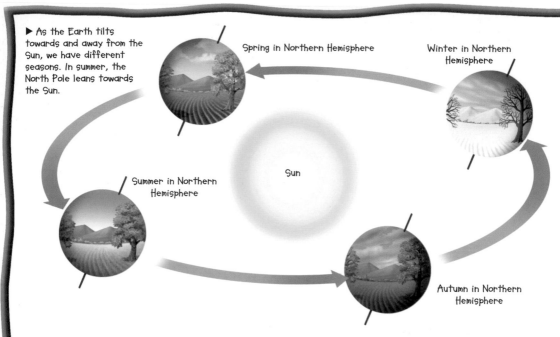

▶ As the Earth tilts towards and away from the Sun, we have different seasons. In summer, the North Pole leans towards the Sun.

Spring in Northern Hemisphere

Winter in Northern Hemisphere

Sun

Summer in Northern Hemisphere

Autumn in Northern Hemisphere

70 **The reason for the seasons lies in space.** Our planet Earth plots a path through space that takes it around the Sun. This path, or orbit, takes one year. The Earth is tilted, so over the year, first one and then the other Pole leans towards the Sun, creating seasons.

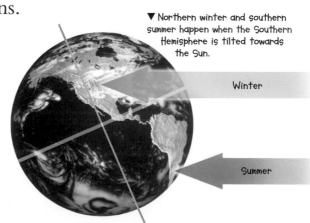

▼ Northern winter and southern summer happen when the Southern Hemisphere is tilted towards the Sun.

Winter

Summer

71 **When it is summer in Argentina, it is winter in Canada.** In December, the South Pole leans towards the Sun. Places in the southern half of the world, such as Argentina, have summer. At the same time, places in the northern half, such as Canada, have winter.

▲ At the North Pole, the Sun never disappears below the horizon at Midsummer's Day.

72 A day can last 21 hours! Night and day happen because Earth is spinning as it circles the Sun. At the height of summer, places near the North Pole are so tilted towards the Sun that it is light almost all day long. In Stockholm, Sweden, Midsummer's Eve lasts 21 hours because the Sun disappears below the horizon for only three hours.

I DON'T BELIEVE IT!

When the Sun shines all day in the far north, there is 24-hour night in the far south.

73 Forests change colour in the autumn. Autumn comes between summer and winter. Trees prepare for the cold winter months ahead by losing their leaves. First, they suck back the precious green chlorophyll, or dye, in their leaves, making them turn shades of red, orange and brown.

◀ Deciduous trees lose their leaves in autumn, but evergreens keep their leaves all year round.

Inside the Earth

74 There are different parts to the Earth. There is a thin, rocky crust, a solid middle called the mantle and a centre called the core. The outer part of the core is liquid but the inner core is made of solid metal.

75 At the centre of the Earth is a huge metal ball called the inner core. It is 2500 kilometres wide and is made mainly from iron, with some nickel. The ball has an incredible temperature of 6000°C – hot enough to make the metals melt. They stay solid because other parts of the Earth push down heavily on them.

76 Around the centre of the Earth flows a hot, liquid layer of iron and nickel. This layer is the outer core and is about 2200 kilometres thick. As the Earth spins, the metal ball and liquid layer move at different speeds.

Crust

Mantle
4500°C

Outer core
6000°C

Inner core
7000°C

◄ The internal structure of the Earth. The centre of the Earth – the inner core – is solid even though it is intensely hot. This is because it is under extreme pressure.

77 The largest part of Earth is a layer called the mantle, which is 2900 kilometres thick. It lies between the core and the crust. Near the crust, the mantle is made of slow-moving rock. When you squeeze an open tube of toothpaste, the toothpaste moves a little like the rocks in the upper mantle.

300 million years ago

200 million years ago

78 The Earth's surface is covered by crust. Land is made of continental crust between 20 and 70 kilometres thick. Most of this is made from a rock called granite. The ocean bed is made of oceanic crust about 8 kilometres thick. It is made mainly from a rock called basalt.

▶ Scientists know that the continents were once joined because matching rocks and fossils are found in places that are now separated by vast oceans

65 million years ago

79 The crust is divided into huge slabs of rock called plates. Most plates have land and seas on top of them but some, like the Pacific Plate, are mostly covered by water. The large areas of land on the plates are called continents. There are seven continents – Africa, Asia, Europe, North America, South America, Oceania and Antarctica.

80 Very, very slowly, the continents are moving. Slow-flowing mantle under the crust moves the plates across the Earth's surface. As the plates move, so do the continents. In some places, the plates push into each other. In others, they move apart. North America is moving 3 centimetres away from Europe every year!

Massive mountains

Mount Everest
8850 metres
(Asia)

Mount Kilimanjaro
5895 metres
(Africa)

Mount Cook
3754 metres
(Oceania)

81 **The Earth is covered with a thick layer of rocky crust.** In some places, sections of crust have squeezed together, forcing their way upwards to make mountains. Mountains often form in a long line or group, called a mountain range. High up, it is cold and windy. This means that the tops of mountains are very icy, snowy and stormy.

82 **Mount Everest is the world's highest mountain.** It's on the border between Nepal and China, in the Himalayas mountain range. It is about 8850 metres high. The first people to climb to the top of Everest were Edmund Hillary and Tenzing Norgay, on May 29, 1953.

83 **The highest mountain on Earth isn't the hardest to climb.** Another peak, K2, is much tougher for mountaineers. At 8611 metres, it's the world's second-highest mountain. Its steep slopes and swirling storms make it incredibly dangerous. Fewer than 300 people have ever climbed it, and over 65 have died in the attempt.

▶ Mount Everest is so high that climbers have to climb it over several days, stopping at camps along the way.

Mount Aconcagua
6959 metres (South America)

Mount Mckinley
6194 metres
(North America)

Mount Blanc 4807 metres (Europe)

I DON'T BELIEVE IT!

Mountains seem big to us, but they're very small compared to the whole planet. If the world was shrunk to the size of a football, it would feel totally smooth.

◀ This diagram shows a height comparison of the highest mountains by continent.

84 Most mountains are shaped like big humps — but a cliff is a sheer drop. The east face of Great Trango, a mountain in Pakistan, is 1340 metres high, making it the tallest vertical cliff in the world. There's another giant cliff on Mount Thor in Canada, with a drop of 1250 metres. If a pebble fell off one of these cliffs, it would take more than 15 seconds to reach the bottom!

85 Some people don't just climb to the tops of high mountains — they live there! The town of Wenzhuan in Tibet, China, is the highest in the world. It is in the Himalayas, 5100 metres up — that's over 5 kilometres above sea level! The highest capital city is La Paz, in the Andes in Bolivia, South America. It has an altitude (height) of around 3600 metres.

▶ There are three types of mountain — volcanic, fold and block.

1. Volcanic mountains form when hot, liquid rock (lava) erupts through the Earth's crust. As the lava cools, it forms a rocky layer. With each new eruption, another layer is added.

2. Fold mountains occur when sections of the Earth's crust push against each other, making the land buckle and fold upwards.

3. Block mountains occur when sections of the crust split and crack, forming faults where some sections are pushed up higher than others.

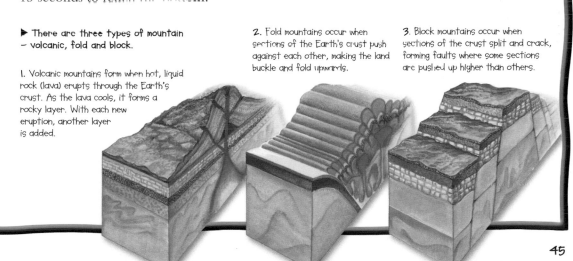

Hot volcanoes

86 **Volcanoes happen because the Earth is hot inside.** The surface is cool, but it gets hotter the deeper you go into the Earth. Under the crust, magma is under so much pressure that it is almost solid. Sometimes the pressure is released by the shifting of the crust and the magma melts. Then it can bubble up through the cracks in the crust as volcanoes.

▼ Here, an oceanic plate dips below a continental plate. The thinner oceanic plate is pushed down into the mantle.

Plates move together

Subducted plate melts into mantle

A volcano has formed along the edge of the overlying plate

I DON'T BELIEVE IT!

Tectonic plates move at about the same speed as your fingernails grow. That is just a few centimetres each year.

▼ Constructive boundaries often occur in the middle of oceans, forming ocean ridges.

Plates move apart

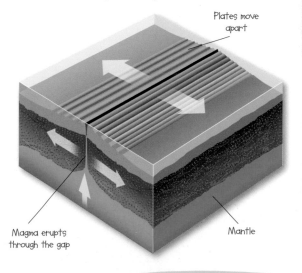

87 **The Earth's crust is cracked into giant pieces called tectonic plates.** There are about 60 plates, and the seven largest are thousands of kilometres across. Tectonic plates move slowly across the Earth's surface. This movement, called continental drift, has caused the continents to move apart over millions of years.

Magma erupts through the gap

Mantle

88 About 250 million years ago there was just one continent, known as Pangaea. The movement of tectonics plates broke Pangaea apart and moved the land around to form the continents we recognize today.

89 Most volcanoes erupt along plate boundaries. These are the cracks separating tectonic plates. On a world map of plate boundaries (below) you can see there are often rows of volcanoes along boundaries.

90 Volcanoes also happen at 'hot spots'. These are places where especially hot magma being driven upwards in the mantle, burns through the middle of a plate to form volcanoes. The most famous hot-spot volcanoes are those of the Hawaiian islands.

▼ Most active volcanoes occur along the 'Ring of Fire' (tinted red). Five volcanoes from around the world are highlighted on the map below.

Mount Bromo, Asia

Hawaii, Pacific Ocean

Mount Rainier, North America

EURASIAN PLATE

RING OF FIRE

NORTH AMERICAN PLATE

AFRICAN PLATE

PACIFIC PLATE

SOUTH AMERICAN PLATE

INDO AUSTRALIAN PLATE

ANTARCTIC PLATE

Mount Kilimanjaro, Africa

Arenal, South America

Parts of a volcano

91 Material erupted from a volcano can build up to form a mountain. Beneath the surface is a system of pipes and chambers that supply the volcano with magma from below the crust.

93 A magma chamber is a store of molten rock under a volcano. As magma moves through cracks in the Earth's crust, it collects in huge reservoirs underground. Magma chambers are usually 1–10 kilometres underground. Some volcanoes have several magma chambers.

92 Magma rises up through a conduit. This is a giant pipe that leads from the magma chamber to the surface. Usually there is one main conduit that leads to the summit of a volcano. The hole at the top of the conduit is called a vent. There are often side vents on a volcano's slopes that have branched off the main conduit.

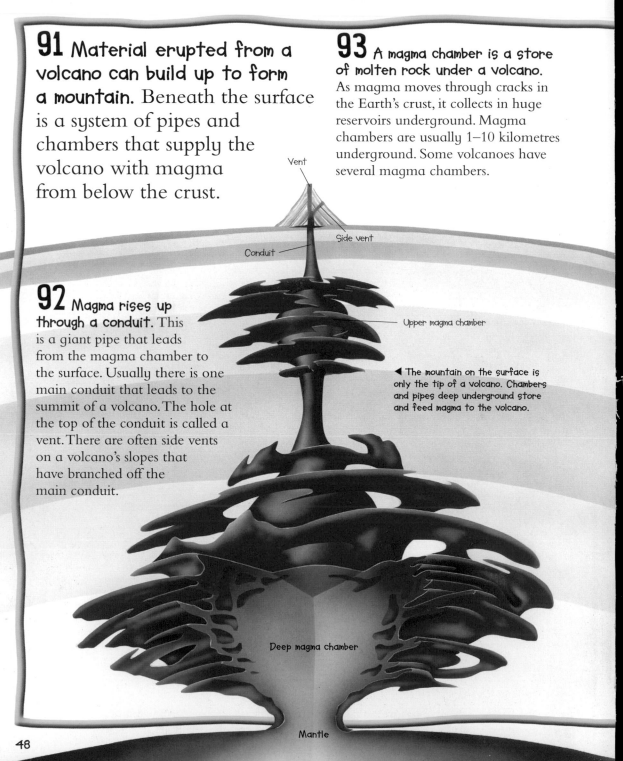

Vent

Side vent

Conduit

Upper magma chamber

◄ The mountain on the surface is only the tip of a volcano. Chambers and pipes deep underground store and feed magma to the volcano.

Deep magma chamber

Mantle

A composite volcano (also known as a stratovolcano) has steep sides built up of layers of lava and ash.

A shield volcano has a low, wide shape, with gently sloping sides.

▶ Volcanoes come in different shapes and sizes. Here are three common examples.

A caldera is a huge crater left after an old eruption. New cones often grow again inside.

94 A crater can form around the vent of a volcano. As magma is blasted out during an eruption, the material forms a rim around the top of the vent. Sometimes several vents may erupt into the same crater. A crater can fill with lava during an eruption. When this forms a pool it is known as a lava lake.

▼ Crater Lake in Oregon, USA. It formed in the caldera of Mount Mazama and is around 9 kilometres across.

95 Lakes can form in the craters of dormant (inactive) volcanoes. When a volcano stops erupting and cools down, its crater can slowly fill with rainwater, creating a lake. Crater lakes also form in calderas – huge craters that form when a volcano collapses into its empty magma chamber.

QUIZ

Which of these are parts of a volcano?
1. Conduit
2. Bed chamber
3. Side vent
4. Ventricle
5. Crater

Answers:
Only 1, 3 and 5 are parts of a volcano

Eruptions

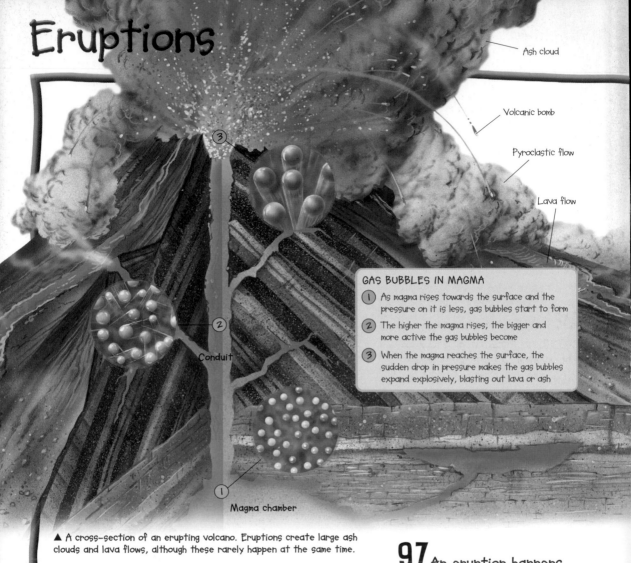

Ash cloud

Volcanic bomb

Pyroclastic flow

Lava flow

3

GAS BUBBLES IN MAGMA

1 As magma rises towards the surface and the pressure on it is less, gas bubbles start to form

2 The higher the magma rises, the bigger and more active the gas bubbles become

3 When the magma reaches the surface, the sudden drop in pressure makes the gas bubbles expand explosively, blasting out lava or ash

Conduit

2

1

Magma chamber

▲ A cross-section of an erupting volcano. Eruptions create large ash clouds and lava flows, although these rarely happen at the same time.

96 At any time, about 20 volcanoes are erupting around the world. On average, 60 volcanoes erupt each year. Eruptions can go on for just a few days or for years on end. A single eruption can spew out millions of tonnes of material.

97 An eruption happens when magma swells beneath the Earth's surface. Magma is a mixture of molten rock and other materials, including dissolved water and gases. As magma rises, the pressure on it lessens. This allows the dissolved gas and water to form bubbles. This makes the magma swell quickly, causing an eruption.

▲ The island of Stromboli, Italy, is an active volcano that erupts almost continuously.

98 **As well as lava and hot gases, explosive eruptions throw out pieces of solid magma.** As the volcano erupts, the pieces of rock are blasted into billions of fragments called pyroclasts. These fragments mainly form vast clouds of ash during an eruption.

99 **A volcano can be active or dormant.** An active volcano is one that is erupting now or seems likely to erupt. Some scientists define an active volcano as one that has erupted in the last 10,000 years. A dormant volcano is one that is not active at the moment, but might become so in the future.

100 **Volcanoes that seem unlikely to erupt again are described as extinct.** Some say that a volcano that has not erupted in the last 10,000 years is extinct. But experts cannot always be sure that a volcano will never erupt again.

GASES IN MAGMA

You will need:
bottle of fizzy drink

Shake the bottle of fizzy drink a little, but not too much, and put it in the sink. As you gradually open the cap, watch the drink in the bottle closely. Bubbles of gas will form, rush upwards and force the drink out of the bottle. The gas stays dissolved in the drink until the pressure on the drink is released. This is the same as what happens when the pressure on magma is released.

▶ Sugar Loaf Mountain in Brazil is a volcanic plug – the solidified core of an extinct volcano.

Lava

◀ A slow-moving lava flow engulfs a road. A person could walk away from a lava flow like this without any danger.

101 Lava is liquid rock ejected from a volcano. Some lava is very runny and flows downhill quickly. Another type is thick and gooey and flows very slowly. The temperature, consistency and thickness of lava affect the way it is erupted.

102 A lava flow is a river of lava. Thin, runny lava can flow downhill at speeds up to 100 kilometres an hour. Lava flows follow the natural contours of the land. They can reach many kilometres from the volcano before the lava cools and stops. Lava often spreads out to form lava fields.

▼ Sometimes lava keeps flowing below the surface through a 'lava tunnel', under a solidified crust.

TRUE OR FALSE?

1. Aa lava is fast flowing.
2. Igneous rock is made when lava cools down.
3. A shortcrust bomb is made from lava.

Answers:
1. True – aa lava is thick, slow-moving lava 2. True – all igneous rocks are formed when magma, lava or ash cools 3. False – but a breadcrust bomb is

103 When lava or magma cools, it forms rock. This kind of rock is called igneous rock. Basalt – a dark-coloured rock – is one common type of igneous rock. Over time, lava flows build up on top of each other forming deep layers of igneous rock.

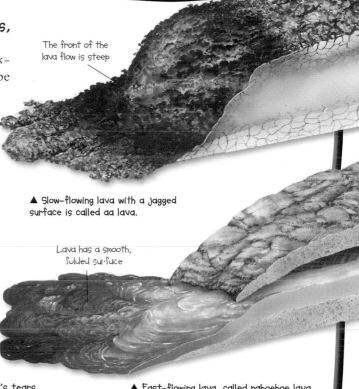

The front of the lava flow is steep

▲ Slow-flowing lava with a jagged surface is called aa lava.

104 Pahoehoe and aa are the two main types of lava. Thick lava that flows slowly cools to form jagged blocks. This is called aa (say ah) lava. Fast-flowing, runny lava cools to form rock with a smooth surface. This is called pahoehoe (say pa-hoey-hoey) lava.

Lava has a smooth, folded surface

▲ Fast-flowing lava, called pahoehoe lava, cools to form smooth, rope-like rock.

▶ Pele's tears are tiny lava bombs often produced in Hawaiian eruptions.

Pele's tears

Breadcrust bomb

Spindle bomb

Cowpat bomb

Ribbon bomb

105 A volcanic bomb is a flying lump of lava. Lumps of lava, usually bigger than the size of a fist, are thrown upwards by jets of gas from the vent during an eruption. Sometimes the outside of a bomb solidifies while it is in the air and splits open when it lands. This is called a breadcrust bomb. If the bomb is still soft when it lands, the bomb splats like a cowpat.

◀ Lumps of lava blasted into the air by a volcano form different shapes in the air.

Hot springs and fountains

106 **There are natural hot baths and showers all over the world.** You might think water outdoors is cold, but in some places, water meets hot rock under the ground and gets heated up. It sometimes even boils. The hot water can then make a lake or spring – or even shoot out of the ground like a fountain, forming a geyser.

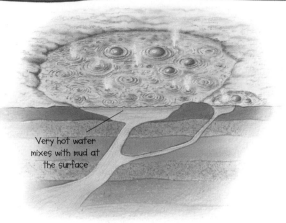

▲ A mudpot forms when hot water from underground mixes with clay at the surface to make hot mud.

▼ A mudpot, like this one in Myvatn Geothermal Area in Iceland, is a pool of hot, bubbling mud. Some mudpots are boiling hot. Others bubble as hot gases burst up through them.

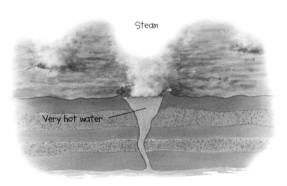

Steam

Very hot water

▲ Sometimes, hot underground water forms steam, which escapes through a hole or crack in the ground. These are called steam vents, or fumaroles.

107 **You shouldn't stand too close to a geyser – even if nothing's happening!** A geyser is a hole in the ground that suddenly shoots out hot water and steam. Under the hole there is a water-filled chamber. Hot rock beneath it heats the water until it rises back to the surface and erupts in a giant jet of water and steam.

108 Old Faithful is one of the world's most famous geysers. Found in Yellowstone National Park USA, it gets its name because it erupts on average once every 94 minutes. Its jet of steam and water can reach 55 metres high – as high as a 15-storey building.

109 Soap helps geysers to erupt. People discovered this when they tried to use hot water pools and geysers to wash their clothes in. Soap disturbs the cold water in the chamber, helping the hot water to burst through.

▶ Strokkur (Icelandic for 'churn') is a geyser in Iceland. It erupts regularly, every 5–10 minutes, and can shoot water up to 25 metres in the air.

110 Besides geysers, the Earth's hot water can form amazing thermal (hot) springs and pools. They often occur in places where there are lots of volcanoes, such as New Zealand and Japan. Some thermal pools are famous for their beautiful colours. These are caused by millions of bacteria (tiny living things) that live in the very hot water.

I DON'T BELIEVE IT!

Japanese macaque monkeys use thermal springs as hot baths! They live in the mountains of Japan where winters are very cold. They climb into the natural hot pools to keep themselves warm.

▼ When rainwater seeps into the earth, it can be heated by hot rocks underground before rising back up to the surface as hot springs, pools and geysers.

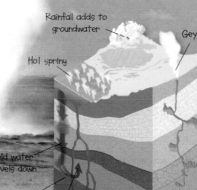

Rainfall adds to groundwater

Geyser

Hot spring

Cold water travels down

Water is heated by hot rocks

Heated water starts to move upwards

Heat from Earth's interior

The rock cycle

111 All rock goes through a cycle over millions of years. During the rock cycle rocks form deep in the Earth, move and sometimes change, go up to the surface and eventually return below the ground. There are three kinds of rock – igneous, sedimentary and metamorphic. They form in different ways and have different features.

112 Rocks can go around the cycle in lots of ways. Igneous rocks were once molten (liquid), and have hardened beneath or above the surface. Metamorphic rock forms when rock is changed by heat, pressure or a combination of the two. Sedimentary rocks are formed when sediment – small particles of rock – becomes buried.

113 When rocks change from one form to another, they can be used for different things. For example, when mudstone is squashed and heated it changes to slate. Crystals begin to line up in layers. This makes it easy to split the rock into thin sheets. Slate makes a good roof material. The smooth sheets are also used to make the bases of pool tables.

Weathering of rocks at surface

Erosion and transport

Laying down of sediment

Burial and becoming more compact under pressure

SEDIMENTARY ROCK

Deep burial and metamorphism (changing structure)

▼ The rock cycle is the long, slow journey of rocks down from the surface and then up again. Rocks are often changed during this process.

IGNEOUS ROCK

Magma forms crystals as it cools

METAMORPHIC ROCK

Melting to form magma

I DON'T BELIEVE IT!

Pumice is solidified lava. It is so light it will float until water soaks into it. It has tiny holes with sharp edges all over it, making it ideal for rubbing down rough surfaces and cleaning skin.

114 **Exposed rock is eroded (worn away) over time.** This is a process in which tiny pieces (particles) of rock are loosened and transported as a result of gravity, wind, water or ice. Gradually these particles may become buried under more rock particles, forming sediment. If the sediment is buried deep enough to reach the mantle it will be heated by magma (hot molten rock), which may melt or bake it. Uplift and erosion can then expose them again.

Formed in fire

115 Rock that forms when hot molten rock (magma or lava) cools and hardens is called **igneous rock.** Igneous rock is divided into two types, extrusive and intrusive, depending on where it forms.

◄ When the pressure in the magma chamber is high enough, the volcano erupts and spews out its lava with incredible force.

116 Igneous rock is known as 'extrusive' if it forms above Earth's surface. This can happen if it erupts or flows from a volcano as lava. Sometimes lava settles, sealing the volcano until pressure builds for another eruption. Extrusive rock can form over thousands or even millions of years. As extrusive rock cools, its fine grains grow into larger crystals.

117 Intrusive rock cools and solidifies inside the Earth's crust below the surface. It only becomes visible when the rocks above it wear away. Granite and dolerite are two examples of intrusive rock.

118 **The most common type of igneous rock is basalt, which often cools in hexagonal columns.** At the Giant's Causeway in Northern Ireland, thousands of these columns were created as lava cooled and shrank over millions of years. Legend says that the columns, some as much as 2 metres in height, are stepping stones for giants to walk across the sea.

QUIZ

1. What is igneous rock before it hardens?
2. Where does 'extrusive' rock form?
3. How were the columns at the Giant's Causeway formed?

Answers:
1. Molten rock, or magma
2. Above ground 3. They formed as lava cooled and shrank

119 **Sometimes gas creates holes in rock.** Crystals form inside the holes, creating geodes – dull-looking stones from the outside, lined with brilliant crystals on the inside. Geodes are often sold cut in half and polished to reveal their glittering insides.

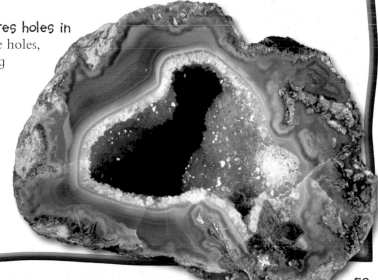

▶ Geodes are rock cavities with crystal formations or circular bands inside them.

59

Lots of layers

120 When rocks are weathered or eroded they break into tiny pieces called sediment. This sediment is eventually buried and compacted (packed tightly together) under pressure until it becomes solid, forming sedimentary rock. It is found in layers known as strata.

▼ The Grand Canyon was formed by two billion years of erosion from the Colorado River exposing countless layers of sedimentary rock.

I DON'T BELIEVE IT!

Uluru in Australia is the most famous block of freestanding rock. It is a 348-metre-high lump of sandstone and is 300 million years old.

121 The walls of the Grand Canyon in Arizona, USA, are sedimentary rock. The canyon is 350 kilometres long and has a depth of 1.6 kilometres in places. It was created by the flowing force of the Colorado River, which wore away the rock. Rock layers are clearly visible along the sides of the canyon.

122 Limestone is a sedimentary rock mostly formed from crushed shells. It contains the remains of millions of sea creatures that have piled up over millions of years, and so it often contains fossils.

123 Some sedimentary rocks are formed when saline (salt) water evaporates. This can happen when a bay or gulf is cut off from the sea and starts to dry up. These mineral-rich rocks are known as evaporites and include gypsum, rock salt (halite) and potash.

124 Coal is a sedimentary rock formed over millions of years. Vegetation from swampy forests died and rotted away. As the water dried out, the vegetation became first peat and eventually coal. Both peat and coal can be mined and burned as fuel.

The rock that changes

125 Metamorphic rock is rock that has been changed by heat or pressure (or both) into a new form deep underground. Pressure from movement of the Earth's crust, the weight of the rocks above and heat from magma cause metamorphic changes. Most of these happen at temperatures of 200–500°C. The rock does not melt – that would make igneous rock – but it is altered.

▼ Part of a slate landscape on Valencia Island off the coast of Ireland. This useful rock has been quarried and mined for thousands of years.

126 The appearance and texture of rock changes as a result of heat and pressure. Crystals break down and form, and a rock's chemical structure can change as its minerals react together. If the change is made under pressure, the rock crystals grow flat and form layers. If shale is compressed it forms slate.

▼ Slate forms when fine clay settles in layers and is then compressed and heated.

1. Bands of shale form solid layers

Shale

2. Movement creates curves

Slate

127 Sometimes rocks don't stop changing. For example, over centuries shale becomes slate, which looks the same as shale but is far harder and is more likely to split into sheets. However, if slate is then heated and squeezed it will be transformed again into phyllite, then schist and finally gneiss. This is the incredibly hard rock that forms the Alps.

I DON'T BELIEVE IT!
Gneiss found in northern Canada is the world's oldest rock. It was created under the volcanoes that made the first landmasses around four billion years ago.

▼ The Alps is a long mountain range stretching from east to west across Europe, formed about 40–20 million years ago.

128 Eclogite is one of the rarest but most interesting metamorphic rocks. It is full of crystals and minerals so it is very coarse-grained. Eclogite is green and often studded with red garnets, and sometimes even diamonds. It forms deep in the Earth's mantle, reaching the surface through volcanoes.

▼ No other rock contains as many interesting crystals and minerals as eclogite, which is formed by extremely high pressures and temperatures.

What are minerals?

129 Minerals are natural substances that form crystals. There are more than 4000 different minerals but only about 30 are found all over the world. Quartz and feldspar are two of the most common types of mineral.

Cubic

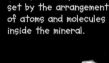
▼ Crystal shapes are set by the arrangement of atoms and molecules inside the mineral.

Tetragonal

Orthorhombic

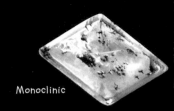
Monoclinic

130 A mineral is a chemical compound (a combination of two or more substances) or element (a single fundamental substance). Rocks are made from minerals. Limestone is made mainly of the mineral calcite (calcium carbonate), and granite contains quartz, mica and feldspar.

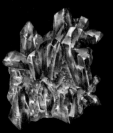
Triclinic

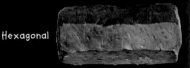
Hexagonal

Trigonal

131 Minerals form crystals. They can do this in several ways. Some are formed as hot molten magma cools. Others come from water (the white powder left when water evaporates is a mineral deposit). Crystals can also be formed when minerals are altered by heat or pressure.

132 Crystals have seven basic shapes. Some just look like a jumble of different surfaces and angles. They have flat, often shiny faces and sharp edges.

133 The tiny grains you can see in most rocks are actually minerals, often forced together. Large crystals form in cracks and holes in rocks, where they have space to grow. The deeper the rock, the longer it generally takes to reach the surface, and the more time the crystal has to grow.

134 Some minerals are so valuable that they are mined. This might mean scraping them from the ground, or blowing up the rocks that hold them. Minerals buried deep underground are reached by drilling down and digging tunnels. People have mined minerals for thousands of years.

▶ Miners have to follow the direction of the mineral-rich band in the seam of rock.

Fossils

135 Fossils are time capsules buried in rock. They form when a dead animal or plant is buried in sediment, which slowly turns into rock. Sometimes the plant or animal dissolves, leaving a gap of the same shape. This gap is then filled by minerals that create a perfect replica in the mould.

136 More animals have become extinct (died out) than are living today and we only know about them from fossils. For example, no one has ever seen a living dinosaur, but through fossils we have learned about the many types of these reptiles that ruled the earth for 175 million years.

I DON'T BELIEVE IT!

Not all fossils are stone. Tree sap hardens into amber, and sometimes insects and tiny animals become trapped in sap. When the sap hardens, the animal is preserved inside the amber forever.

▼ Only a tiny number of animals and plants have been fossilized because the conditions have to be just right.

I. The animal dies and its soft parts rot or are eaten

2. It is covered by sediment, slowing its decay

3. More layers form and the skeleton is replaced by minerals

4. The upper rocks wear away and the fossil is exposed

137 The study of fossils is called palaeontology. One of its first experts was Georges Cuvier (1769–1832). He could work out what a prehistoric animal looked like from studying its fossils and comparing them with the anatomies of living animals, and proved that there were animals alive in the past that are now extinct.

138 Fossils can tell us the age of rocks.
If scientists can identify a fossilized animal or
plant, they will be able to identify the time
period in which it lived, so the rock that the
fossil has been found in must also date from
that period.

139 Sometimes footprints,
burrows and animal droppings are
fossilized. These 'trace fossils' are
created when mud or sand fills
cavities before they are washed
away. Scientists can work out
the size and speed of
dinosaurs from trace
fossils of their
footprints.

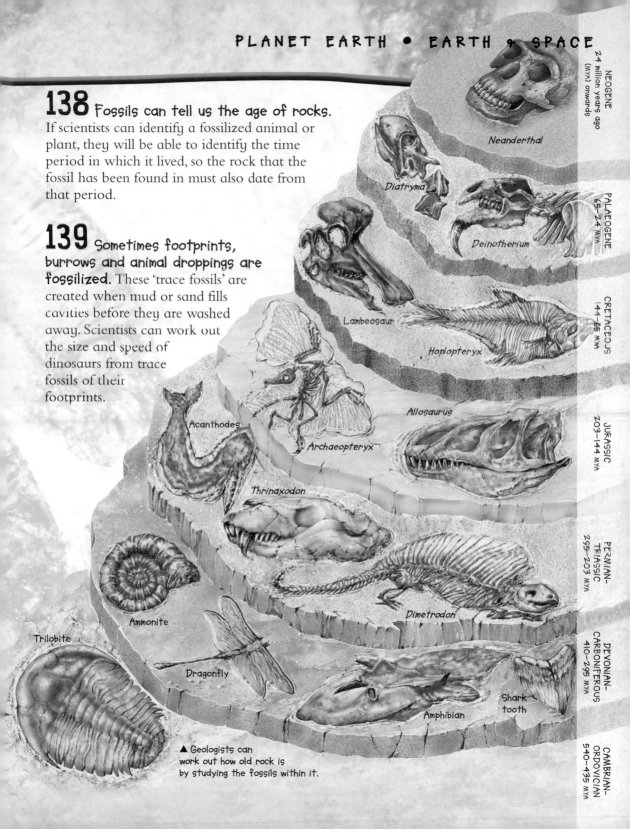

Neanderthal

Diatryma

Deinotherium

Lambeosaur

Hoplopteryx

Acanthodes

Archaeopteryx

Allosaurus

Thrinaxodon

Ammonite

Dimetrodon

Trilobite

Dragonfly

Amphibian

Shark
tooth

▲ Geologists can
work out how old rock is
by studying the fossils within it.

NEOGENE
24 million years ago
(MYA) onwards

PALAEOGENE
65–24 MYA

CRETACEOUS
144–65 MYA

JURASSIC
203–144 MYA

PERMIAN–
TRIASSIC
295–203 MYA

DEVONIAN–
CARBONIFEROUS
410–295 MYA

CAMBRIAN–
ORDOVICIAN
540–435 MYA

Forming waterways

140 **A mighty river can start from a spring.**
This is a place where water flows from the
ground. Rain soaks into the ground, through
the soil and rock, until it gushes out on the side
of a hill. The trickle of water from a spring is
called a stream. Many streams join
together to make a river.

Oxbow lake

Meander

Delta

141 Water wears rocks down to
make a waterfall. When a river flows
off a layer of hard rock onto softer rock,
it wears the softer rock away. The rocks
and pebbles in the water grind the soft
rock away to make a cliff face. At the
bottom of the waterfall they make a
deep pool called a plunge pool.

▶ High in the
mountains, streams join
to form the headwater of a
river. From here the river flows
through the mountains then more slowly
across the plains to the sea.

◀ Waterfalls may only be a few centimetres high, or come
crashing over a cliff with a massive drop. Angel Falls in
Venezuela form the highest falls in the world. One of the drops
is an amazing 807 metres.

142 A river changes as it flows to the
sea. Rivers begin in hills and mountains.
They are narrow and flow quickly there.
When the river flows through flatter land it
becomes wider and slow-moving. It makes
loops called meanders which may separate
and form oxbow lakes. Where the river meets
the sea is the river mouth. It may be a wide
channel called an estuary or a group of
sandy islands called a delta.

Headwater

145 Lakes form in hollows in the ground. The hollows may be left when glaciers melt or when plates in the crust split open. Some lakes form when a landslide makes a dam across a river.

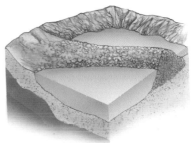

143 A lake can form in the crater of a volcano. A few crater lakes have formed in craters left by meteorites that hit Earth long ago.

▲ A landslide has fallen into the river and blocked the flow of water to make a lake.

144 Some lake water may be brightly coloured. The colours are made by tiny organisms called algae or by minerals dissolved in the water.

▼ Most lakes are just blue but some are green, pink, red or even white. The Laguna Colorado in Chile is red due to tiny organisms (creatures) that live in the water.

▲ A volcano can sometimes form in a lake inside a crater.

Rivers and waterfalls

146 The Earth is laced with thousands of rivers. As well as allowing the rain that falls on the land to drain away. Rivers also provide people and animals with drinking water and a place to wash, swim and fish. A waterfall is a place where a river flows over a rocky ledge and pours down to a lower level.

▼ This aerial photo of the River Amazon shows how it twists and loops as it flows through the Amazon rainforest in South America.

147 The world's longest river is the Nile, in Africa. It starts in the area near Lake Victoria and flows north to Egypt, where it opens into the Mediterranean Sea. The journey covers 6700 kilometres, and about 3470 cubic metres of water flows out of the Nile every second. The Nile provides water, a transport route, and fishing for millions of people. If it wasn't for the Nile, the civilization of ancient Egypt could not have existed.

148 Although the Nile is the longest river, the Amazon is the biggest. The Amazon flows from west to east across South America, and empties into the Atlantic Ocean. It carries 58 times as much water as the Nile, and about 200,000 cubic metres flow out of it each second. In some places, the Amazon is an amazing 60 kilometres wide.

150 Rivers can cut through solid rock. Over thousands of years, as a river flows, it wears away the rock around it. If the stone is quite soft, the river can carve a deep, steep-sided valley, or gorge. The Grand Canyon in Arizona, USA, is a massive gorge cut by the Colorado River. It is about 450 kilometres long, and in areas it is up to 29 kilometres wide and 1.8 kilometres deep.

▼ At Angel Falls, the world's highest waterfall, the water spreads out into a misty spray as it plunges down the cliff.

▲ Part of the Grand Canyon, with the Colorado River visible at the bottom of a deep gorge.

149 Angel Falls in Venezuela is the world's highest waterfall, spilling over a drop 979 metres high. It flows off the side of a very high, flat-topped mountain. Although it's the world's highest waterfall, it's not the biggest. Many waterfalls are much wider and carry more water – including Niagara Falls in North America and Victoria Falls in Africa.

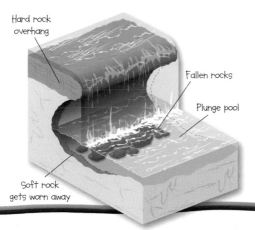

Hard rock overhang

Fallen rocks

Plunge pool

Soft rock gets worn away

◄ A waterfall forms where a river flows from hard rock onto softer rock. The softer rock is worn away faster, while the overhanging ledge of hard rock gradually crumbles away. Over time, the waterfall retreats, or moves upstream.

Record-breaking lakes

151 The Caspian Sea in central Asia is actually the world's biggest lake! It covers 378,000 square kilometres. It isn't connected to true seas and oceans, but because it's so big, and is salty like the sea, some experts say it isn't a proper lake, either. The world's biggest freshwater (non-salty) lake is Lake Superior, in the USA and Canada.

▼ A picture of the Caspian Sea taken from space. Swirling clouds of sediment (sand and mud) and plankton (tiny plants and animals) can be seen.

Plankton and sediment

152 The Dead Sea in Israel is another lake that is referred to as a sea. At 400 metres below sea level, it is the lowest lake in the world. The Dead Sea is very salty because no rivers flow out of it. All the salts and minerals that are washed into it remain there as the water evaporates in the Sun's heat. In fact the Dead Sea is nine times saltier than the real sea. It gets its name because no fish or other animals can live in such salty water.

153 The world's deepest lake is Lake Baikal in Russia. At its deepest point, it's 1700 metres deep. Because of this, it contains far more water than any other lake in the world. Twenty percent of all the unfrozen fresh water on Earth is in Lake Baikal.

▲ The high levels of salt in the Dead Sea mean that people can float easily in the water.

QUIZ

1. Which is the biggest freshwater lake?
2. Which is the deepest lake?
3. Which is the saltiest lake?
4. In which lake might a monster live?

Answers:
1. Lake Superior 2. Lake Baikal 3. The Dead Sea 4. Loch Ness

154 The largest body of fresh water is found in North America. On the border between the United States and Canada are the Great Lakes. They contain one-fifth of the world's fresh water – a staggering 22.8 quadrillion litres!

CANADA

Lake Superior

Lake Huron

Lake Michigan

Lake Ontario

Lake Erie

UNITED STATES

155 Many lakes around the world are believed to be home to mysterious monsters. According to legend, a monster that looks similar to a plesiosaur lives in Loch Ness in Scotland, UK. Plesiosaurs were prehistoric water reptiles that lived at the same time as the dinosaurs. Scientists think they became extinct (died out) 65 million years ago. However some people believe they may still live in Loch Ness.

◀ The five Great Lakes are situated in the USA and Canada. The biggest is Lake Superior, followed by Huron, Michigan, Erie and Ontario.

Cavernous caves

156 Some caves are made from a tube of lava. As lava moves down the side of a volcano, its surface cools down quickly. The cold lava becomes solid but below, the lava remains warm and keeps on flowing. Under the solid surface a tube may form in which liquid lava flows. When the tube empties, a cave is formed.

▲ A cave made by lava is so large that people can walk through it without having to bend down.

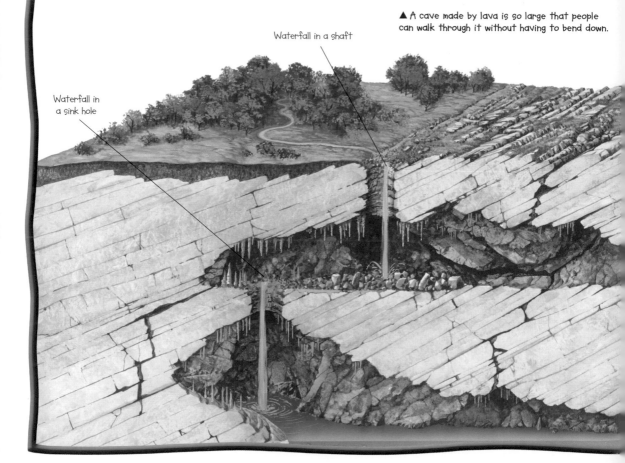

Waterfall in a shaft

Waterfall in a sink hole

1. Water seeps through cracks in rock

157 When rain falls on limestone it becomes a cave-maker. Rainwater can mix with carbon dioxide to form an acid strong enough to attack limestone and make it dissolve. Underground, the action of the rainwater makes caves in which streams and lakes can be found.

▶ Water runs through the caves in limestone rock and makes pools and streams. In wet weather it may flood the caves.

2. Underground stream carves into rock

▼ Water flows through the cracks in limestone and makes them wider to form caves. The horizontal caves are called galleries and the vertical caves are called shafts.

3. Large cave system develops

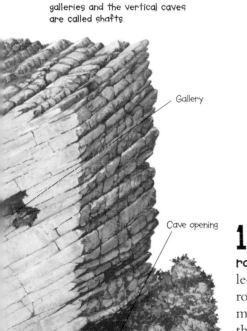

Gallery

Cave opening

I DON'T BELIEVE IT!
The longest stalactite is 59 metres long. The tallest stalagmite is 32 metres tall.

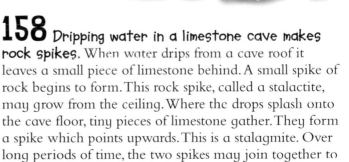

158 Dripping water in a limestone cave makes rock spikes. When water drips from a cave roof it leaves a small piece of limestone behind. A small spike of rock begins to form. This rock spike, called a stalactite, may grow from the ceiling. Where the drops splash onto the cave floor, tiny pieces of limestone gather. They form a spike which points upwards. This is a stalagmite. Over long periods of time, the two spikes may join together to form a column of rock.

Dry deserts

QUIZ

Which of these things would be useful if you were lost in the desert?
1. Mirror 2. Woolly blanket
3. Swimming costume
4. Umbrella

Answers:
1, 2 and 4. You should not wear
swimming gear in case of sunburn.

▶ The Namib Desert in the southwest of Africa contains some of the biggest sand dunes in the world.

159 Deserts occur in places where it's hard for rain to reach. Most rain comes from clouds that form over the sea and blow onto the land. If there's a big mountain range, the clouds never reach the other side. An area called a rainshadow desert forms. Deserts also form in the middle of continents. The land there is so far from the sea, rainclouds rarely reach it.

160 The world's biggest desert used to be a swamp! The Sahara desert takes up most of northern Africa. It is made up of 9 million square kilometres of dry sand, pebbles and boulders. There are some oases too, where freshwater springs flow out of the ground. Animal bones and objects left by ancient peoples show that around 6000 years ago, the Sahara desert was green and swampy. Lots of hippos, crocodiles and humans lived there.

▼ These sand piles show the relative sizes of the world's biggest deserts.

Kalahari Desert
520,000 km²

Gobi Desert
1,040,000 km²

Arabian Desert
1,300,000 km²

Australian Desert
3,800,000 km²

Sahara
9,269,000 km²

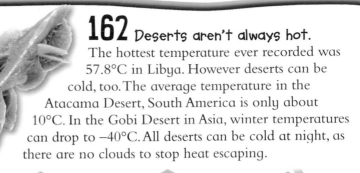

162 Deserts aren't always hot.

The hottest temperature ever recorded was 57.8°C in Libya. However deserts can be cold, too. The average temperature in the Atacama Desert, South America is only about 10°C. In the Gobi Desert in Asia, winter temperatures can drop to −40°C. All deserts can be cold at night, as there are no clouds to stop heat escaping.

▲ Desert roses aren't plants. They occur when desert minerals, such as gypsum, combine with sand to form crystals.

▶ Sand dunes form in different shapes and patterns, depending on the type of wind and sand in the desert. The blue arrows indicate the wind direction.

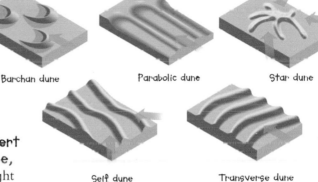

Barchan dune   Parabolic dune   Star dune

Seif dune   Transverse dune

161 The world's driest desert is the Atacama Desert in Chile, South America.

This desert is right next to the sea! It formed because in South America, rainclouds blow from east to west. They drop their rain on the Amazon rainforest, but cannot get past the Andes mountains. On the other side of the Andes, next to the Pacific Ocean, is the Atacama Desert. It is so dry that people who died there 9000 years ago have been preserved as mummies.

163 Even in dry deserts, there is water if you know where to look.

Desert plants, such as cactuses store water in their stems, leaves or spines. When rain does fall, it seeps into the ground and stays there. Desert people and animals chew desert plants or dig into the ground to find enough water.

▶ An oasis is a freshwater spring in a desert. Oases form when water stored deep underground meets a barrier of rock that it can't soak through, and rises to the desert surface.

Fantastic forests

164 There are three main kinds of forest. They are coniferous, temperate and tropical forests. The main forest regions are shown on the world map below.

▲ This map shows the major areas of forest in the world:
① Coniferous forest ② Temperate forest
③ Tropical forest

165 Coniferous trees form huge forests around the northern part of the planet. They have long, green, needle-like leaves covered in wax. These trees stay in leaf throughout the year. In winter, the wax helps snow slide off the leaves so that sunlight can reach them to keep them alive. Coniferous trees produce seeds in cones. These are eaten by squirrels.

166 Most trees in temperate forests have flat, broad leaves and need large amounts of water to keep them alive. In winter, the trees cannot get enough water from the frozen ground, so they lose their leaves and grow new ones in spring.

◀ Temperate forests are found in much of Europe and North America. In autumn, the leaves change colour before they fall in winter.

QUIZ

1. How many kinds of forest are there?

2. Which tree forms forests in the north?

3. What shape are leaves in temperate forests?

Answers:
1. Three 2. Conifer 3. Flat and broad

167 Many animals live in temperate forests, from tiny ants and frogs to large bears and deer. They are able to find plenty to eat here. Rabbits, foxes, mice and deer live on the woodland floor while squirrels, woodpeckers and owls live in the trees.

What is a rainforest?

168 **The third type of forest is a rainforest.** Lots of rain falls here every year – usually more than 2000 millimetres. They are filled with enormous, broad-leaved trees and a bewildering collection of living things. Rainforests usually grow in warm, steamy parts of the world.

169 **Trees provide habitats (homes) for millions of rainforest animals and plants.** Much of the wildlife in these forests cannot survive anywhere else – just one of the reasons why people want to make sure rainforests are kept safe.

Toco toucan

170 **Of all the different habitats found on Earth, rainforests have the biggest range of living things.** They are home to more than 80 percent of all insects and a single rainforest in South America has 18,000 different types of plant. The word 'biodiversity' is used to describe the range of living things that live in one habitat.

Tapir

EMERGENT LAYER

CANOPY

UNDERSTOREY

FOREST FLOOR

Queen Alexandra's birdwing butterfly

◄ Most animals and plants live in the rainforest canopy layer. The understorey is very gloomy because not much sunlight reaches it.

I DON'T BELIEVE IT!

People who live in rainforests can build their entire homes from plant materials. Walls are made from palm stems or bamboo and leaves can be woven to make roofs and floors.

Red-eyed tree frog

171 Rainforests have four main layers. The bottom layers are the dark, dank forest floor and understorey, where the shortest plants live. Here, bugs, frogs, fungi and many other living things thrive. The middle layer is the forest canopy and the top layer is the emergent layer. This is where the tallest trees poke up above a blanket of green leaves. The trees are home to vines, mosses, monkeys, lizards, snakes, insects and thousands of species (types) of bird.

The ends of the Earth

172 The Earth is round, but it has two 'ends' – the North Pole and the South Pole. The Earth is constantly spinning around an imaginary line called the axis. At the ends of this axis are the poles. Here, it is always cold, because the poles are so far from the Sun.

▼ The position of the poles means they receive little heat from the Sun.

North Pole

ARCTIC REGION

ANTARCTIC REGION

Axis

South Pole

173 At the North Pole, the average temperature is –20°C. At the South pole, it's much colder – about –50°C. It's hard for humans to survive in this cold. Water droplets in your breath would freeze on your face. If you were to touch something made of metal with your bare hand, it would freeze onto your skin and stick there.

▼ There are no towns or cities in Antarctica as it's so cold, but people do go there to explore and to study nature. They sometimes use snowmobiles to travel around on the snow and ice.

174 The area around the North Pole is called the Arctic. Parts of Europe, Asia and North America reach into the Arctic, but most of it is actually the Arctic Ocean. Many animals live in the Arctic. Polar bears live on the ice and Arctic foxes live on the land. The sea around the pole is mainly frozen. Scientists have found the ice is melting because of global warming – pollution in the air is trapping heat close to the Earth, making it warm up.

175 The Antarctic is mostly made up of a huge continent, called Antarctica. Much of it is covered in a layer of solid ice up to 4.7 kilometres thick. The Antarctic is colder than the Arctic because its thick ice and mountains make it very high, and the air is colder higher up. Because Antarctica is so big, the seas around it cannot warm it very much. Little wildlife lives here, but it is home to lots of penguins.

▲ There are several different species (types) of penguins living in Antarctica. These emperor penguins and their chicks are the largest species

176 Explorers didn't make it to the poles until the 20th century. US explorer Robert Peary and his team reached the North Pole in 1909. Soon afterwards, two explorers raced to reach the South Pole. Norwegian Roald Amundsen arrived first, in December 1911. British explorer Robert Scott arrived one month later – but he and his men died on their way home.

I DON'T BELIEVE IT!

Explorers at the poles sometimes lose body parts. If they let their fingers, toes or nose get too cold, they can get frostbite. Blood stops flowing to these parts, and they can turn black and fall off.

Glaciers and icebergs

177 About two percent of the water in the world is permanently frozen as ice. The ice is found at the chilly polar regions, and on high mountains where the air is freezing cold. On steep slopes, the ice creeps downhill, like a very slow river. This kind of ice 'river' is called a glacier. On high mountains, glaciers flow downhill until they reach warmer air and start to melt. At the poles, many glaciers flow into the sea.

▶ A glacier develops deep cracks called crevasses as it moves downhill. The lower end of a glacier is called the 'snout'.

Snout

Crevasse

178 One of the world's biggest glaciers, not including the ice at the poles, is the Siachen Glacier in the Himalayas. It is 78 kilometres long and, in places, its ice is over 100 metres thick. India and Pakistan have been fighting a war over who the glacier belongs to since 1984. It has been home to hundreds of soldiers for more than 20 years.

▼ Instead of melting on the way down a mountain, this glacier in Prince William Sound, Alaska is flowing into a fjord.

179 Glaciers have shaped the Earth. As a glacier flows down a mountain, the heavy ice pushes and scrapes at the soil and rocks. This carves a huge, U-shaped valley, known as a glacial valley. 20,000 years ago, when the Earth was in an Ice Age, glaciers covered much more of the land than they do now. Since then, many have melted, revealing their glacial valleys

▲ Due to global warming, glaciers and icebergs are slowly melting and breaking into the sea.

▼ These penguins are on an iceberg in the Southern Ocean, close to Antarctica. A huge mass of ice can be seen below the water's surface.

180 Icebergs are a problem for ships. As an iceberg floats, only about one-tenth of it sticks up out of the sea. The rest is below the surface. Many icebergs have odd, lumpy shapes. This means that a ship can bump into the underwater part of an iceberg, even if the part above water looks far away. Icebergs have damaged and sunk many ships, including the famous ocean liner *Titanic* in 1912.

181 Icebergs exist because of glaciers. At the poles, glaciers flow downhill to the sea. There, the ice is slowly pushed out into the water, where it starts to float. Every so often, a large chunk of the glacier breaks off and floats away into the sea. This is an iceberg and it drifts until it melts.

Amazing oceans

182 About 70 percent of the Earth's surface is covered by ocean. The oceans cover about 361 million square kilometres and they are all connected. The average depth of the ocean is 3750 metres. Over 90 percent of the Earth's species (types) of living things live in the oceans.

184 If you were sitting at the bottom of the deep ocean, you'd be squashed flat. At great depths, the weight of all the water above presses from all sides. At the bottom of Challenger Deep, the water pressure is more than 1000 times stronger than at the surface. It's cold, too – only just above freezing point. People can only go there inside specially built diving machines with thick walls that can resist the pressure and cold.

183 The deepest point in all the world's oceans is called Challenger Deep. It is in the Mariana Trench in the Pacific Ocean and is 10,923 metres deep – almost 11 kilometres. A tower of 3500 elephants, one of top of the next, could stand in it without touching the surface. In 1960, two explorers, Jacques Piccard and Don Walsh, visited the bottom of Challenger Deep in a diving vessel called *Trieste*.

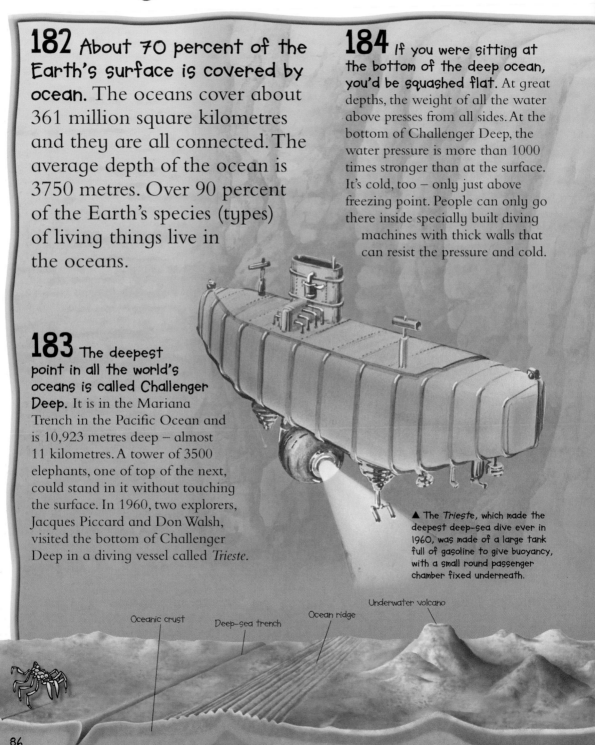

▲ The *Trieste*, which made the deepest deep-sea dive ever in 1960, was made of a large tank full of gasoline to give buoyancy, with a small round passenger chamber fixed underneath.

Oceanic crust

Deep-sea trench

Ocean ridge

Underwater volcano

Challenger Deep

ARCTIC OCEAN

PACIFIC OCEAN

ATLANTIC OCEAN

INDIAN OCEAN

SOUTHERN OCEAN

▶ This map shows the ridges, trenches, plains and mountains within the world's oceans, as well as those on land.

185 One of the world's most extreme environments is found under the sea. At hydrothermal vents, incredibly hot water bubbles out from inside the Earth at temperatures of up to 400°C. Around the hot vents live unusual creatures such as giant tubeworms and sea spiders, and tiny bacteria that feed on the minerals dissolved in the hot water. Hydrothermal vents were only discovered in 1977.

186 Sea level — the height of the sea — is about the same all over the world. It changes over time, as the Earth's temperature varies. About 20,000 years ago, during the Ice Age, the sea level was 130 metres lower than it is now. At the moment, the sea level is rising because global warming is making ice melt at the poles.

▼ A cross-section of the seabed. It usually slopes gently away from the shore, then drops steeply down to a flat plain.

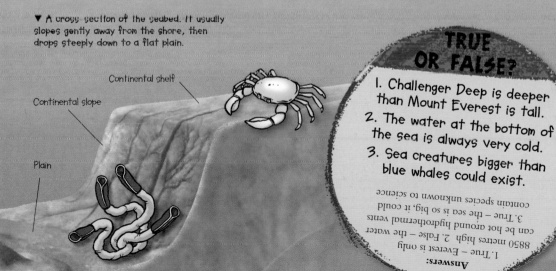

Continental shelf

Continental slope

Plain

TRUE OR FALSE?

1. Challenger Deep is deeper than Mount Everest is tall.
2. The water at the bottom of the sea is always very cold.
3. Sea creatures bigger than blue whales could exist.

Answers:
1.True — Everest is only 8850 metres high. 2. False — the water can be hot around hydrothermal vents 3.True — the sea is so big, it could contain species unknown to science

Tides and shores

187 **The sea level rises and falls twice each day along the coast.** This is known as high and low tides. Tides happen because of the pull of the Moon, which lifts water from the part of the Earth's surface facing it.

▼ At high tide, the sea rises up the shore and dumps seaweed, shells and drift wood. Most coasts have two high tides and two low tides every day.

High tides happen at the same time each day on opposite sides of the Earth

At high tide the water level rises

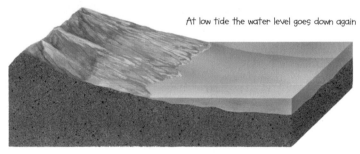

At low tide the water level goes down again

188 **Spring tides are especially high.** They occur twice a month, when the Moon is in line with the Earth and the Sun. Then, the Sun's pulling force joins the Moon's and seawater is lifted higher than usual. The opposite happens when the Moon and Sun are at right angles to the Earth. Then, their pulling powers work against each other causing weak neap tides – the lowest high tides and low tides.

◀ Neap tides occur when the Sun and Moon are at right angles to each other and pulling in different directions.

▶ Spring tides occur when the Sun and the Moon are lined up and pulling together.

190 The sea is strong enough to carve into rock. Pounding waves batter coastlines and erode, or wear away, the rock. Sand can also be found on bars and spits, as well as beaches. It is made up of grains of worn-down rock and shell. Sand collects on shorelines and spits, but also forms on offshore beaches called sand bars. Spits are narrow ridges of worn sand and pebbles.

◀ Waves can create amazing shapes such as pillars called sea stacks.

▼ The stilt-like roots of mangrove trees take in both air and water.

189 Some shores are swampy. This makes the border between land and sea hard to pinpoint. Muddy coastlines include tropical mangrove swamps that are flooded by salty water from the sea.

I DON'T BELIEVE IT!

The biggest tsunami was taller than five Statues of Liberty! It hit the Japanese Ryuku Islands in 1771.

Extreme earthquakes

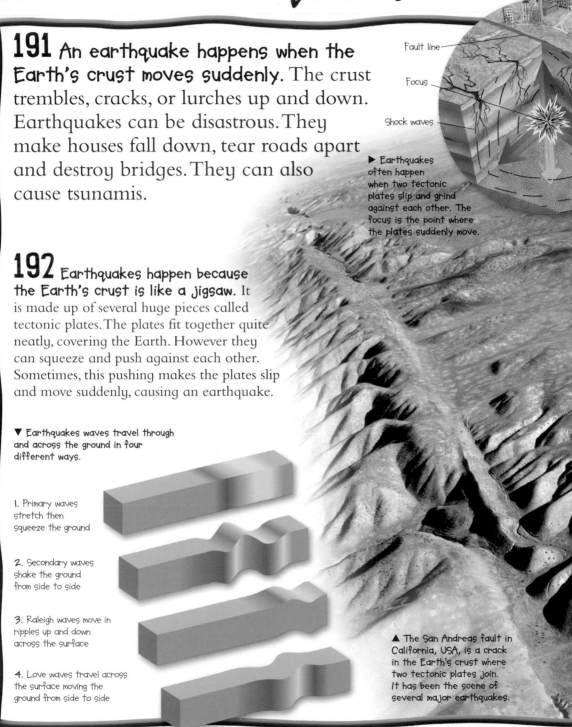

191 **An earthquake happens when the Earth's crust moves suddenly.** The crust trembles, cracks, or lurches up and down. Earthquakes can be disastrous. They make houses fall down, tear roads apart and destroy bridges. They can also cause tsunamis.

Fault line

Focus

Shock waves

▶ Earthquakes often happen when two tectonic plates slip and grind against each other. The focus is the point where the plates suddenly move.

192 Earthquakes happen because the Earth's crust is like a jigsaw. It is made up of several huge pieces called tectonic plates. The plates fit together quite neatly, covering the Earth. However they can squeeze and push against each other. Sometimes, this pushing makes the plates slip and move suddenly, causing an earthquake.

▼ Earthquakes waves travel through and across the ground in four different ways.

1. Primary waves stretch then squeeze the ground

2. Secondary waves shake the ground from side to side

3. Raleigh waves move in ripples up and down across the surface

4. Love waves travel across the surface moving the ground from side to side

▲ The San Andreas fault in California, USA, is a crack in the Earth's crust where two tectonic plates join. It has been the scene of several major earthquakes.

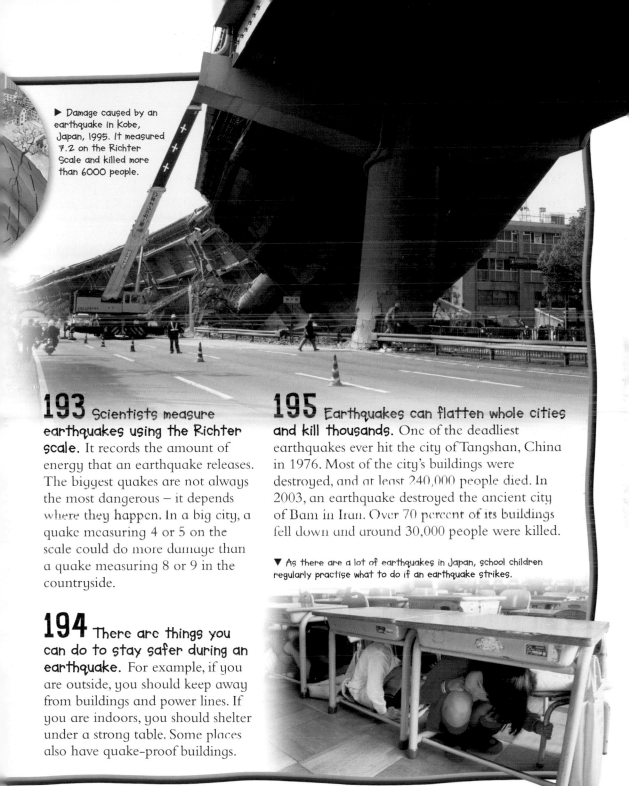

▶ Damage caused by an earthquake in Kobe, Japan, 1995. It measured 7.2 on the Richter Scale and killed more than 6000 people.

193 Scientists measure earthquakes using the Richter scale. It records the amount of energy that an earthquake releases. The biggest quakes are not always the most dangerous – it depends where they happen. In a big city, a quake measuring 4 or 5 on the scale could do more damage than a quake measuring 8 or 9 in the countryside.

194 There are things you can do to stay safer during an earthquake. For example, if you are outside, you should keep away from buildings and power lines. If you are indoors, you should shelter under a strong table. Some places also have quake-proof buildings.

195 Earthquakes can flatten whole cities and kill thousands. One of the deadliest earthquakes ever hit the city of Tangshan, China in 1976. Most of the city's buildings were destroyed, and at least 240,000 people died. In 2003, an earthquake destroyed the ancient city of Bam in Iran. Over 70 percent of its buildings fell down and around 30,000 people were killed.

▼ As there are a lot of earthquakes in Japan, school children regularly practise what to do if an earthquake strikes.

Terrifying tsunamis

196 A tsunami is a giant wave, or series of waves. Tsunamis form when a large amount of water in a sea or lake is moved suddenly. This sets up a circular wave, a bit like the ripples you see when you throw a pebble into a pond. The wave then zooms outwards until it hits land.

▶ A tsunami begins as fast-travelling waves far out at sea. As they approach land, the waves slow down, but become much taller.

As the tall tsunami reaches shallow water, it surges forwards onto the shore

▼ A tsunami wave crashes onto the promenade on Ao Nang Beach, Thailand, in 2004. The power and speed of a tsunami can easily sweep away cars and even entire buildings.

197 When a tsunami hits, it can smash the coast to smithereens. Out in the ocean, tsunami waves are very long, low and fast-moving. However as a tsunami moves into shallow water, the wave slows down. All the water in it piles up, forming a powerful wall of water, often between 10 and 30 metres high. As it crashes onto the shore, it can flood towns, tear up trees and sweep away cars, buildings and people.

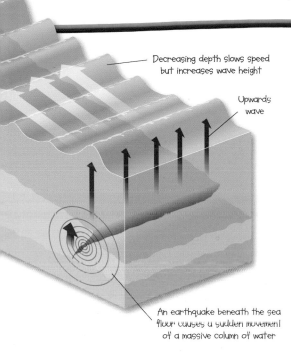

Decreasing depth slows speed but increases wave height

Upwards wave

An earthquake beneath the sea floor causes a sudden movement of a massive column of water

199 The tallest tsunami was higher than a skyscraper. It occurred at Lituya Bay, in Alaska, USA, in 1958. An earthquake triggered a landslide, and rock and soil plunged into the sea. A giant tsunami, more than 500 metres high, zoomed down the bay. Luckily, there were no towns there, but the wave stripped the coast of trees. A giant tsunami such as this is sometimes called a mega tsunami.

198 Most tsunamis are caused by earthquakes under the sea. A section of seabed shifts suddenly and the water above it is jolted upwards. Tsunamis can also happen when a landslide or volcanic eruption throws a large amount of rock into the sea, pushing the water aside. This happened when Krakatau, a volcano in Indonesia, erupted in 1883. The tsunamis it caused killed 36,000 people.

200 A tsunami in the Indian Ocean in 2004 was the deadliest ever recorded. It was caused by a huge undersea earthquake near the coast of Indonesia. Tsunami waves spread across the ocean and swamped coasts in Indonesia, Thailand, Sri Lanka, India and the Maldive Islands. Around 230,000 people were killed.

▼ The town of Kalutara in Sri Lanka, shown in satellite images before (left) and after (right), being swamped by the deadly 2004 tsunami.

Our atmosphere

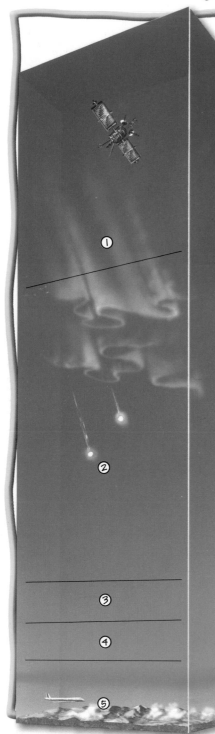

201 Our planet is wrapped in a blanket of air. We call this blanket the atmosphere. It stretches hundreds of kilometres above our heads. The blanket keeps in heat, especially at night when part of the planet faces away from the Sun. During the day, the blanket becomes a sunscreen instead. Without an atmosphere, there would be no weather.

202 Most weather happens in the troposphere. This is the layer of atmosphere that stretches from the ground to around 10 kilometres above your head. The higher in the troposphere you go, the cooler the air. Because of this, clouds are most likely to form here. Clouds with flattened tops show just where the troposphere meets the next layer, the stratosphere.

KEY
① Exosphere 190 to 960 kilometres
② Thermosphere 80 to 190 kilometres
③ Mesosphere 50 to 80 kilometres
④ Stratosphere 10 to 50 kilometres
⑤ Troposphere 0 to 10 kilometres

◀ The atmosphere stretches right into space. Scientists have split it into five layers, or spheres, such as the troposphere.

203 **Air just cannot keep still.** Tiny particles in air, called molecules, are always bumping into each other! The more they smash into each other, the greater the air pressure. Generally, there are more smashes lower in the troposphere, because the pull of gravity makes the molecules fall towards the Earth's surface. The higher you go, the lower the air pressure, and the less oxygen there is in the air.

▶ At high altitudes there is less oxygen. That is why mountaineers often wear breathing equipment.

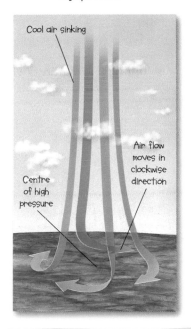

High pressure

Cool air sinking

Air flow moves in clockwise direction

Centre of high pressure

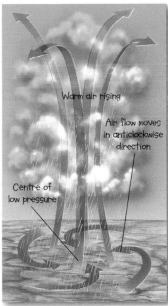

Low pressure

Warm air rising

Air flow moves in anticlockwise direction

Centre of low pressure

204 **Warmth makes air move.** When heat from the Sun warms the molecules in air, they move faster and spread out more. This makes the air lighter, so it rises in the sky, creating low pressure. As it gets higher, the air cools. The molecules slow down and become heavier again, so they start to sink back to Earth.

◀ A high pressure weather system gives us warmer weather, while low pressure gives us cooler more unsettled weather.

95

Clouds and rain

205 Rain comes from the sea. As the Sun heats the surface of the ocean, some seawater turns into water vapour and rises into the air. As it rises, it cools and turns back into water droplets. Lots of water droplets make clouds. The droplets join together to make bigger and bigger drops that eventually fall as rain. Some rain is soaked up by the land, but a lot finds its way back to the sea. This is called the water cycle.

RAIN GAUGE

You will need:

jam jar   waterproof marker pen
ruler   notebook   pen

Put the jar outside. At the same time each day, mark the rainwater level on the jar with your pen. At the end of a week, empty the jar. Measure and record how much rain falls each day and over the whole week.

206 Some mountains are so tall that their summits (peaks) are hidden by cloud. Really huge mountains even affect the weather. When moving air hits a mountain slope it is forced upwards. As it travels up, the temperature drops, and clouds form.

◀ Warm, rising air may be forced up the side of a mountain. At a certain level, lower temperatures make the water form clouds.

▼ The water cycle involves all the water on Earth. Water vapour rises from lakes, rivers and the sea to form clouds in the atmosphere.

④ Rain falls, filling rivers

③ Water is given off by forests

② Clouds form

① Water evaporates from the sea

⑤ The rivers run back to the sea, and the cycle starts again

▼ Virga happens when rain reaches a layer of dry air. The rain droplets turn back into water vapour in mid-air, and seem to disappear.

207 **Some rain never reaches the ground.** The raindrops turn back into water vapour because they hit a layer of super-dry air. You can actually see the drops falling like a curtain from the cloud, but the curtain stops in mid-air. This type of weather is called virga.

208 Clouds gobble up heat and keep the Earth's temperature regular. From each 2-metre-square patch of land, clouds can remove the equivalent energy created by a 60-Watt light bulb.

Lightning strikes

209 **Lightning is a giant spark of electricity.** It happens when tiny droplets of water and ice swirl around inside a stormcloud. This makes the cloud develop a strong electrical charge. Eventually, a spark jumps between the base of the cloud and the ground. This allows electricity to flow, releasing the electrical charge. We see the spark as a flash or 'bolt' of lightning.

Negative charge

Negative charge from the cloud meets a positive charge from the ground to create lightning

Positive charge

▲ During a thunderstorm, negative electrical charge builds up at the base of a cloud, while the ground has a positive charge. A lightning spark jumps between them to release the charge.

210 **Thunder and lightning go together.** In fact, thunder is the sound of lightning. When a lightning bolt jumps through the air, it is very hot. It can reach a temperature of 30,000°C. It heats the air around it very quickly. Heat makes air expand (get bigger). It expands so suddenly that it pushes against the air around it, and creates a shock wave. The wave travels through the air and our ears detect it as a loud boom.

I DON'T BELIEVE IT!

At any one time, there are around 2000 thunderstorms happening on Earth. Lightning strikes somewhere in the world about 100 times every second.

211 Long ago, people used to think lightning was a punishment sent by their gods. However from the 1500s, scientists began learning about electricity and how it worked. Around 1750, US scientist Benjamin Franklin found that lightning was a kind of electricity. He invented the lightning conductor to protect buildings from lightning damage. It is a metal pole that can be fixed to tall buildings. If lightning strikes, the electrical charge runs down the pole and down a metal wire, then flows safely into the ground.

▶ Fulgarites occur when lightning strikes sand. The high temperature makes the sand melt. It eventually cools into hollow tubes.

◀ You can clearly see the lightning conductor on the spire of this cathedral in Liverpool, UK.

212 Lightning can strike the same person twice – or more. A US park ranger named Roy Sullivan was struck by lightning seven times during his life. It is quite rare for lightning to strike people, and most of those who are struck, survive. However lightning does kill over 2000 people around the world each year.

213 Lightning can make glass. Glass is made by heating up sand. When lightning strikes in a sandy desert or on a sandy beach, this happens naturally. At the place where the lightning hits the ground, it creates a tubelike tunnel of glass in the sand. These natural glass tubes are called fulgurites.

Extreme snow and ice

214 An ice storm isn't stormy – but it is dangerous. Cold rain falls onto freezing cold surfaces. The rain freezes solid, forming a thick layer of ice on the ground, trees and other objects. Ice storms cause 'black ice'– invisible ice on roads that causes accidents. Ice-laden trees fall down, breaking power lines and cutting off roads.

◀ Overburdened by the weight of ice from an ice storm, this tree has collapsed across a road.

▲ An avalanche thunders downhill in Silverton, Colorado, USA. This avalanche was started deliberately by dropping explosives, in order to make the mountains safer for visitors.

215 An avalanche is a massive pile of snow crashing down a mountainside. Avalanches can happen whenever lots of snow piles up at the top of a slope. They can be deadly if the snow lands on top of mountain walkers or skiers. Sometimes, big avalanches bury whole houses or even whole villages.

216 A blizzard, or snowstorm, is even more dangerous than an ice storm. If you get caught outdoors in a blizzard, it's very easy to get lost. Falling snow fills the air, making it impossible to see. Thick snowdrifts build up, making it hard to walk or drive. People have lost their way and died in blizzards, just a short distance from safety.

▲ Ice can form beautiful crystal patterns as it freezes across a window or car windscreen.

QUIZ

Which of these things could help you survive if you were lost in the snow?

1. Woolly hat
2. Magazine
3. Chocolate
4. Torch
5. Metal camping plate

Answer:
All of them!

217 **If you get stuck in a blizzard or avalanche, a hole in the snow can keep you warm.** Snow is a great insulator as heat does not flow through it very well. If you curl up inside a hole dug in the snow, it traps the heat from your body and keeps it close to you. Many people have survived blizzards by making snow holes.

218 **We put food in a freezer to keep it fresh – and the same thing happens in nature.** Snow and ice can stop dead bodies from rotting away. Woolly mammoths that lived 10,000 years ago have been dug out of the ice in northern Russia, perfectly preserved. In 1991, the body of a 5000-year-old man was found in the ice in mountains in Austria. He was nicknamed Ötzi the Iceman.

Howling hurricanes

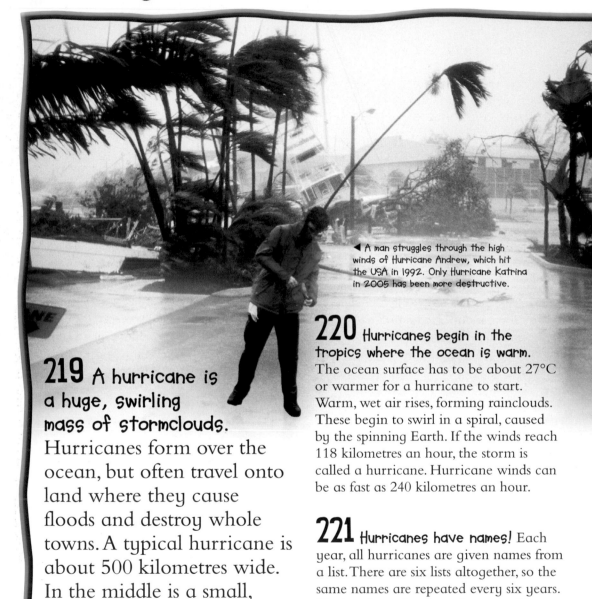

◄ A man struggles through the high winds of Hurricane Andrew, which hit the USA in 1992. Only Hurricane Katrina in 2005 has been more destructive.

219 **A hurricane is a huge, swirling mass of stormclouds.** Hurricanes form over the ocean, but often travel onto land where they cause floods and destroy whole towns. A typical hurricane is about 500 kilometres wide. In the middle is a small, circular area with no clouds in it, about 70 kilometres wide. This is called the 'eye' of the hurricane.

220 **Hurricanes begin in the tropics where the ocean is warm.** The ocean surface has to be about 27°C or warmer for a hurricane to start. Warm, wet air rises, forming rainclouds. These begin to swirl in a spiral, caused by the spinning Earth. If the winds reach 118 kilometres an hour, the storm is called a hurricane. Hurricane winds can be as fast as 240 kilometres an hour.

221 **Hurricanes have names!** Each year, all hurricanes are given names from a list. There are six lists altogether, so the same names are repeated every six years. If a hurricane becomes famous – like Hurricane Katrina in 2005 – the list is changed so that name does not reappear.

222 The word 'hurricane' is only used to describe storms in the Atlantic Ocean. The scientific name for this type of storm is a tropical cyclone. The same type of storm in the Indian Ocean is known as a cyclone, and in the Pacific Ocean it is called a typhoon.

▲ A satellite view from space showing a hurricane swirling across the Gulf of Mexico.

223 Hurricanes and other tropical cyclones can cause terrible disasters. When Hurricane Katrina struck the southern coast of the USA in August 2005, it damaged many cities on the coasts of Mississippi and Louisiana. In New Orleans, huge waves broke through the flood barriers and more than 80 percent of the city was flooded. The hurricane killed more than 1800 people and caused damage costing over $80 billion. The Bhola cyclone, which hit Bangladesh in 1970, killed over 300,000 people.

224 Scientists think hurricanes are getting worse. Global warming means that the Earth's temperature is rising, so the seas are getting warmer. This means that more hurricanes are likely. Hurricanes are also becoming bigger and more powerful, as there is more heat energy to fuel them.

▼ These buildings near Lake Pontchartrain, Louisiana, USA, were destroyed by Hurricane Katrina in 2005.

Twisting tornadoes

225 **Tornadoes are also called twisters.** A tornado is an incredibly powerful windstorm that twists around in a swirling 'vortex' shape. It forms a narrow funnel or tube, stretching from the clouds to the ground. Tornadoes often look dark because of all the dirt, dust and broken objects that they pick up as they travel across the land.

226 **You can sometimes tell when a tornado is coming, because the sky turns green.** Tornadoes usually develop from thunderclouds. Scientists are not sure exactly how they form. They think that as warm, damp air rises, drier, colder air is pulled in and begins to swirl around it. This creates a spinning tube of wind that moves along the ground. A tornado can travel at up to 80 kilometres an hour.

227 **Tornadoes contain some of the fastest winds on the planet.** Wind inside a tornado can move at up to 500 kilometres an hour. This powerful wind can cause terrible damage. Tornadoes smash buildings, tear off roofs, make bridges collapse, and suck out doors and windows. They can pick up people, animals and cars, and carry them through the air. In 2006, a tornado in Missouri, USA picked up 19-year-old Matt Suter and carried him nearly 400 metres. He survived with only cuts and bruises.

Cold front

Warm front

◀ Tornadoes often form where a front, or mass, of cold air meets warm air. They spin around each other and form a funnel shape.

TORNADO IN A BOTTLE

You will need:
2 plastic drinks bottles, the same size
water   sticky tape

1. Fill one of the bottles almost full with water.

2. Position the second bottle upside-down on top of the first, so that their necks join together. Tape them together firmly.

3. Turn both bottles over and swirl them around in a circle as fast as you can.

4. When you hold them still, you should see a tornado shape as the water forms a vortex.

▲ A large, terrifying tornado snakes down to the ground from the base of a big thundercloud.

228 Damaging tornadoes happen most often in Tornado Alley. This is an area that stretches across the middle of the USA, between the states of Texas and Illinois. Tornadoes are most common there in the tornado season, from April to August. The Great Tri-State Tornado of 1925 was one of the worst ever. It roared through Missouri, Illionois and Indiana, travelling 350 kilometres. It destroyed 15,000 homes and killed 695 people.

◀ The shaded area on this map shows the part of the USA known as Tornado Alley, where tornadoes are most common.

229 Sometimes, tornadoes occur in deserts, or over the sea. In sandy deserts, small tornadoes pick up sand and carry it along in a whirling tower. They are called sand devils or dust devils. Tornadoes over the sea can suck up water in the same way, and carry it for long distances. They are known as waterspouts.

Flooding the land

230 A flood happens when water overflows and covers what is normally land. Floods can be caused by rivers overflowing their banks after heavy rain. The sea can also flood the land with large waves or tsunamis. Floods can be useful – some rivers flood every year in the rainy season, bringing water and mud that make farmland moist and fertile. However most floods are bad news.

▲ A satellite image of the River Nile in Egypt flowing into the Mediterranean Sea. The green triangular area is the Nile Delta. The Nile used to flood each summer, spreading fertile silt across the land. These floods are now controlled by the Aswan Dam in southern Egypt.

▼ A woman carries a precious pot of clean drinking water through dirty floodwaters during a flood in Bangladesh in 1998.

231 Floods can cause death and destruction. When floodwater flows into houses, it fills them with mud, rubbish and sewage (smelly waste from drains and toilets). It ruins electrical appliances, carpets and furniture. After a flood, homes have to be completely cleaned out and repaired – costing huge amounts of money. Even worse, fast-flowing floodwater can sweep away people, cars and even buildings.

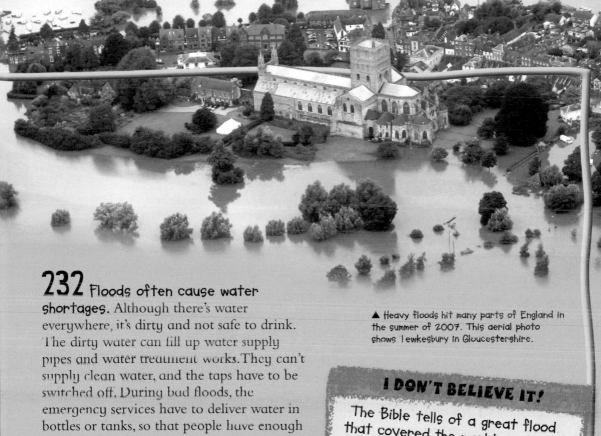

232 **Floods often cause water shortages.** Although there's water everywhere, it's dirty and not safe to drink. The dirty water can fill up water supply pipes and water treatment works. They can't supply clean water, and the taps have to be switched off. During bad floods, the emergency services have to deliver water in bottles or tanks, so that people have enough clean water to drink.

▲ Heavy floods hit many parts of England in the summer of 2007. This aerial photo shows Tewkesbury in Gloucestershire.

I DON'T BELIEVE IT!

The Bible tells of a great flood that covered the world in water. Some scientists think flood stories may be based on flooding that happened around 10,000 years ago, as sea levels rose when ice melted after the last Ice Age.

233 **More floods are coming.** Because of global warming, the Earth is heating up. In some areas, this means more water will evaporate into the air, causing more clouds and more rain. Global warming also means higher sea levels, so more areas of land are at risk of being flooded.

▼ This car was caught in a flash flood (a sudden, unexpected flood) in Texas, USA. Flash floods can wash entire towns away.

Disastrous droughts

▼ During drought conditions, the land becomes dry, hard and cracked.

234 A drought is a shortage of rainfall that leaves the land dry. Deserts hardly ever get rain, and are dry and dusty all the time. A drought happens when a place gets much less rain than usual. Scientists don't always know why weather patterns change. However, this can be caused by changes in the oceans. Every few years, a change in sea temperatures in the Pacific, called El Niño, affects weather around the world and causes droughts.

235 Droughts are disastrous for people, animals and plants. A shortage of rain means crops can't grow properly, and herds of animals can't get enough drinking water. So people face food and water shortages. Dried-out grass and trees can easily catch fire, and loose dust can blow up into blinding dust storms. Droughts can also cause wars, when people are forced to leave their lands and flock into other areas.

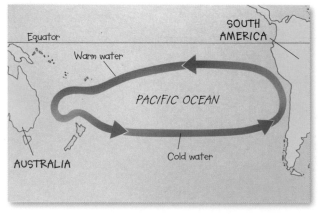

▲ El Niño is a warming of surface ocean waters in the eastern Pacific that can lead to flooding and drought around the world.

▲ Part of the Murray River in southern Australia, usually flowing with water, lies empty during a drought.

237 Droughts have always happened. They are mentioned in many ancient books, such as the Bible and the writings of the ancient Mesopotamians, who lived in the area around what is now Iraq. However, scientists think that today, global warming is making some droughts worse. As the world gets warmer, weather patterns are changing. Some areas, such as eastern Australia, are now having worse droughts than they used to.

236 The 'Dust Bowl' was a great drought disaster that hit the USA in the 1930s. Several years of drought dried out farm soil in the central states of the USA, such as Oklahoma and Kansas. It blew away in huge dust storms, and farmers could not grow their crops. Hundreds of thousands of people had to leave the area. Many trekked west in search of new lives and jobs.

TRUE OR FALSE?

1. Droughts make forest fires more likely.
2. The Dust Bowl is a volcano in the USA.
3. El Niño is a temperature change in the Indian Ocean.

Answers:
1. True. Droughts make forests drier so they burn more easily 2. False. The Dust Bowl was a drought 3. False El Niño is in the Pacific Ocean

◀ A massive dust storm about to engulf a farm during the Dust Bowl years. Caused by drought conditions, these storms devastated the American prairies.

Global warming

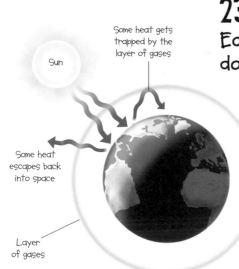

Sun

Some heat gets trapped by the layer of gases

Some heat escapes back into space

Layer of gases

▲ Global warming happens when greenhouse gases collect in the Earth's atmosphere. They let heat from the Sun through, but as it bounces back, it gets trapped close to the Earth, making the planet heat up.

238 Throughout its history, the Earth has warmed up and cooled down. Experts think that today's warming is down to humans – and it's happening faster than normal. Carbon dioxide and methane gases are released into the air as pollution. They are known as greenhouse gases and can stop the Sun's heat escaping from the atmosphere.

239 Global warming tells us that the climate is changing. Weather changes every day – we have hot days and cold days – but on average the climate is warming up. Scientists think that average temperatures have risen by one degree Celsius in the last 100 years, and that they will keep rising.

I DON'T BELIEVE IT!

Scientists think that sea levels could rise by one metre by 2100 – maybe even more. Three million years ago when the Earth was hotter, the sea was 200 metres higher than today. We could be heading that way again.

240 Warmer temperatures mean wilder weather. Wind happens when air is heated and gets lighter. It rises up and cold air is sucked in to replace it. Rain occurs when heat makes water in rivers and seas turn into vapour in the air. It rises up and forms rain clouds. Warmer temperatures mean more wind, rain and storms.

▼ The ice in the Arctic Ocean is melting so fast that scientists think over half of it could be gone by 2100.

ARCTIC OCEAN

KEY

Average area of sea covered by ice from 1980–2000

Predicted area of sea covered by ice for 2080–2100

▲ Huge chunks of ice often break off into the sea at Paradise Bay, at the Antarctic.

241 As the Earth heats up, its ice melts.
Vast areas of the Earth are covered in ice. It is found around the North and South Poles, and on high mountains. Now, because of global warming, more and more of this ice is melting. It turns into water and flows into the sea. Also, as the water gets warmer, it expands (gets bigger) and the sea takes up more space, making sea levels rise.

▶ Polar bears depend on large chunks of ice to hunt and rest on. Melting ice in the Arctic is making life much harder for them.

242 We pump greenhouse gases into the atmosphere because we burn fuels to make energy. Cars, planes and trains run on fuel, and we also burn it in power stations to produce electricity. The main fuels – coal, oil and gas – are called fossil fuels because they formed underground over millions of years.

243 Fossil fuels are running out. Because they take so long to form, we are using up fossil fuels much faster than they can be replaced. Eventually, they will become so rare that it will be too expensive to find them. Experts think this will happen before the end of the 21st century.

▶ Oil and natural gas formed from the remains of tiny prehistoric sea creatures that collected on the seabed. Layers of rock built up on top and squashed them. Over time, they became underground stores of oil, with pockets of gas above.

Oil platform drilling for oil and gas

Hard rock layer

Gas

Oil

Oil and gas move upwards through soft rock layers until reaching a hard rock layer

The layer of dead sea creatures is crushed by rock that forms above, and turns into oil and gas

Tiny sea creatures die and sink to the seabed

QUIZ

Which of these things are used to supply electricity?
A. Burning coal B. Wind
C. The flow of rivers
D. Hamsters on wheels E. Sunshine
F. The energy of earthquakes

Answers:
A, B, C and E. Hamsters could turn tiny turbines, but would make very little electricity. Earthquakes contain vast amounts of energy, but we have not found a way to use it.

244 One thing we can do is find other fuels. Besides fossil fuels, we can burn fuels that come from plants. For example, the rape plant contains oil that can be burned in vehicle engines. However, burning these fuels still releases greenhouse gases.

245 Nuclear power is another kind of energy. By splitting apart atoms – the tiny units that all materials are made of – energy is released, which can be turned into electricity. However, producing this energy creates toxic waste that can make people ill, and may be accidentally released into the air. Safer ways to use nuclear power are being researched.

▲ The Hoover Dam, on the border of Arizona and Nevada, USA, holds back a river, creating a lake, or reservoir. Water is let through the dam to turn turbines, which create electricity.

246 Lots of energy is produced without burning anything. Hydroelectric power stations use the pushing power of flowing rivers to turn turbines. Hydroelectricity is a renewable, or green, energy source – it doesn't use anything up or cause pollution. Scientists are also working on ways to turn the movement of waves and tides into usable energy.

247 The wind and the Sun are great renewable sources of energy, too. Wind turbines turn generators, which convert the 'turning movement' into electricity. Solar panels work by collecting sunlight and turning it into an electrical current.

◄ Solar panels are made of materials that soak up sunlight and turn its energy into a flow of electricity.

Rotor blade

▲ Modern wind turbines usually have three blades, which spin around at speed in high winds.

113

Pollution problems

248 **Pollution means dirt, waste and other substances that damage our surroundings.** Our farms and factories often release harmful chemicals into rivers and lakes, and cars, lorries and other road vehicles give out poisonous, polluting gases. Litter and rubbish are pollution, too.

▼ A thick layer of smog hangs over the city of Bangkok, the capital of Thailand.

249 **Humans make waste — when we go to the toilet.** The waste and water from our toilets is called sewage. This usually ends up at sewage works where we process it to make it safe, but in some places sewage flows straight into rivers or the sea. It is smelly and dirty and can contain deadly germs.

250 **Pollution can harm our health.** Smog is a mixture of smoke from factories and motor vehicles, and fog, and it collects over some cities. It makes it harder to breathe, worsening illnesses such as asthma.

▼ People in Kuala Lumpur, the capital of Malaysia, wear masks to avoid breathing in smog.

◀ People who live near airports have to put up with the sound of low-flying planes flying over their houses.

251 **Even noise is a kind of pollution.** Noise from airports disturbs the people who live nearby, and loud noises from ships and submarines can disturb whales. They rely on their own sounds to find their way and send messages, so other noises can confuse them.

252 **The more we throw away, the more rubbish piles up.** When we drop rubbish just anywhere, it becomes litter. If we put rubbish in the bin, some of it may get recycled, and the rest gets taken away and dumped in a big hole in the ground, called a landfill site. Either way, there's too much of it!

253 **Air pollution can cause acid rain.** The waste gases from power stations and factories mix with water droplets in clouds and form weak acid. This makes soil, rivers and lakes more acidic, which can kill fish and plants. Acid rain can even make rock crumble and dissolve.

TRUE OR FALSE?

1. Rubbish isn't a problem if you put it in a bin.
2. Acid rain can make your nose fall off.
3. Loud noises in the ocean can make whales get lost.

Answers:
1. FALSE – it still piles up in landfill sites. 2. FALSE – the acid is not very strong, but it can dissolve away the stone nose of a statue. 3. TRUE – according to some scientists.

▶ At landfill sites, rubbish piles up making huge mountains of waste that have to be flattened down by rollers.

Saving habitats

254 To save wildlife, we need to save habitats. Humans are taking up more and more space and if we don't slow down, there'll be no wild, natural land left. We need to leave plenty of natural areas for wildlife to live in.

▼ Tourists in a jeep approach a pride of lions in a nature reserve in South Africa.

255 One hundred years ago, people went on safari to hunt animals. Today, more tourists go to watch wild animals and plants in their natural habitat – this is called ecotourism and it helps wildlife. Local people can make enough money from tourism, so they don't need to hunt. However, ecotourism can disturb wildlife, so tourists have to take care where they go.

256 Nature reserves and national parks are safe homes for wildlife. The land is kept wild and unspoiled to preserve natural habitats. There are also guards or wardens to protect the wildlife and watch out for hunters.

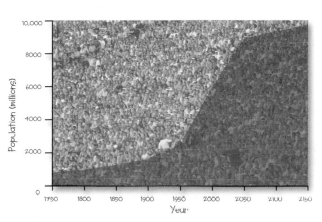

▲ As the human population continues to rise, more and more wild, natural land is being taken over.

258 It can be hard for humans to preserve habitats because we need space too. There are nearly 7 billion (7,000,000,000) humans on Earth today. Experts think this will rise to at least 9 billion. Some countries have laws to limit the number of children people are allowed to have to try to control the population.

▼ A diver explores a coral reef. The corals are home to many species of fish, crabs and shellfish.

257 You can help to keep habitats safe. In the countryside, don't take stones, shells or flowers. Visit nature reserves – your money helps to run them. Don't buy souvenirs made of coral, or other animals or plants, as this encourages hunting and habitat destruction.

I DON'T BELIEVE IT!

The river Thames in London has just 10 percent of the pollution it had in the 1950s because of pollution prevention, and is home to more than 100 species of fish.

SCIENCE

259 Even one hundred books like this could not explain all the reasons why we need science. Toasters, bicycles, mobile phones, computers, cars, light bulbs – all the gadgets and machines we use every day are the results of scientific discoveries. Houses, skyscrapers, bridges and rockets are built using science. Our knowledge of medicines, illnesses and the human body comes from science.

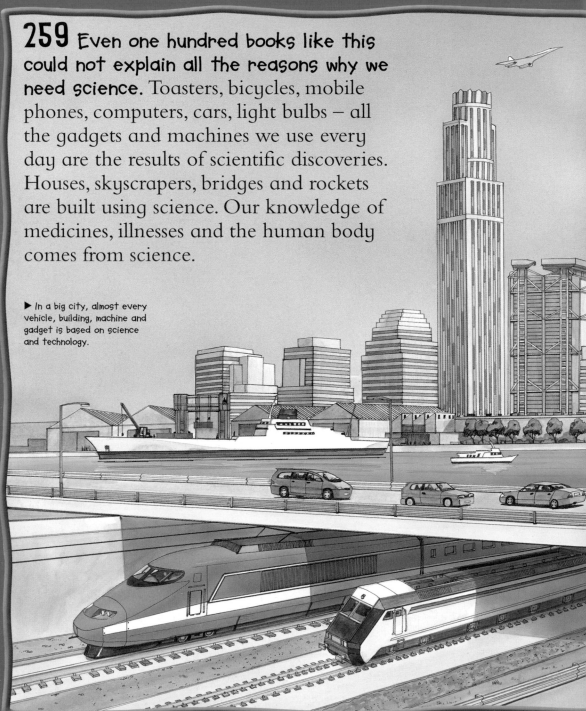

▶ In a big city, almost every vehicle, building, machine and gadget is based on science and technology.

Small science

260 **Atoms are the smallest bits of a substance and they make up everything – from this book to a building.** They are so tiny, even a billion atoms would be too small to see. But scientists have carried out experiments to find out what's inside an atom. The answer is – even smaller bits. These are sub-atomic particles, and there are three main kinds.

261 **At the centre of each atom is the nucleus.** It contains an equal number of two kinds of sub-atomic particles. These are protons and neutrons. Protons are positive, or plus. Neutrons are neither positive or negative.

Electron

Nucleus

I DON'T BELIEVE IT!

One hundred years ago, people thought the electrons were spread out in an atom, like the raisins in a raisin pudding.

262 Atoms of the various elements have different numbers of protons and neutrons. An atom of hydrogen has just one proton. An atom of helium, the gas put in party balloons to make them float, has two protons and two neutrons. An atom of the heavy metal, lead, has 82 protons and 124 neutrons.

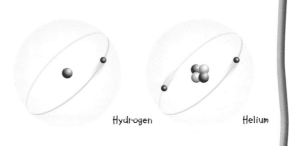

Hydrogen   Helium

▶ The bits inside an atom give each substance its features, from exploding hydrogen to life-giving oxygen.

● Electron
● Proton
○ Neutron

Oxygen

263 Around the centre of each atom are sub-atomic particles called electrons. They whizz round and round the nucleus. In the same way that a proton in the nucleus is positive or plus, an electron is negative or minus. The number of protons and electrons is usually the same, so the plus and minus numbers are the same.

Movement of electrons

264 It is hard to imagine that atoms are so small. A grain of sand, smaller than this 'o', contains at least 100 billion billion atoms. If you could make the atoms bigger, so that each one becomes as big as a pin head, the grain of sand would be 2 kilometres high!

◀ Uranium is a tough, heavy, dangerous metal. Each atom of uranium has 92 electrons whizzing around its nucleus.

Science on the move

265 **Without science, we would have to walk everywhere, or ride a horse.** Luckily, scientists and engineers have developed many methods of transport, most importantly, the car. Lots of people can travel together in a bus, train, plane or ship. This uses less energy and resources, and makes less pollution.

Passenger terminal

Underground trains to take passengers to and from the terminal

▶ Modern airports are enormous. They can stretch for several miles, and they have a constant flow of planes taking off and landing. Hundreds of people are needed to make sure that everything runs smoothly and on time.

266 Jetways are extending walkways that stretch out like telescopic fingers, right to the plane's doors. Their supports move along on wheeled trolleys driven by electric motors.

 ► The radar screen shows each aircraft as a blip, with its flight number or identity code.

Jetway

267 Every method of transport needs to be safe and on time. In the airport control tower, air traffic controllers track planes on radar screens. They talk to pilots by radio. Beacons send out radio signals, giving the direction and distance to the airport.

268 On the road, drivers obey traffic lights. On a railway network, train drivers obey similar signal lights of different colours, such as red for stop. Sensors by the track record each train passing and send the information by wires or radio to the control room. Each train's position is shown as a flashing light on a wall map.

▼ Train signals show just two colours — red for stop and green for go.

D-27

QUIZ

On traffic lights, what do these colours mean?
1. Green 2. Amber 3. Red
4. Red and amber

Answers:
1. Go 2. Get ready to stop 3. Stop 4. Get ready to go

How do planes fly?

269 A plane flies by moving through the air. The engines drive the plane forwards with a force called thrust. However, air pushes in the opposite direction and slows the plane down. This is called drag. Weight is the force that tries to pull the plane down. When moving through the air, the wings give an upwards force called lift.

Direction of air flow around wing

▲ As the wing moves forwards, air streams under and over it, lifting it up.

270 Air flowing over the wings gives an upwards lift. The wings are a special shape called an aerofoil. The top curves upwards while the bottom is flatter. As the plane moves forwards, air flowing over the top has further to go and is more spread out than the air beneath. The air beneath pushes the wing harder than the air above it, so the wing lifts, taking the plane with it.

A force called lift pulls the plane up

LIFTING FORCE

Wrap a strip of narrow paper around a pencil. Holding one end of the strip, blow hard over the top of it. Watch the free end of the paper lift upwards. This shows how an aircraft wing lifts as it moves through the air, keeping the heavy aircraft in the air. The faster you blow, the higher the paper lifts.

A force called thrust pulls the plane forwards

A force called weight pulls the plane down

▲ A flying plane is pushed and pulled by four different forces in four different directions.

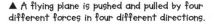

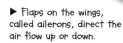

Aileron

▶ Flaps on the wings, called ailerons, direct the air flow up or down.

271 The engines give the thrust that drives the plane forwards in the air. As the plane travels faster, the lifting force grows stronger. This force must be equal to the weight of the plane before it can rise into the air and fly. This means that the thrust from the engines must drive the plane quickly to give it enough lift to fly

272 As the plane moves forwards it pushes against the air. The air pushes back, which slows the plane down and makes it use more fuel. Aircraft builders try to make the drag as minimal as possible by designing the plane to be smooth and streamlined so it cuts cleanly through the air.

273 The weight of a plane is always trying to pull it down. For this reason, planes are built to be as light as possible, using light but strong materials. Even so, a Boeing 747 jumbo jet with all its passengers and luggage can weigh as much as 360 tonnes and still take off.

A force called drag pulls the plane backwards

▼ Jet engines or propellers thrust a plane forwards.

Propeller engine

274 Planes get thrust from jet engines or propellers. Jet engines are more powerful and better for flying high up where the air is thinner. Airliners and fighter planes have jet engines. Propellers are more useful for planes that fly slower and nearer the ground. Most small private planes and some large planes that carry heavy cargo use propeller engines.

Jet engine

Powerful engines

275 **A jet engine thrusts a plane forwards by shooting out a jet of hot gases.** A turbojet engine uses spinning blades called a compressor to suck air into the front of the engine and squeeze it tightly. This air is then mixed with fuel inside the engine, as the fuel requires air to burn. The burning fuel creates hot gases that shoot out of a nozzle at the back of the engine.

BALLOON JET

Blow up a balloon then let it go. Watch the balloon shoot away as the air rushes out. In the same way, a plane shoots forwards when gases rush out of its jet engines.

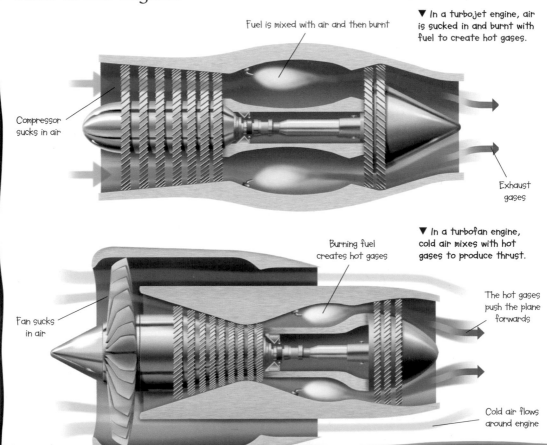

Fuel is mixed with air and then burnt

▼ In a turbojet engine, air is sucked in and burnt with fuel to create hot gases.

Compressor sucks in air

Exhaust gases

▼ In a turbofan engine, cold air mixes with hot gases to produce thrust.

Burning fuel creates hot gases

The hot gases push the plane forwards

Fan sucks in air

Cold air flows around engine

276 A turbofan engine is another type of jet engine used by modern airliners. These are less noisy than turbojet engines and cheaper to run. A large fan at the front sucks in air, but not all of it is squeezed and mixed with fuel. Some of the air flows around the outside of the engine and mixes with the hot gases shooting out of the back.

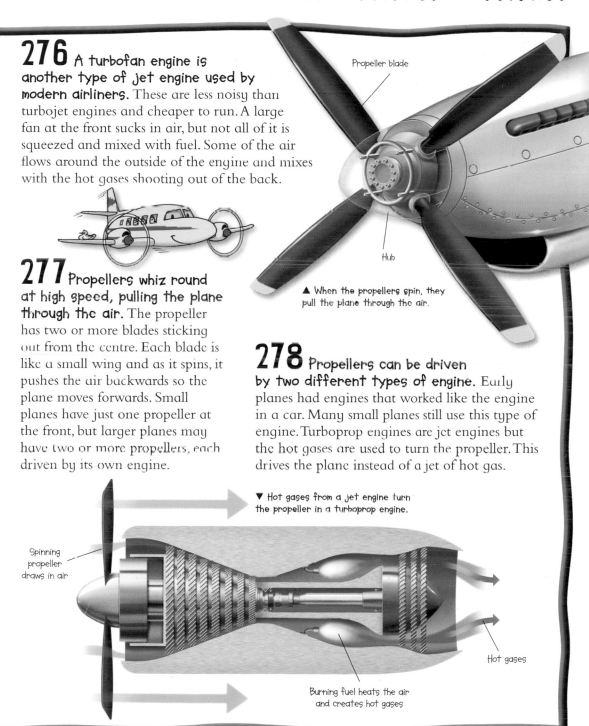

Propeller blade

Hub

▲ When the propellers spin, they pull the plane through the air.

277 Propellers whiz round at high speed, pulling the plane through the air. The propeller has two or more blades sticking out from the centre. Each blade is like a small wing and as it spins, it pushes the air backwards so the plane moves forwards. Small planes have just one propeller at the front, but larger planes may have two or more propellers, each driven by its own engine.

278 Propellers can be driven by two different types of engine. Early planes had engines that worked like the engine in a car. Many small planes still use this type of engine. Turboprop engines are jet engines but the hot gases are used to turn the propeller. This drives the plane instead of a jet of hot gas.

▼ Hot gases from a jet engine turn the propeller in a turboprop engine.

Spinning propeller draws in air

Hot gases

Burning fuel heats the air and creates hot gases

When science is hot!

279 Fire! Flames! Burning! Heat! The science of heat is important in all kinds of ways. Not only do we cook with heat, but we also warm our homes and heat water. Burning happens in all kinds of engines in cars, trucks, planes and rockets. It is also used in factory processes, from making steel to shaping plastics.

280 Heat moves by conduction. A hot object will pass on, or transfer, some of its heat to a cooler one. Dip a metal spoon in a hot drink and the spoon handle soon warms up. Heat is conducted from the drink, through the metal.

▲ A firework burns suddenly as an explosive, with heat, light and sound... BANG!

◄ Metal is a good conductor of heat. Put a teaspoon in a hot drink and feel how quickly it heats up.

281 Heat moves by invisible 'heat rays'. This is called thermal radiation and the rays are infrared waves. The Sun's warmth radiates through space as infrared waves, to reach Earth.

282 **Burning, also called combustion, is a chemical process.** Oxygen gas from the air joins to, or combines with, the substance being burned. The chemical change releases lots of heat, and usually light too. If this happens really fast, we call it an explosion.

283 **Temperature is a measure of how hot or cold something is.** It is usually measured in degrees Fahrenheit (°F) or Celsius (°C). Water freezes at 32°F (0°C), and boils at 212°F (100°C). We use a thermometer to take temperatures. Your body temperature is about 98.6°F (37°C).

▶ A thermometer may be filled with alcohol and red dye. As the temperature goes up, the liquid rises up its tube to show how hot it is. It sinks back down if the temperature falls.

CARRYING HEAT

You will need:

wooden ruler   metal spoon
plastic spatula   heatproof jug
frozen peas   some butter

Find a wooden ruler, a metal spoon and a plastic spatula, all the same length. Fix a frozen pea to one end of each with butter. Put the other ends in a heatproof jug. Ask an adult to fill the jug with hot water. Heat is conducted from the water, up the object, to melt the butter. Which object is the best conductor?

284 **Heat moves by convection, especially through liquids and gases.** Some of the liquid or gas takes in heat, gets lighter and rises into cooler areas. Then other, cooler, liquid or gas moves in to do the same. You can see this as 'wavy' hot air rising from a flame.

▶ See how hot air shimmers over a candle.

Noisy science

285 Listening to the radio or television, playing music, shouting at each other – they all depend on the science of sound – acoustics. Sounds are carried by invisible waves in the air. A loudspeaker moves in and out. When it moves out it squashes the air, causing high pressure. When it moves back in there is a region of low pressure.

◄ Workmen need to wear ear protection so the noise made by the pneumatic drill doesn't damage their hearing.

► The decibel scale measures the intensity, or energy, in sound.

286 Scientists measure the loudness or intensity of sound in decibels, dB. A very quiet sound like a ticking watch is 10 dB. Ordinary speech is 50–60 dB. Loud music is 90 dB. A jet plane taking off is 120 dB. Too much noise damages the ears.

287 Whether a sound is high or low is called its pitch, or frequency. It is measured in Hertz, Hz. A singing bird or whining motorcycle has a high pitch. A rumble of thunder or a massive truck has a low pitch. People can hear frequencies from 25 to 20,000 Hz.

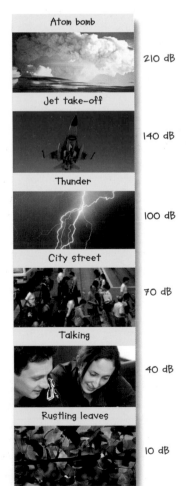

Atom bomb — 210 dB

Jet take-off — 140 dB

Thunder — 100 dB

City street — 70 dB

Talking — 40 dB

Rustling leaves — 10 dB

288 Sound waves spread out from a vibrating object that is moving rapidly to and fro. Stretch an elastic band between your fingers and twang it. As it vibrates, it makes a sound. When you speak, vocal cords in your neck vibrate. You can feel them through your skin.

289 Sound waves travel about 330 metres every second. This is fast, but it is one million times slower than light waves. Sound waves also bounce off hard, flat surfaces. This is called reflection. The returning waves are heard as an echo.

290 Loudspeakers change electrical signals into sounds. The signals in the wire pass through a wire coil inside the speaker. This turns the coil into a magnet, which pushes and pulls against another magnet. The pushing and pulling make the cone vibrate, which sends sound waves into the air.

BOX GUITAR

You will need:
shoebox   elastic band
split pins   some card

Cut a hole about 10 centimetres across on one side of an empy shoebox. Push split pins through either side of the hole, and stretch an elastic band between them. Pluck the band. Hear how the air and box vibrate. Cover the hole with card. Is the 'guitar' as loud?

▼ A loudspeaker turns electrical signals from the mp3 player into sound waves, so we can listen to music.

Large loudspeaker for low sounds

Small loudspeaker for high sounds

Stand

Mp3 player on a dock

Looking at light

291 Almost everything you do depends on light and the science of light, which is called optics. Light is a form of energy that you can see. Light waves are made of electricity and magnetism – and they are tiny. About 2000 of them laid end to end would stretch across this full stop.

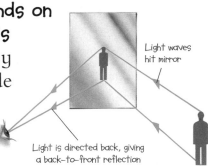

Light waves hit mirror

Light is directed back, giving a back-to-front reflection

▲ Light waves bounce off a mirror.

▼ A prism of clear glass or clear plastic separates the colours in white light.

293 Like sound, light bounces off surfaces that are very smooth. This is called reflection. A mirror is smooth, hard and flat. When you look at it, you see your reflection.

292 Ordinary light from the Sun or from a light bulb is called white light. But when white light passes through a prism, a triangular block of clear glass, it splits into seven colours. These colours are known as the spectrum. Each colour has a different length of wave. A rainbow is made when raindrops split sunlight like millions of tiny prisms.

294 Light passes through certain materials, such as clear glass and plastic. Materials that let light pass through, to give a clear view, are transparent. Those which do not allow light through, such as wood and metal, are opaque.

▶ Glass and water bend, or refract, light waves. This makes a drinking straw look bent where it goes behind the glass and then into the water.

295 Mirrors and lenses are important parts of many optical (light–using) gadgets. They are found in cameras, binoculars, microscopes, telescopes and lasers. Without them, we would have no close-up photographs of tiny microchips or insects or giant planets – in fact, no photos at all.

▼ A concave lens, which is thin in the middle, makes things look smaller.

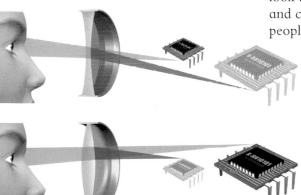

▲ A convex lens, which bulges in the middle, makes things look larger.

296 Light does not usually go straight through glass. It bends slightly where it goes into the glass, then bends back as it comes out. This is called refraction. A lens is a curved piece of glass or plastic that bends light to make things look bigger, smaller or clearer. Spectacle and contact lenses bend light to help people see more clearly.

I DON'T BELIEVE IT!

Light is the fastest thing in the Universe. It travels through space at 300,000 kilometres per second. That's seven times around the world in less than one second!

Mystery magnets

297 **Without magnets there would be no electric motors, computers or loudspeakers.** Magnetism is an invisible force to do with atoms – tiny particles that make up everything. Atoms are made of even smaller particles, including electrons. Magnetism is linked to the way that these line up and move. Most magnetic substances contain iron. As iron makes up a big part of the metallic substance steel, steel is also magnetic.

▼ An electromagnet attracts the body of a car, which is made of iron-based steel.

298 **A magnet is a lump of iron or steel which has all its electrons and atoms lined up.** This means that their magnetic forces all add up. The force surrounds the magnet, in a region called the magnetic field. This is strongest at the two parts of the magnet called the poles. In a bar or horseshoe magnet, the poles are at the ends.

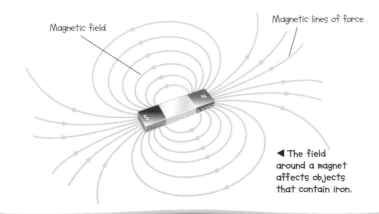

Magnetic field

Magnetic lines of force

◄ The field around a magnet affects objects that contain iron.

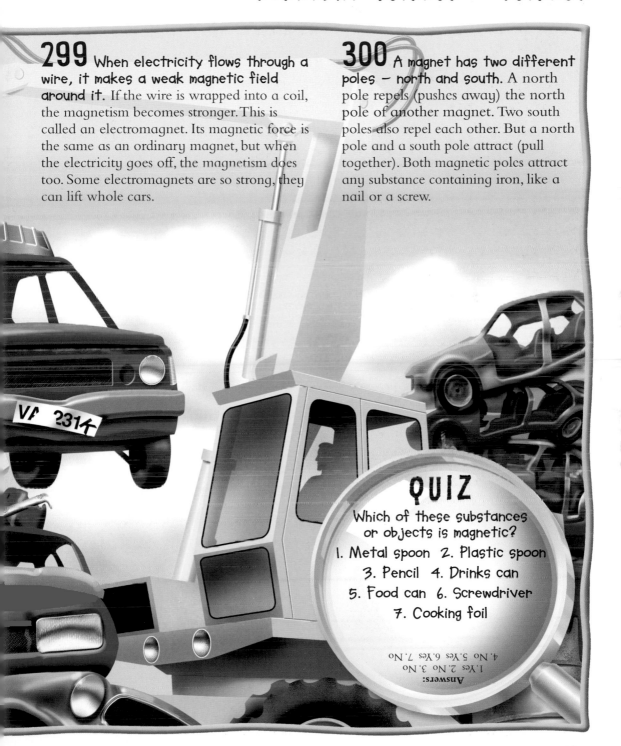

299 When electricity flows through a wire, it makes a weak magnetic field around it. If the wire is wrapped into a coil, the magnetism becomes stronger. This is called an electromagnet. Its magnetic force is the same as an ordinary magnet, but when the electricity goes off, the magnetism does too. Some electromagnets are so strong, they can lift whole cars.

300 A magnet has two different poles – north and south. A north pole repels (pushes away) the north pole of another magnet. Two south poles also repel each other. But a north pole and a south pole attract (pull together). Both magnetic poles attract any substance containing iron, like a nail or a screw.

VA 2314

QUIZ
Which of these substances or objects is magnetic?
1. Metal spoon 2. Plastic spoon
3. Pencil 4. Drinks can
5. Food can 6. Screwdriver
7. Cooking foil

Answers:
1.Yes 2.No 3.No
4.No 5.Yes 6.Yes 7.No

Electric sparks!

301 **Flick the switch and things happen.** The television goes off, the computer comes on, lights shine and music plays. Electricity is our favourite form of energy. We send it along wires and plug hundreds of machines into it. Imagine no washing machine, no electric light and no vacuum cleaner!

▶ Electricity is bits of atoms moving along a wire.

Atom

Electron

302 **Electricity depends on electrons, tiny parts of atoms.** In certain substances, when electrons are 'pushed', they hop from one atom to the next. When billions do this every second, electricity flows. The 'push' is from a battery or the generator at a power station. Electricity only flows if it can go in a complete loop or circuit. Break the circuit and the flow stops.

304 **Electricity flows easily through some substances, including water and metals.** These are electrical conductors. Other substances do not allow electricity to flow. They are insulators. Insulators include wood, plastic, glass, card and ceramics. Metal wires and cables have coverings of plastic, to stop the electricity leaking away.

303 **A battery makes electricity from chemicals.** Two different chemicals next to each other, such as an acid and a metal, swap electrons and get the flow going. Electricity's pushing strength is measured in volts. Most batteries are about 1.5, 3, 6 or 9 volts, with 12 volts in cars.

Positive contact

◀ A battery has a chemical paste inside a metal casing.

1.5v

Negative contact on base

305 Electricity from power stations
is carried along cables on high pylons, or
buried underground. This is known as the
distribution grid. At thousands of volts, this
electricity is extremely dangerous. For use in
the home, it is changed to 220 volts (in
Britain), but it can still easily kill a person.

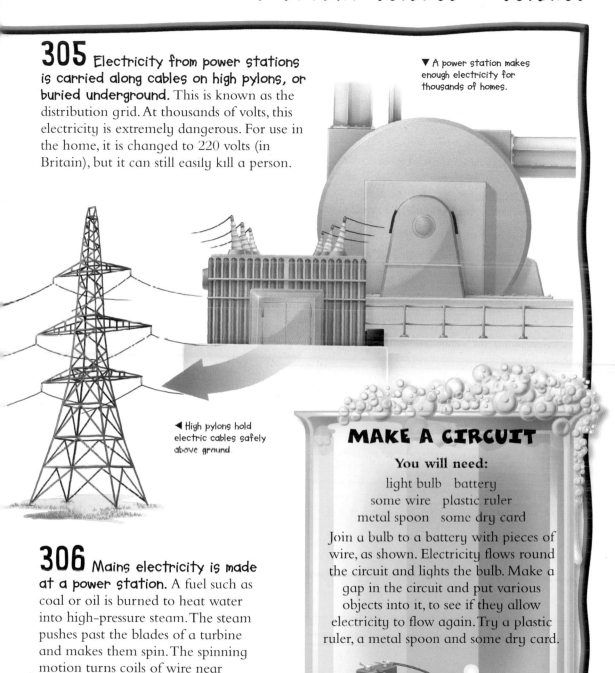

▼ A power station makes
enough electricity for
thousands of homes.

◄ High pylons hold
electric cables safely
above ground.

MAKE A CIRCUIT

You will need:

light bulb   battery
some wire   plastic ruler
metal spoon   some dry card

Join a bulb to a battery with pieces of
wire, as shown. Electricity flows round
the circuit and lights the bulb. Make a
gap in the circuit and put various
objects into it, to see if they allow
electricity to flow again. Try a plastic
ruler, a metal spoon and some dry card.

306 Mains electricity is made
at a power station. A fuel such as
coal or oil is burned to heat water
into high-pressure steam. The steam
pushes past the blades of a turbine
and makes them spin. The spinning
motion turns coils of wire near
powerful magnets, and this makes
electricity flow in the coils.

Making sounds and pictures

307 **The air is full of waves we cannot see or hear, unless we have the right machine.** Radio waves are a form of electrical and magnetic energy, just like heat and light waves, microwaves and X-rays. All of these are called electromagnetic waves and they travel at an equal speed – the speed of light.

Satellite

Radio waves

309 **Radio waves carry their information by being altered, or modulated, in a certain pattern.** The height of a wave is called its amplitude. If this is altered, it is known as AM (amplitude modulation). Look for AM on the radio display.

308 **Radio waves are used for both radio and television.** They travel vast distances. Long waves curve around the Earth's surface. Short waves bounce between the Earth and the sky.

310 **The number of waves per second is called the frequency.** If this is altered, it is known as FM (frequency modulation). FM radio is clearer than AM, and less affected by weather and thunderstorms.

▼ All these waves are the same form of energy. They all differ in length.

▲ A radio set picks up radio waves using its long aerial or antenna.

Long radio waves	Shorter radio waves (TV)	Microwaves	Light waves	X-rays	Short X-rays	Gamma rays

311 Radio and TV programmes may be sent out as radio waves from a tall tower on the ground. The tower is called a transmitter. Sometimes waves may be broadcast (sent) by a satellite in space. Or the programmes may not even arrive as radio waves. They can come as flashes of laser light, as cable TV and radio.

I DON'T BELIEVE IT!

You can listen to a radio on the Moon, but not in a submarine. Radio waves travel easily though space, but they hardly pass at all through water.

312 Inside a TV set, the pattern of radio waves is changed into electrical signals. Some go to the loudspeaker to make the sounds. Others go to the screen to make the pictures.

▶ A dish-shaped receiver picks up radio waves for TV channels.

▼ In a plasma screen, small electric pulses heat a gas into a form called 'plasma'. It then glows for a split second and shows the different colours you see on your screen.

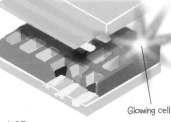

Glowing cell

◀ Flat-screen TVs can be LCD or plasma. They use less electricity than cathode-ray tvs and produce a better picture.

139

Compu-science

313 Computers are amazing machines. But they have to be told exactly what to do. So we put in instructions and information, by various means. These include typing on a keyboard, inserting a disc, using a joystick or games board, or linking up a camera, scanner or another computer.

CD or DVD drive (reader)

Microchips on circuit board

Main computer case

314 Most computers are controlled by instructions from a keyboard and a mouse. The mouse moves a pointer around on the screen and its click buttons select choices from lists called menus.

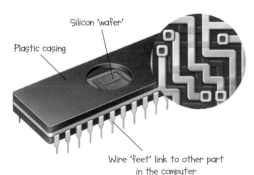

Silicon 'wafer'

Plastic casing

Wire 'feet' link to other part in the computer

◄ This close up of a slice of silicon 'wafer' shows the tiny parts that receive and send information in a computer.

315 Some computers are controlled by talking to them! They pick up the sounds using a microphone. This is VR, or voice recognition technology.

316 The 'main brain' of a computer is its Central Processing Unit. It is usually a microchip – millions of electronic parts on a chip of silicon, hardly larger than a fingernail. It receives information and instructions from other microchips, carries out the work, and sends back the results.

Flat screen monitor

QUIZ

You may have heard of these sets of letters. Do you know what they mean? Their full written-out versions are all here on these two pages.

1. RAM 2. ROM
3. CPU 4. DVD

Answers:
1.Random Access Memory
2.Read Only Memory
3.Central Processing Unit
4.Digital Versatile Disc

Mouse

◄ This is a PC, or personal computer. The keyboard is like a typewriter, but has extra keys called function keys. These make the computer do certain tasks. By using the mouse to move a pointer (cursor) around the screen, certain instructions can be clicked on. This can be quicker than using the keyboard.

Keyboard

317 Information and instructions are contained in the computer in two kinds of memory microchip. Random Access Memory is like a jotting pad. It keeps changing as the computer carries out its tasks. Read Only Memory is like an instruction book. It usually contains the instructions for how the computer starts up and how all the microchips work together.

318 Once the computer has done its task, it feeds out the results. These usually go to a screen called a monitor, where we see them. But they can also go to a printer, a loudspeaker or even a robot arm. Or they can be stored on a disc such as a magnetic disc, compact disc or Digital Versatile Disc (DVD).

What's it made of?

319 **You would not make a bridge out of straw, or a cup out of thin paper!** Choosing the right substance or material for the job is part of materials science. All the substances in the world can be divided into several groups. The biggest group is metals such as iron, copper, silver, and gold. Most metals are strong, hard and shiny, and carry heat and electricity well. They are used where materials must be tough and long-lasting.

320 **Plastics are made mainly from the substances in petroleum (crude oil).** There are so many kinds – some are hard and brittle while others are soft and bendy. They are usually long-lasting, not affected by weather or damp, and they resist heat and electricity.

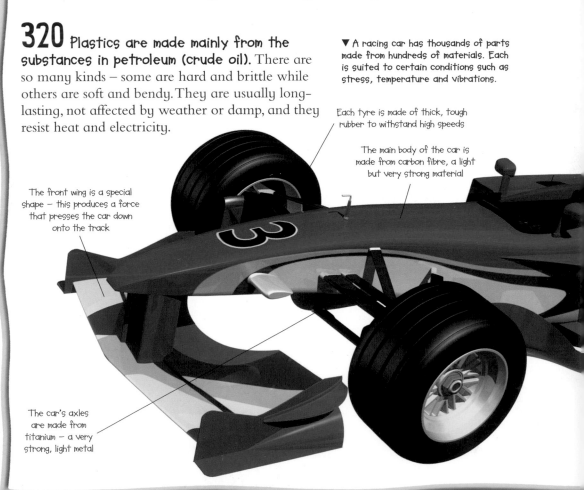

▼ A racing car has thousands of parts made from hundreds of materials. Each is suited to certain conditions such as stress, temperature and vibrations.

Each tyre is made of thick, tough rubber to withstand high speeds

The main body of the car is made from carbon fibre, a light but very strong material

The front wing is a special shape – this produces a force that presses the car down onto the track

The car's axles are made from titanium – a very strong, light metal

321 Ceramics are materials based on clay or other substances dug from the Earth. They can be shaped and dried, like a clay bowl. Or they can be fired – baked in a hot oven called a kiln. This makes them hard and long-lasting, but brittle and prone to cracks. Ceramics resist heat and electricity very well.

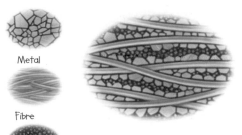

Metal

Fibre

Ceramic

◀ Metal, fibre and ceramic can combine to make a composite material (above). The way all of these ingredients are arranged can affect the composite's strength.

322 Glass is produced from the raw substances limestone and sand. When heated at a high temperature, these substances become a clear, gooey liquid, which sets hard as it cools. Its great advantage is that you can see through it.

323 Composites are mixtures or combinations of different materials. For example, glass strands are coated with plastic to make GRP – glass-reinforced plastic. This composite has the advantages of both materials.

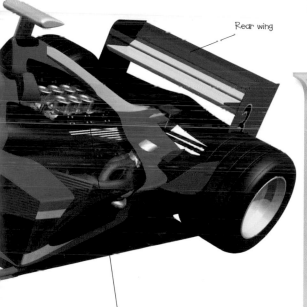

Rear wing

The engine can produce about ten times as much power as an ordinary car – but it needs to be as light as possible

MAKE YOUR OWN COMPOSITE

You will need:
flour   newspaper strips
water   balloon   pin

You can make a composite called pâpier maché from flour, newspaper and water. Tear newspaper into strips. Mix flour and water into a paste. Dip each strip in the paste and place it around a blown-up balloon. Cover the balloon and allow it to dry. Pop the balloon with a pin, and the composite should stay in shape.

Pure science

324 The world seems to be made of millions of different substances – such as soil, wood, concrete, plastics and air. These are combinations of simpler substances. If you could take them apart, you would see that they are made of pure substances called elements.

H Hydrogen 1											
Li Lithium 3	Be Beryllium 4										
Na Sodium 11	Mg Magnesium 12										
K Potassium 19	Ca Calcium 20	Sc Scandium 21	Ti Titanium 22	V Vanadium 23	Cr Chromium 24	Mn Manganese 25	Fe Iron 26	Co Cobalt 27	Ni Nickel 28	Cu Copper 29	Zn Zinc 30
Rb Rubidium 37	Sr Strontium 38	Y Yttrium 39	Zr Zirconium 40	Nb Niobium 41	Mo Molybdenum 42	Tc Technetium 43	Ru Ruthenium 44	Rh Rhodium 45	Pd Palladium 46	Ag Silver 47	Cd Cadmium 48
Cs Caesium 55	Ba Barium 56		Hf Hafnium 72	Ta Tantalum 73	W Tungsten 74	Re Rhenium 75	Os Osmium 76	Ir Iridium 77	Pt Platinum 78	Au Gold 79	Hg Mercury 80
Fr Francium 87	Ra Radium 88		Rf Rutherfordium 104	Db Dubnium 105	Sg Seaborgium 106	Bh Bohrium 107	Hs Hassium 108	Mt Meitnerium 109	Ds Darmstadtium 110	Rg Roentgenium 111	Uub Ununbium 112

▲ The Periodic Table is a chart of all the elements and their chemical symbols. The elements can be arranged in a table. Each has a letter, such as C for carbon. It also has a number showing how big or heavy its atoms are compared to those of other elements.

325 Hydrogen is the simplest element and it is the first element in the Periodic Table. This means it has the smallest atoms. It is a very light gas, which floats upwards in air. Hydrogen was once used to fill giant airships. But there was a problem – hydrogen catches fire easily and explodes.

► Stars are made mainly of burning hydrogen, which is why they are so hot and bright.

326 About 90 elements are found naturally on and in the Earth. In an element, all of its particles, called atoms, are exactly the same as each other. Just as important, they are all different from the atoms of any other element.

KEY

- Hydrogen, simplest element
- Alkali metals
- Alkali earth metals
- Transition metals
- Poor metals
- Non-metals
- Halogens
- Noble gases

He					
Helium					
2					

B	C	N	O	F	Ne
Boron	Carbon	Nitrogen	Oxygen	Fluorine	Neon
5	6	7	8	9	10

Al	Si	P	S	Cl	Ar
Aluminium	Silicon	Phosphorus	Sulphur	Chlorine	Argon
13	14	15	16	17	18

Ga	Ge	As	Se	Br	Kr
Gallium	Germanium	Arsenic	Selenium	Bromine	Krypton
31	32	33	34	35	36

In	Sn	Sb	Te	I	Xe
Indium	Tin	Antimony	Tellurium	Iodine	Xenon
49	50	51	52	53	54

Tl	Pb	Bi	Po	At	Rn
Thalium	Lead	Bismuth	Polonium	Astatine	Radon
81	82	83	84	85	86

QUIZ

1. Where does petrol come from?

2. What usually happens when you mix an acid and a base?

3. Which element makes up stars?

4. What do diamonds and coal have in common?

Answers:
1. Petroleum 2. They react to form a salt 3. Hydrogen 4. They are both made of pure carbon

328 Uranium is a heavy and dangerous element. It gives off harmful rays and tiny particles. This process is called radioactivity and it can cause sickness, burns and diseases such as cancer. Radioactivity is a type of energy and, under careful control, it may be used as fuel in nuclear power stations.

▶ Aluminium is a strong but light metal that is ideal for forming the body of vehicles such as planes.

327 Carbon is a very important element in living things — including our own bodies. It joins easily with atoms of other elements to make large groups of atoms called molecules. When it is pure, carbon can be two different forms. These are soft, powdery soot, and hard, glittering diamond. The form depends on how the carbon atoms join to each other.

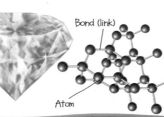

▶ Carbon can be hard diamond or soft soot, which is made of sheets of joined atoms.

Bond (link)

Atom

329 Aluminium is an element that is a metal, and it is one of the most useful in modern life. It is light and strong, it does not rust, and it is resistant to corrosion. Saucepans, drinks cans, cooking foil and jet planes are made mainly of aluminium.

Baby body

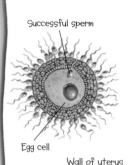

Successful sperm

Egg cell

330 A full-grown human body is made of billions of microscopic parts, called cells. But in the beginning, the body is a single cell, smaller than this full stop. Yet it contains all the instructions, known as genes, for the whole body to grow and develop.

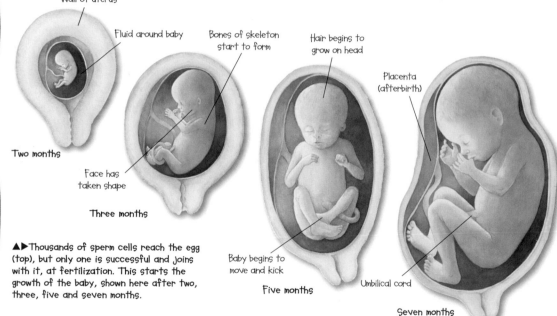

Wall of uterus

Fluid around baby

Bones of skeleton start to form

Hair begins to grow on head

Placenta (afterbirth)

Two months

Face has taken shape

Three months

▲▶Thousands of sperm cells reach the egg (top), but only one is successful and joins with it, at fertilization. This starts the growth of the baby, shown here after two, three, five and seven months.

Baby begins to move and kick

Five months

Umbilical cord

Seven months

331 The body begins when an egg cell inside the mother joins up with sperm from the father. The egg cell splits into two cells, then into four cells, then eight, and so on. The bundle of cells embeds itself in the mother's womb (uterus), which protects and nourishes it. Soon there are thousands of cells, then millions, forming a tiny embryo. After two months the embryo has grown into a tiny baby, as big as your thumb, with arms, legs, eyes, ears and a mouth.

332 After nine months in the womb, the baby is ready to be born. Strong muscles in the walls of the womb tighten, or contract. They push the baby through the opening, or neck of the womb, called the cervix, and along the birth canal. The baby enters the outside world.

333 A newborn baby may be frightened and usually starts to cry. Inside the womb it was warm, wet, dark, quiet and cramped. Outside there are lights, noises, voices, fresh air and room to stretch. The crying is also helpful to start the baby breathing, using its own lungs.

I DON'T BELIEVE IT!

The human body never grows as fast again as it does during the first weeks in the womb. If the body kept growing at that rate every day for 50 years, it would be bigger than the biggest mountain in the world!

Wall of womb is stretched

Placenta

◄ Inside the womb, the baby cannot breathe air or eat food. Nutrients and oxygen pass from mother to baby through the blood vessels in the ropelike umbilical cord.

Umbilical cord

Nine months

334 Being born can take an hour or two — or a whole day or two. It is very tiring for both the baby and its mother. After birth, the baby starts to feel hungry and it feeds on its mother's milk. Finally, mother and baby rest and sleep.

Baby is born head-first

Cervix (neck of womb)

The growing body

335 **A new baby just seems to eat, sleep and cry.** It feeds on milk when hungry and sleeps when tired. Also, it cries when it is too hot, too cold, or when its nappy needs changing.

336 **A new baby is not totally helpless.** It can do simple actions called reflexes, to help it survive. If something touches the baby's cheek, it turns its head to that side and tries to suck. If the baby hears a loud noise, it opens its eyes wide, throws out its arms and cries for help. If something touches the baby's hand and fingers, it grasps tightly.

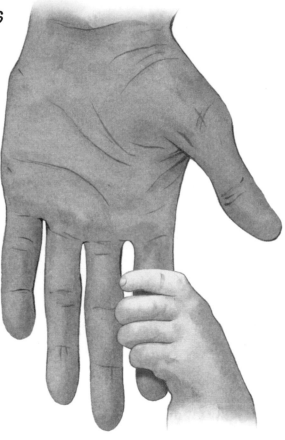

▲ In the grasping reflex, the baby tightly holds anything that touches its hand or fingers. Its grip is surprisingly strong!

WHAT HAPPENS WHEN?

Most babies learn to do certain actions in the same order. The order is mixed up here. Can you put it right?

walk, crawl, roll over, sit up, smile, stand

Answers:
smile, roll over, sit up, crawl, stand, walk

337 **A new baby looks, listens, touches and quickly learns.** Gradually it starts to recognize voices, faces and places. After about six weeks, it begins to smile. Inside the body, the baby's brain is learning very quickly. The baby soon knows that if it laughs, people will laugh back. If it cries, someone will come to look after it.

▼ Most babies crawl before they walk, but some go straight from sitting or 'bottom–shuffling' to walking.

339 As a baby grows into a child, at around 18 months, it learns ten new words every day, from 'cat' and 'dog' to 'sun' and 'moon'. There are new games such as piling up bricks, new actions such as throwing and kicking, and new skills such as using a spoon at mealtimes and scribbling on paper.

338 At about three months old, most babies can reach out to hold something, and roll over when lying down. By the age of six months, most babies can sit up and hold food in their fingers. At nine months, many babies are crawling well and perhaps standing up. By their first birthday, many babies are learning to walk and starting to talk.

340 At the age of five, when most children start school, they continue to learn an amazing amount. This includes thinking or mental skills such as counting and reading, and precise movements such as writing and drawing. They learn out of the classroom too – how to play with friends and share.

► Playing is lots of fun, but it's learning too, as children develop control over the muscles in their fast-growing bodies.

On the body's outside

341 Skin's surface is made of tiny cells that have filled up with a hard, tough substance called keratin, and then died. So when you look at a human body, most of what you see is 'dead'! The cells get rubbed off as you move, have a wash and get dry.

▲ Skin may feel smooth, but its surface is made of millions of tiny flakes, far too small to see.

342 Skin rubs off all the time, and grows all the time, too. Just under the surface, living cells make more new cells that gradually fill with keratin, die and move up to the surface. It takes about four weeks from a new skin cell being made to when it reaches the surface and is rubbed off. This upper layer of skin is called the epidermis.

▼ This view shows skin magnified (enlarged) about 50 times.

343 Skin's lower layer, the dermis, is thicker than the epidermis. It is made of tiny, bendy, threadlike fibres of the substance collagen. The dermis also contains small blood vessels, tiny sweat glands, and micro-sensors that detect touch.

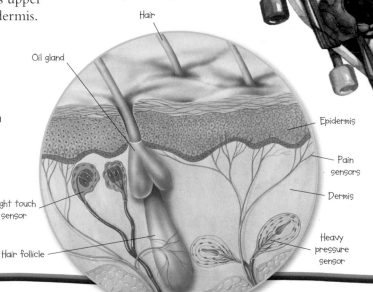

Oil gland

Hair

Light touch sensor

Hair follicle

Epidermis

Pain sensors

Dermis

Heavy pressure sensor

345 Skin helps to keep the body at the same temperature.

If you become too hot, sweat oozes onto your skin and, as it dries, draws heat from the body. Also, the blood vessels in the lower layer of skin widen, to lose more heat through the skin. This is why a hot person looks sweaty and red in the face.

346 Skin gives us our sense of touch.

Millions of microscopic sensors in the lower layer of skin, the dermis, are joined by nerves to the brain. Different sensors detect different kinds of touch, from a light stroke to heavy pressure, heat or cold, and movement. Pain sensors detect when skin is damaged.

▼ Skin is tough, but it sometimes needs help to protect the body. Otherwise it, and the body parts beneath, may get damaged.

Safety helmet protects head and brain

Elbow-pads cushion fall

Knee pads prevent hard bumps

Gloves save fingers from scrapes and breaks

344 One of skin's important jobs is to protect the body.

It stops the delicate inner parts from being rubbed, knocked or scraped. Skin also prevents body fluids from leaking away and it keeps out dirt and germs.

SENSITIVE SKIN

You will need:
a friend   sticky-tack
two used matchsticks   ruler

1. Press some sticky-tack on the end of the ruler. Press two matchsticks into the sticky-tack, standing upright, about one centimetre apart.

2. Make your friend look away. Touch the back of their hand with both matchstick ends. Ask your friend, "Is that one matchstick or two?" Sensitive skin can detect both ends

3. Try this at several places, such as on the finger, wrist, forearm, neck and cheek.

The bony body

347 The human body is strengthened, supported and held up by parts that we cannot see – bones. Without bones, the body would be as floppy as a jellyfish!

348 Bones do many jobs. The long bones in the arms work like levers to reach out the hands. The finger bones grasp and grip. The leg bones are also levers when we walk and run. Bones protect softer body parts. The domelike skull protects the brain. The ribs in the chest are like the bars of a cage to protect the heart and lungs inside.

▶ The skeleton forms a strong framework inside the body. The only artificial (man-made) substances that can match bone for strength and lightness are some of the materials used to make racing cars and jet planes.

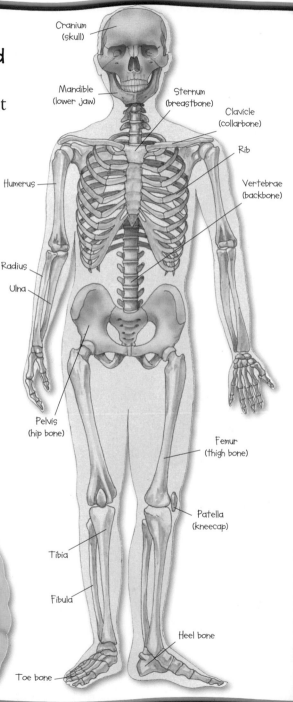

Cranium (skull)

Mandible (lower jaw)

Sternum (breastbone)

Clavicle (collarbone)

Rib

Humerus

Vertebrae (backbone)

Radius

Ulna

Pelvis (hip bone)

Femur (thigh bone)

Patella (kneecap)

Tibia

Fibula

Heel bone

Toe bone

NAME THE BONE!

Every bone has a scientific name and an ordinary name. Can you match up the names for these bones?

1. Mandible 2. Femur 3. Clavicle
4. Pelvis 5. Patella 6. Sternum

a. Thigh bone b. Breastbone
c. Kneecap d. Hip bone
e. Collarbone f. Lower jaw bone

Answers:
1f 2a 3e 4d 5c 6b

349 All the bones together make up the skeleton. Most people have 206 bones, from head to toe.
- 8 in the upper part of the skull, the cranium or braincase
- 14 in the face
- 6 tiny ear bones, 3 deep in each ear
- 1 in the neck, which is floating and not directly connected to any other bone
- 26 in the spinal column or backbone
- 25 in the chest – 24 ribs and the breastbone
- 32 in each arm, from shoulder to fingertips (8 in each wrist)
- 31 in each leg, from hip to toetips (7 in each ankle)

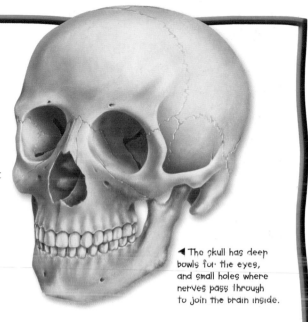

◄ The skull has deep bowls for the eyes, and small holes where nerves pass through to join the brain inside.

350 Bone contains threads of the tough, slightly bendy substance called collagen. It also has hard minerals such as calcium and phosphate. Together, the collagen and minerals make a bone strong and rigid, yet able to bend slightly under stress.

351 Bones have blood vessels for nourishment and nerves to feel pressure and pain. Also, some bones are not solid. They contain a jellylike substance called marrow. This makes tiny parts for the blood, called red and white blood cells.

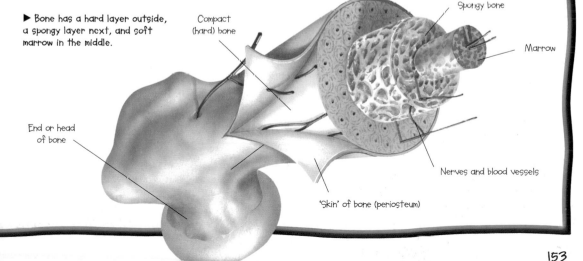

▶ Bone has a hard layer outside, a spongy layer next, and soft marrow in the middle.

Compact (hard) bone

Spongy bone

Marrow

End or head of bone

Nerves and blood vessels

'Skin' of bone (periosteum)

153

When muscles pull

352 Almost half the body's weight is muscles, and there are more than 640 of them! Muscles have one simple but important job, which is to get shorter, or contract. A muscle cannot get longer.

353 A muscle is joined to a bone by its tendon. This is where the end of the muscle becomes slimmer or tapers, and is strengthened by strong, thick fibres of collagen. The fibres are fixed firmly into the surface of the bone.

▼ A tendon is stuck firmly into the bone it pulls, with a joint stronger than superglue!

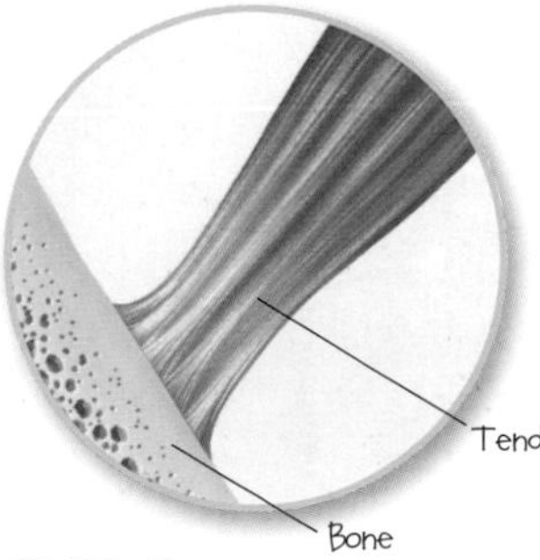

Tendon

Bone

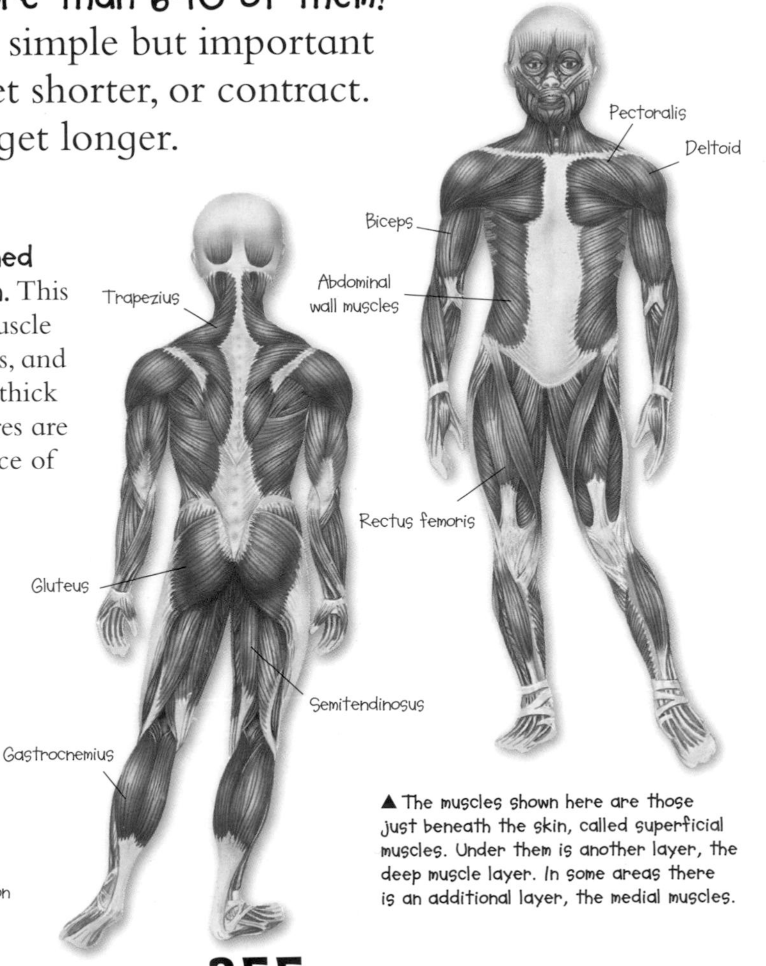

Trapezius

Gluteus

Semitendinosus

Gastrocnemius

Pectoralis

Deltoid

Biceps

Abdominal wall muscles

Rectus femoris

▲ The muscles shown here are those just beneath the skin, called superficial muscles. Under them is another layer, the deep muscle layer. In some areas there is an additional layer, the medial muscles.

354 Some muscles are wide or broad, and shaped more like flat sheets or triangles. These include the three layers of muscles in the lower front and sides of the body, called the abdominal wall muscles. If you tense or contract them, they pull your tummy in to make you look thinner.

355 Most muscles are long and slim, and joined to bones at each end. As they contract they pull on the bones and move them. As this happens, the muscle becomes wider, or more bulging in the middle. To move the bone back again, a muscle on the other side of it contracts, while the first muscle relaxes and is pulled longer.

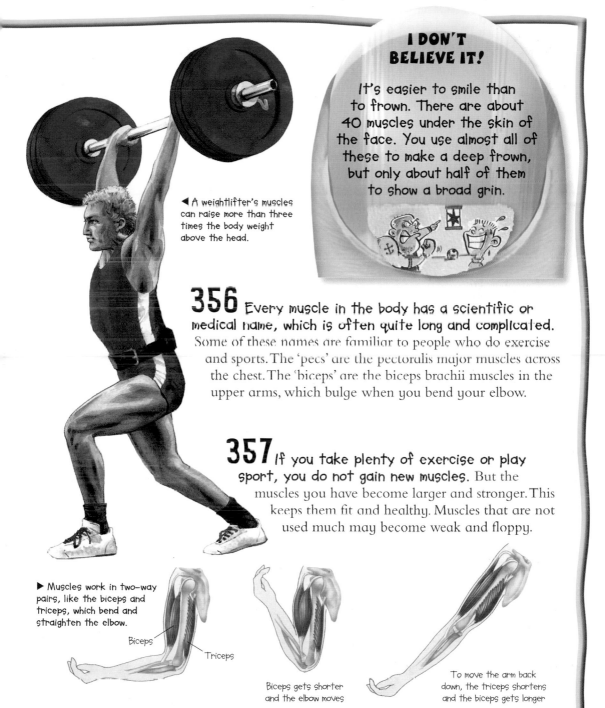

◄ A weightlifter's muscles can raise more than three times the body weight above the head.

I DON'T BELIEVE IT!

It's easier to smile than to frown. There are about 40 muscles under the skin of the face. You use almost all of these to make a deep frown, but only about half of them to show a broad grin.

356 Every muscle in the body has a scientific or medical name, which is often quite long and complicated. Some of these names are familiar to people who do exercise and sports. The 'pecs' are the pectoralis major muscles across the chest. The 'biceps' are the biceps brachii muscles in the upper arms, which bulge when you bend your elbow.

357 If you take plenty of exercise or play sport, you do not gain new muscles. But the muscles you have become larger and stronger. This keeps them fit and healthy. Muscles that are not used much may become weak and floppy.

► Muscles work in two-way pairs, like the biceps and triceps, which bend and straighten the elbow.

Biceps

Triceps

Biceps gets shorter and the elbow moves

To move the arm back down, the triceps shortens and the biceps gets longer

Muscle power

358 **Muscles have many shapes and sizes, but inside they are all similar.** They have bundles of long, hairlike threads called muscle fibres, or myofibres. Each muscle fibre is slightly thinner than a hair. A big muscle has many thousands of them. Most are about 3 or 4 centimetres long. In a big muscle, many fibres of different lengths lie alongside each other and end-to-end.

Muscle fibre

Nerve branches

Muscle fibre

Muscle fibril

▶ While arm muscles prepare to make the racket hit the ball, hundreds of other muscles keep the body poised and balanced.

359 Each muscle fibre is made of dozens or hundreds of even thinner parts, called muscle fibrils or myofibrils. There are millions of these in a large muscle. And, as you may guess, each fibril contains hundreds of yet thinner threads! There are two kinds, actin and myosin. As the actins slide past and between the myosins, the threads get shorter – and the muscle contracts.

360 Muscles are controlled by the brain, which sends messages to them along stringlike nerves. When a muscle contracts for a long time, its fibres 'take turns'. Some of them shorten powerfully while others relax, then the contracted ones relax while others shorten, and so on.

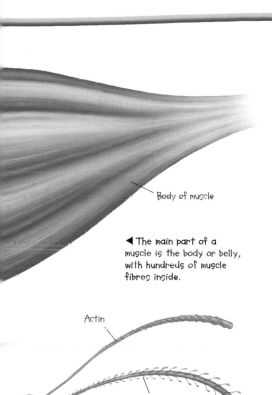

Body of muscle

◀ The main part of a muscle is the body or belly, with hundreds of muscle fibres inside.

Actin

Myosin

▼ Dozens of arm and hand muscles move a pen precisely, a tiny amount each time.

WHICH MUSCLES?

Can you match the names of these muscles with different parts of the body?

a. Gluteus maximus b. Masseter
c. Sartorius d. Cardiac muscle
e. Pectoralis major

1. Heart 2. Chest 3. Front of thigh
4. Buttock 5. Mouth

Answers:
a4 b5 c3 d1 e2

361 The body's biggest muscles are the ones you sit on – the gluteus maximus muscles in the buttocks. The longest muscle is the sartorius, across the front of the thigh. Some of its fibres are more than 30 centimetres in length. The most powerful muscle, for its size, is the masseter in the lower cheek, which closes the jaws when you chew.

The breathing body

362 **The body cannot survive more than a minute or two without breathing.** This action is so important, we do it all the time without thinking. We breathe to take air into the body. Air contains the gas oxygen, which is needed to get energy from food to power all of the body's vital life processes.

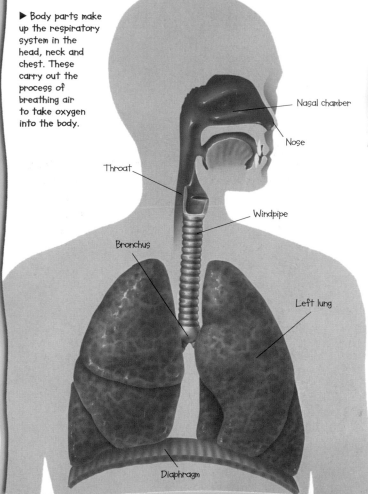

▶ Body parts make up the respiratory system in the head, neck and chest. These carry out the process of breathing air to take oxygen into the body.

Nasal chamber

Nose

Throat

Windpipe

Bronchus

Left lung

Diaphragm

▲ Scuba divers wear special breathing apparatus called 'aqua lungs'. They control their breathing to make their oxygen supply last as long as possible.

363 Parts of the body that work together to carry out a main task are called a system – so the parts that carry out breathing are the respiratory system. These parts are the nose, throat, windpipe, the air tubes or bronchi in the chest, and the lungs.

364 The nose is the entrance for fresh air to the lungs — and the exit for stale air from the lungs. The soft, moist lining inside the nose makes air warmer and damper, which is better for the lungs. Tiny bits of floating dust and germs stick to the lining or the hairs in the nose, making the air cleaner.

365 The windpipe, or trachea, is a tube leading from the back of the nose and mouth, down to the lungs. It has about 20 C-shaped hoops of cartilage in its wall to keep it open, like a vacuum cleaner hose. Otherwise the pressure of body parts in the neck and chest would squash it shut.

◄ The human voice can make a wide range of sounds, from loud to soft, and low to high.

HUMMMMMM!

You will need:
stopwatch

Do you think making sounds with your voice-box uses more air than breathing? Find out by following this experiment.

1. Take a deep breath in, then breathe out at your normal rate, for as long as you can. Time the out-breath.

2. Take a similar deep breath in, then hum as you breathe out, again for as long as you can. Time the hum.

3. Try the same while whispering your favourite song, then again when singing.

366 At the top of the windpipe, making a bulge at the front of the neck, is the voice box or larynx. It has two stiff flaps, vocal cords, which stick out from its sides. Normally these flaps are apart for easy breathing. But muscles in the voice-box can pull the flaps almost together. As air passes through the narrow slit between them it makes the flaps shake or vibrate — and this is the sound of your voice.

▼ The vocal cords are held apart for breathing (left) and pulled together for speech (right).

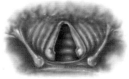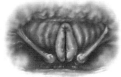

Breathing parts

367 The main parts of the respiratory (breathing) system are the two lungs in the chest. Each one is shaped like a tall cone, with the pointed end at shoulder level.

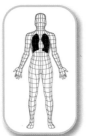

368 Air comes in and out of the lungs along the windpipe, which branches at its base to form two main air tubes, the bronchi. One goes to each lung. Inside the lung, each bronchus divides again and again, becoming narrower each time. Finally the air tubes, thinner than hairs, end at groups of tiny 'bubbles' called alveoli.

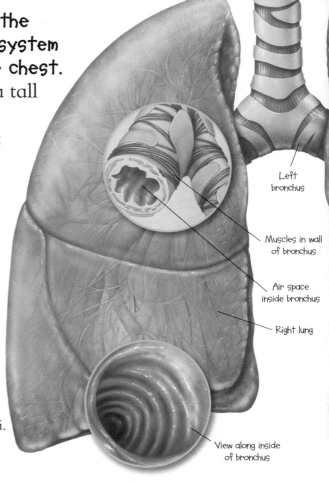

Left bronchus

Muscles in wall of bronchus

Air space inside bronchus

Right lung

View along inside of bronchus

I DON'T BELIEVE IT!

On average, the air breathed in and out through the night by a sleeping person, would fill an average-sized bedroom. This is why some people like to sleep with the door or window open!

369 There are more than 100 million tiny air bubbles, or alveoli, in each lung. Inside, oxygen from breathed-in air passes through the very thin linings of the alveoli to equally tiny blood vessels on the other side. The blood carries the oxygen away, around the body. At the same time a waste substance, carbon dioxide, seeps through the blood vessel, into the alveoli. As you breathe out, the lungs blow out the carbon dioxide.

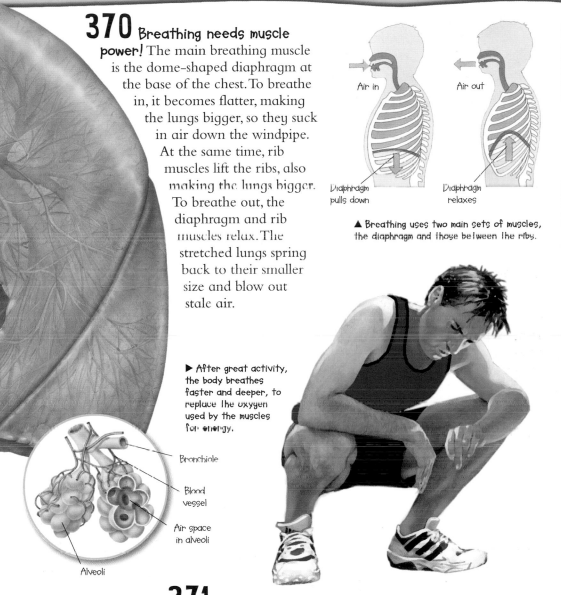

370 Breathing needs muscle power! The main breathing muscle is the dome-shaped diaphragm at the base of the chest. To breathe in, it becomes flatter, making the lungs bigger, so they suck in air down the windpipe. At the same time, rib muscles lift the ribs, also making the lungs bigger. To breathe out, the diaphragm and rib muscles relax. The stretched lungs spring back to their smaller size and blow out stale air.

Air in

Air out

Diaphragm pulls down

Diaphragm relaxes

▲ Breathing uses two main sets of muscles, the diaphragm and those between the ribs.

▶ After great activity, the body breathes faster and deeper, to replace the oxygen used by the muscles for energy.

Bronchiole

Blood vessel

Air space in alveoli

Alveoli

▲ Inside each lung, the main bronchus divides again and again, into thousands of narrower airways called bronchioles.

371 As you rest or sleep, each breath sends about half a litre of air in and out, 15 to 20 times each minute. After great activity, such as running a race, you need more oxygen. So you take deeper breaths faster – 3 litres or more of air, 50 times or more each minute.

Bite, chew, gulp

372 The hardest parts of your whole body are the ones that make holes in your food – teeth. They have a covering of whitish or yellowish enamel, which is stronger than most kinds of rocks! Teeth need to last a lifetime of biting, nibbling, gnashing, munching and chewing. They are your own food processors.

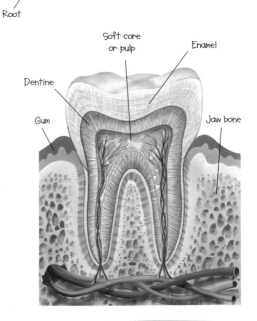

Incisor

Canine

Premolar

Molar

Jaw bone

Root

▲ In an adult, each side (left and right) of each jaw (upper and lower) usually has eight different-shaped teeth, of four main types.

373 There are four main shapes of teeth. The front ones are incisors, and each has a straight, sharp edge, like a spade or chisel, to cut through food. Next are canines, which are taller and more pointed, used mainly for tearing and pulling. Behind them are premolars and molars, which are lower and flatter with small bumps, for crushing and grinding.

Soft core or pulp

Enamel

Dentine

Gum

Jaw bone

374 A tooth may look almost dead, but it is very much alive. Under the enamel is slightly softer dentine. In the middle of the tooth is the dental pulp. This has blood vessels to nourish the whole tooth, and nerves that feel pressure, heat, cold and pain. The lower part of the tooth, strongly fixed in the jaw bone, is the root. The enamel-covered part above the gum is the crown.

▶ At the centre of a tooth is living pulp, with many blood vessels and nerve endings that pass into the jaw bone.

375 Teeth are very strong and tough, but they do need to be cleaned properly and regularly. Germs called bacteria live on old bits of food in the mouth. They make waste products which are acid and eat into the enamel and dentine, causing holes called cavities. Which do you prefer – cleaning your teeth after main meals and before bedtime, or the agony of toothache?

▶ Clean your teeth by brushing in different directions and then flossing between them. They will look better and stay healthier for longer.

▼ The first set of teeth lasts about ten years, while the second set can last ten times longer.

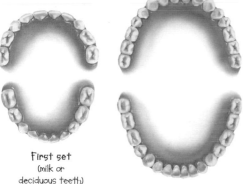

First set
(milk or
deciduous teeth)

Second set
(adult or
permanent set)

377 Teeth are designed to last a lifetime. Well, not quite, because the body has two sets. There are 20 small teeth in the first or baby set. The first ones usually appear above the gum by about six months of age, the last ones at three years old. As you and your mouth grow, the baby teeth fall out from about seven years old. They are replaced by 32 larger teeth in the adult set.

376 After chewing, food is swallowed into the gullet (oesophagus). This pushes the food powerfully down through the chest, past the heart and lungs, into the stomach.

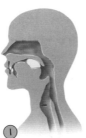

① tongue pushes food to the back of the throat

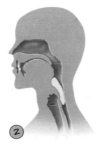

② throat muscles squeeze the food downwards

③ the oesophagus pushes food to the stomach

Food's long journey

378 The digestive system is like a tunnel about 9 metres long, through the body. It includes parts of the body that bite food, chew it, swallow it, churn it up and break it down with natural juices and acids, take in its goodness, and then get rid of the leftovers.

379 The stomach is a bag with strong, muscular walls. It stretches as it fills with food and drink, and its lining makes powerful digestive acids and juices called enzymes, to attack the food. The muscles in its walls squirm and squeeze to mix the food and juices.

380 The stomach digests food for a few hours into a thick mush, which oozes into the small intestine. This is only 4 centimetres wide, but more than 5 metres long. It takes nutrients and useful substances through its lining, into the body.

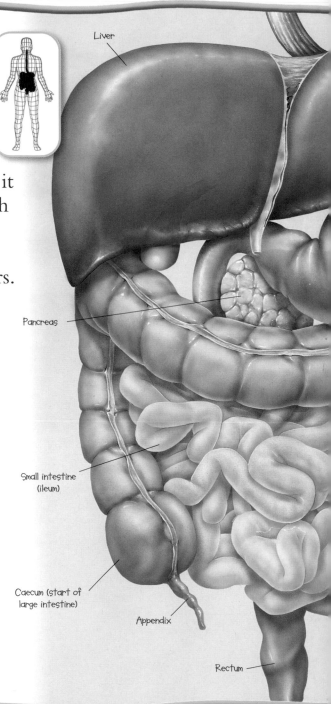

Liver

Pancreas

Small intestine (ileum)

Caecum (start of large intestine)

Appendix

Rectum

381 The large intestine follows the small one, and it is certainly wider, at about 6 centimetres, but much shorter, only 1.5 metres. It takes in fluids and a few more nutrients from the food, and then squashes what's left into brown lumps, ready to leave the body.

Stomach

Large intestine

▶ The lining of the small intestine has thousands of tiny finger-like parts called the villi, which take nutrients from food, into the blood and lymph system.

◀ The digestive parts almost fill the lower part of the main body, called the abdomen.

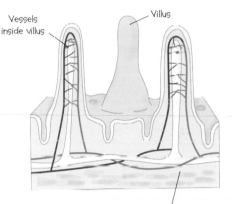

Vessels inside villus

Villus

Vessels in intestine lining

382 The liver and pancreas are also parts of the digestive system. The liver sorts out and changes the many nutrients from digestion, and stores some of them. The pancreas makes powerful digestive juices that pass to the small intestine to work on the food there.

I DON'T BELIEVE IT!

What's in the leftovers? The brown lumps called bowel motions or faeces are only about one-half undigested or leftover food. Some of the rest is rubbed-off parts of the stomach and intestine lining. The rest is millions of 'friendly' but dead microbes (bacteria) from the intestine. They help to digest our food for us, and in return we give them a warm, food-filled place to live.

Blood in the body

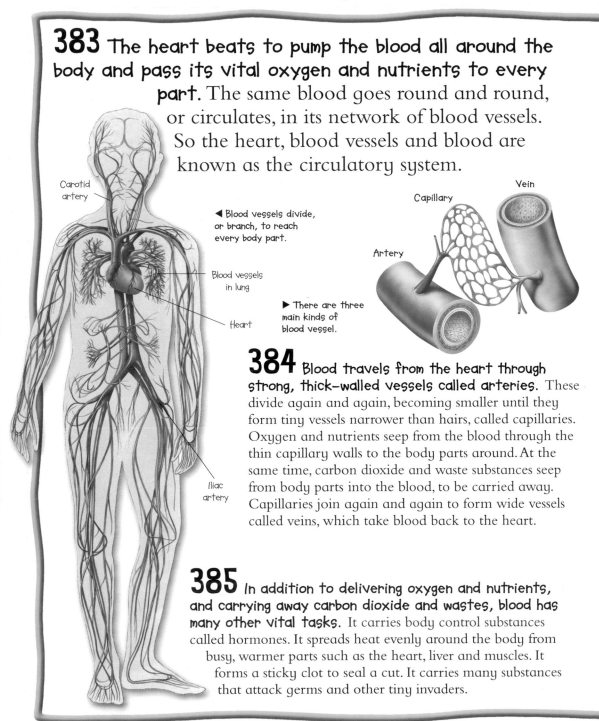

383 The heart beats to pump the blood all around the body and pass its vital oxygen and nutrients to every part. The same blood goes round and round, or circulates, in its network of blood vessels. So the heart, blood vessels and blood are known as the circulatory system.

Carotid artery

◀ Blood vessels divide, or branch, to reach every body part.

Blood vessels in lung

Heart

▶ There are three main kinds of blood vessel.

Iliac artery

Vein

Capillary

Artery

384 Blood travels from the heart through strong, thick-walled vessels called arteries. These divide again and again, becoming smaller until they form tiny vessels narrower than hairs, called capillaries. Oxygen and nutrients seep from the blood through the thin capillary walls to the body parts around. At the same time, carbon dioxide and waste substances seep from body parts into the blood, to be carried away. Capillaries join again and again to form wide vessels called veins, which take blood back to the heart.

385 In addition to delivering oxygen and nutrients, and carrying away carbon dioxide and wastes, blood has many other vital tasks. It carries body control substances called hormones. It spreads heat evenly around the body from busy, warmer parts such as the heart, liver and muscles. It forms a sticky clot to seal a cut. It carries many substances that attack germs and other tiny invaders.

386 Blood has four main parts. The largest is billions of tiny, saucer-shaped red cells, which make up almost half of the total volume of blood and carry oxygen. Second is the white cells, which clean the blood, prevent disease and fight germs. The third part is billions of tiny platelets, which help blood to clot. Fourth is watery plasma, in which the other parts float.

QUIZ

Can you match these blood parts and vessels with their descriptions?
a. Artery b. Vein c. White blood cell
d. Red blood cell e. Platelet f. Capillary

1. Large vessel that takes blood back to the heart
2. Tiny vessel allowing oxygen and nutrients to leave blood
3. Large vessel carrying blood away from the heart
4. Oxygen-carrying part of the blood
5. Disease-fighting part of the blood
6. Part that helps blood to clot

Answers:
a3 b1 c5 d4 e6 f2

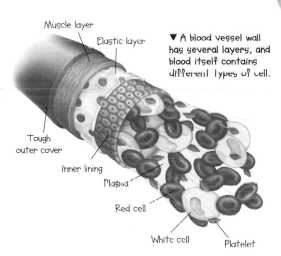

Muscle layer
Elastic layer
Tough outer cover
Inner lining
Plasma
Red cell
White cell
Platelet

▼ A blood vessel wall has several layers, and blood itself contains different types of cell.

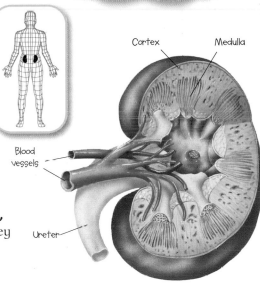

Cortex
Medulla
Blood vessels
Ureter

387 Blood is cleaned by two kidneys, situated in the middle of your back. They filter the blood and make a liquid called urine, which contains unwanted and waste substances, plus excess or 'spare' water. The urine trickles from each kidney down a tube, the ureter, into a stretchy bag, the bladder. It's stored here until you can get rid of it – at your convenience.

▲ Each kidney has about one million tiny filters, called nephrons, in its outer layer, or cortex.

The beating body

388 **The heart is about as big as its owner's clenched fist.** It is a hollow bag of very strong muscle, called cardiac muscle or myocardium. This muscle never tires. It contracts once every second or more often, all through life. The contraction, or heartbeat, squeezes blood inside the heart out into the arteries. As the heart relaxes it fills again with blood from the veins.

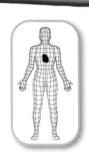

389 **Inside, the heart is not one baglike pump, but two pumps side by side.** The left pump sends blood all around the body, from head to toe, to deliver its oxygen (systemic circulation). The blood comes back to the right pump and is sent to the lungs, to collect more oxygen (pulmonary circulation). The blood returns to the left pump and starts the whole journey again.

▶ The heart is two pumps side by side, and each pump has two chambers, the upper atrium and the lower ventricle.

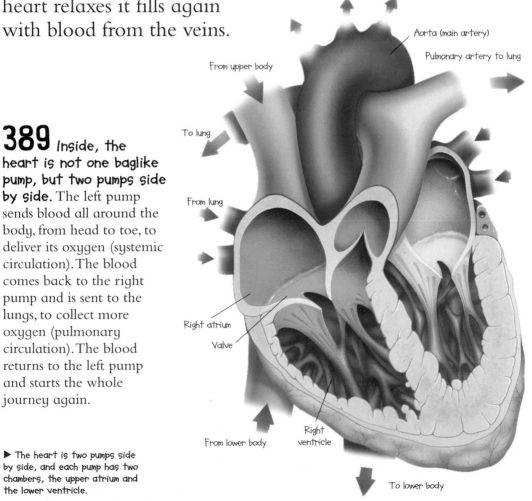

To upper body

Aorta (main artery)

Pulmonary artery to lung

From upper body

To lung

From lung

Right atrium

Valve

From lower body

Right ventricle

To lower body

390 Inside the heart are four sets of bendy flaps called valves. These open to let blood flow the right way. If the blood tries to move the wrong way, it pushes the flaps together and the valve closes. Valves make sure the blood flows the correct way, rather than sloshing to and fro, in and out of the heart, with each beat.

▶ The heartbeat is the regular squeezing of the heart muscle to pump blood around the body.

1. Upper chambers fill with blood

Left atrium

Right atrium

Red: oxygenated blood to body

Blue: deoxygenated blood to lungs

2. Blood passes through valves into lower chambers

4. Blood starts to fill up the relaxed upper chambers from the veins

3. The lower chambers contract, pushing blood into the arteries

391 The heart is the body's most active part, and it needs plenty of energy brought by the blood. The blood flows through small vessels, which branch across its surface and down into its thick walls. These are called the coronary vessels.

392 The heart beats at different rates, depending on what the body is doing. When the muscles are active they need more energy and oxygen, brought by the blood. So the heart beats faster, 120 times each minute or more. At rest, the heart slows to 60 to 80 beats a minute.

HOW FAST IS YOUR HEARTBEAT?

You will need:
plastic funnel   tracing paper
plastic tube (like hosepipe)   sticky-tape

You can hear your heart and count its beats with a sound-funnel device called a stethoscope.

1. Stretch the tracing paper over the funnel's wide end and tape in place. Push a short length of tube over the funnel's narrow end.

2. Place the funnel's wide end over your heart, on your chest, just to the left, and put the tube end to your ear. Listen to and count your heartbeat.

Looking and listening

393 The body finds out about the world around it by its senses — and the main sense is eyesight. The eyes detect the brightness, colours and patterns of light rays, and change these into patterns of nerve signals that they send to the brain. More than half of the knowledge, information and memories stored in the brain come into the body through the eyes.

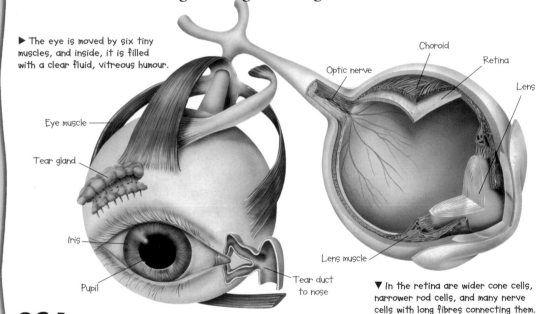

▶ The eye is moved by six tiny muscles, and inside, it is filled with a clear fluid, vitreous humour.

Choroid

Retina

Optic nerve

Lens

Eye muscle

Tear gland

Iris

Pupil

Lens muscle

Tear duct to nose

394 Each eye is a ball about 2.5 centimetres across. At the front is a clear dome, the cornea, which lets light through a small, dark-looking hole just behind it, the pupil. The light then passes through a pea-shaped lens, which bends the rays so they shine a clear picture onto the inside back of the eye, the retina. This has 125 million tiny cells, rods and cones, which detect the light and make nerve signals to send along the optic nerve to the brain.

▼ In the retina are wider cone cells, narrower rod cells, and many nerve cells with long fibres connecting them.

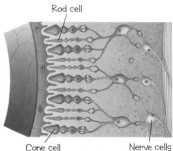

Rod cell

Cone cell

Nerve cells

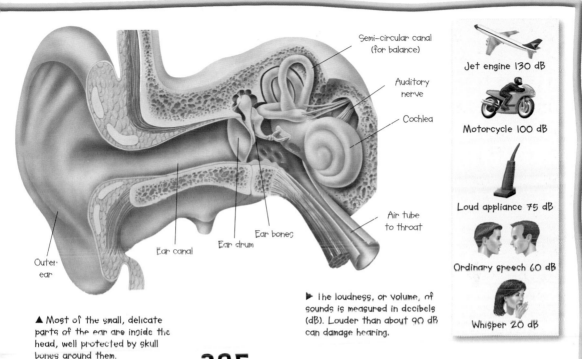

Semi-circular canal
(for balance)

Auditory
nerve

Cochlea

Air tube
to throat

Ear bones

Ear drum

Ear canal

Outer
ear

Jet engine 130 dB

Motorcycle 100 dB

Loud appliance 75 dB

Ordinary speech 60 dB

Whisper 20 dB

▲ Most of the small, delicate parts of the ear are inside the head, well protected by skull bones around them.

▶ The loudness, or volume, of sounds is measured in decibels (dB). Louder than about 90 dB can damage hearing.

395 **The ear is far more than the bendy, curly flap on the side of the head.** The ear flap funnels sound waves along a short tunnel, the ear canal, to a fingernail-sized patch of tight skin, the eardrum. As sound waves hit the eardrum it shakes or vibrates, and passes the vibrations to a row of three tiny bones. These are the ear ossicles, the smallest bones in the body. They also vibrate and pass on the vibrations to another part, the cochlea, which has a curly, snail-like shape.

396 **Inside the cochlea, the vibrations pass through fluid and shake rows of thousands of tiny hairs that grow from specialized hair cells.** As the hairs vibrate, the hair cells make nerve signals, which flash along the auditory nerve to the brain.

BRIGHT AND DIM

Look at your eyes in a mirror. The small, dark hole, the pupil, lets in light. The coloured part around the pupil, the iris, is a ring of muscle.

Close your eyes, then open them and look carefully. Does the pupil quickly get smaller? While the eyes were closed, the iris made the pupil bigger, to try and let in more light, so you could try to see in the darkness. As you open your eyes, the iris makes the pupil smaller again, to prevent too much light from dazzling you.

Smelling and tasting

▼ The parts that carry out smelling are in the roof of the large chamber inside the nose.

Olfactory cells

Mucus lining

Nasal cavity

397 You cannot see smells, which are tiny particles floating in the air — but your nose can smell them. Your nose is more sensitive than you realize. It can detect more than 10,000 different scents, odours, fragrances, pongs and niffs. Smell is useful because it warns us if food is bad or rotten, and perhaps dangerous to eat. That's why we sniff a new or strange food item, almost without thinking, before trying it.

▼ Olfactory (smell) cells have micro-hairs facing down into the nasal chamber, which detect smell particles landing on them.

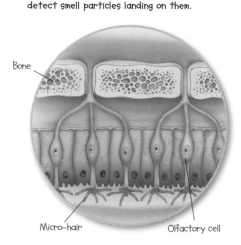

Bone

Micro-hair

Olfactory cell

398 Smell particles drift with breathed-in air into the nose and through the nasal chamber behind it. At the top of the chamber are two patches of lining, each about the area of a thumbnail and with 250 million microscopic hairs. The particles land on the sticky hairs, and if they fit into landing sites called receptors there, like a key into a lock, then nerve signals flash along the olfactory nerve to the brain.

400 The body's most flexible muscle is also the one that is coated with 10,000 micro-sensors for taste – the tongue. Each micro-sensor is a taste bud, shaped like a tiny onion. Most taste buds are along the tip, sides and rear upper surface of the tongue. They are scattered around the much larger flaps and lumps on the tongue, which are called papillae.

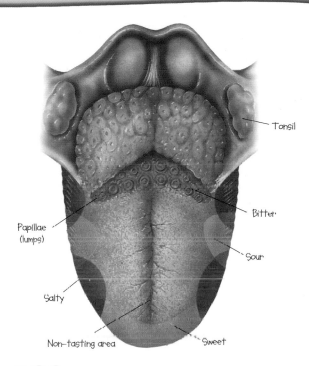

Tonsil

Bitter

Sour

Papillae (lumps)

Salty

Non-tasting area

Sweet

◄ The taste buds are mainly around the edges of the tongue, not on the main middle area.

399 Taste works in a similar way to smell, but it detects flavour particles in foods and drinks. The particles touch tiny hairs sticking up from hair cells in the taste buds. If the particles fit into receptors there, then the hair cell makes nerve signals, which go along the facial and other nerves to the brain.

SWEET AND SOUR

The tongue detects only four basic flavours – sweet at the tip, salty along the front sides, sour along the rear sides, and bitter across the back.

Which of these foods is sweet, salty, bitter or sour?

1. Coffee 2. Lemon 3. Bacon 4. Ice cream

Answers:
1. bitter 2. sour 3. salty 4. sweet

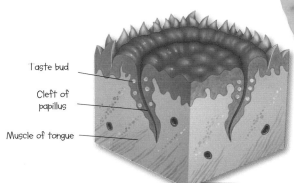

Taste bud

Cleft of papillus

Muscle of tongue

◄ The large pimple-like lumps at the back of the tongue, called papillae, have tiny taste buds in their deep clefts.

The nervous body

Brain

Spinal cord

401 The body is not quite a 'bag of nerves', but it does contain thousands of kilometres of these pale, shiny threads. Nerves carry tiny electrical pulses known as nerve signals or neural messages. They form a vast information-sending network that reaches every part, almost like the body's own Internet.

402 Each nerve is a bundle of much thinner parts called nerve fibres. Like wires in a telephone cable, these carry their own tiny electrical nerve signals. A typical nerve signal has a strength of 0.1 volts (one-fifteenth as strong as a torch battery). The slowest nerve signals travel about half a metre each second, the fastest at more than 100 metres a second.

Axon

Sciatic nerve

Tibial nerve

▲ Nerves branch from the brain and spinal cord to every body part.

Dendrites

Synapse (junction between nerve cells)

403 All nerve signals are similar, but there are two main kinds, depending on where they are going. Sensory nerve signals travel from the sensory parts (eyes, ears, nose, tongue and skin) to the brain. Motor nerve signals travel from the brain out to the muscles, to make the body move about.

TIME TO REACT!

You will need:
friend   ruler

1. Ask your friend to hold the ruler by the end with the highest measurement, letting it hang down. Put your thumb and fingers level with the other end, ready to grab.

2. Get your friend to let the ruler go, for you to grasp it as it falls. Measure where your thumb is on the ruler. Swap places so your friend has a go.

3. The person who grabs the ruler nearest its lower end has the fastest reaction. To grab the ruler, nerve signals travel from the eye, to the brain, and back out to the muscles in the arm and hand.

404 Hormones are part of the body's inner control system. A hormone is a chemical made by a gland. It travels in the blood and affects other body parts, for example, making them work faster or release more of their product.

▼ Female and male bodies have much the same hormone making glands, except for the reproductive parts – ovaries in the female (left) and testes in the male (right).

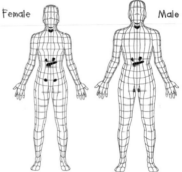

Female   Male

405 The main hormonal gland, the pituitary, is also the smallest. Just under the brain, it has close links with the nervous system. It mainly controls other hormonal glands. One is the thyroid in the neck, which affects the body's growth and how fast its chemical processes work. The pancreas controls how the body uses energy, by its hormone, insulin. The adrenal glands are involved in the body's balance of water, minerals and salts, and how we react to stress and fear.

◄ The brain and nerves are made of billions of specialized cells, nerve cells or neurons. Each has many tiny branches, dendrites, to collect nerve messages, and a longer, thicker branch, the axon or fibre, to pass on the messages.

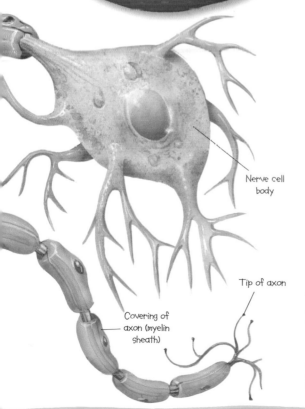

Nerve cell body

Tip of axon

Covering of axon (myelin sheath)

The brainy body

406 Your brain is as big as your two fists side by side. It's the place where you think, learn, work out problems, remember, feel happy and sad, wonder, worry, have ideas, sleep and dream.

Cerebral hemisphere

▶ The two wrinkled hemispheres (halves) of the cerebrum, where thinking happens, are the largest brain parts.

Cerebellum

Brain stem

Thalamus

Hippocampus

408 The main part of the brain is its bulging, wrinkled upper part, the cerebrum. Different areas of its surface (cerebral cortex) deal with nerve signals to and from different parts of the body. For example, messages from the eyes pass to the lower rear part of the cerebrum, called the visual centre. They are sorted here as the brain cells work out what the eyes are seeing. There are also areas for touch, hearing, taste and other body processes.

407 The brain looks like a wrinkly lump of grey-pink jelly! On average, it weighs about 1.4 kilograms. It doesn't move, but its amazing nerve activity uses up one-fifth of all the energy needed by the body.

409 The cerebellum is the rounded, wrinkled part at the back of the brain. It processes messages from the motor centre, sorting and coordinating them in great detail, to send to the body's hundreds of muscles. This is how we learn skilled, precise movements such as writing, skateboarding or playing music (or all three), almost without thinking.

▼ Different areas or centres of the brain's outer layer, the cerebral cortex, deal with messages from and to certain parts of the body.

Touch area   Movement area

Thought area

410 The brain stem is the lower part of the brain, where it joins the body's main nerve, the spinal cord. The brain stem controls basic processes vital for life, like breathing, the heart beating, digesting food and removing wastes.

Vision area

Speech area

Hearing area

411 The brain really does have 'brain waves'. Every second it receives, sorts and sends millions of nerve signals. Special pads attached to the head can detect these tiny electrical pulses. They are shown on a screen or paper strip as wavy lines called an EEG, electro-encephalogram.

▼ The brain's 'waves' or EEG recordings change, depending on whether the person is alert and thinking hard, resting, falling asleep or deeply asleep.

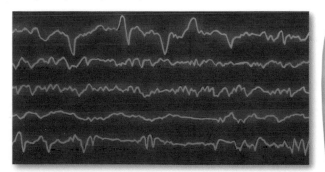

I DON'T BELIEVE IT!

The brain never sleeps! EEG waves show that it is almost as busy at night as when we are awake. It still controls heartbeat, breathing and digestion. It also sifts through the day's events and stores memories.

PREHISTORIC LIFE

412 The Earth was once covered by huge sheets of ice. This happened several times during Earth's history and we call these frozen times ice ages. However, the ice ages are a tiny part of prehistory. Before then, the world was warm and lakes and seas covered the land. Even earlier than this, there was little rain for thousands of years, and the land was covered in deserts. Over millions of years, weather and conditions changed. Living things changed, too, in order to survive. This change is called 'evolution'.

Woolly
rhinoceros

Cave lion

▼ A scene from the last ice age, about 10,000 years ago. Animals grew thick fur coats to protect themselves from the cold. Many animals, such as woolly mammoths, survived on plants such as mosses. Others, such as cave lions, were fierce hunters, needing meat to survive.

Aurochs

Woolly mammoth

Megaloceros

Life begins

413 Life began a very, very long time ago. We know this from the remains of prehistoric life forms that died and were buried. Over millions of years, their remains turned into shapes in rocks, called fossils. The first fossils are over 3000 million years old. They are tiny 'blobs' called bacteria – living things that still survive today.

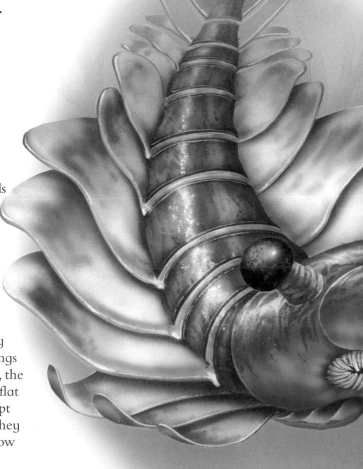

▼ Fossils of *Anomalocaris* have been found in Canada. It had a circular mouth and finlike body parts. Its body was covered by a shell.

414 The first plants were seaweeds, which appeared about 1000 million years ago. Unlike bacteria and blue-green algae, which each had just one living cell, these plants had thousands of cells. Some seaweeds were many metres long. They were called algae – the same name that scientists use today.

415 By about 800 million years ago, some plants were starting to grow on land. They were mixed with other living things called moulds, or fungi. Together, the algae (plants) and fungi formed flat green-and-yellow crusts that crept over rocks and soaked up rain. They were called lichens. These still grow on rocks and trees today.

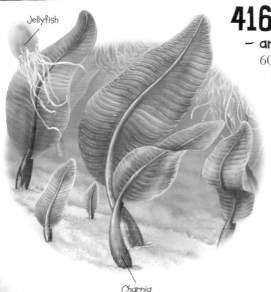

Jellyfish

Charnia

416 The first animals lived in the sea – and they were as soft as jelly! Over 600 million years ago, some of the first animals were jellyfish, floating in the water. On the seabed lived groups of soft, feathery-looking creatures called *Charnia*. This animal was an early type of coral. Animals need to take in food by eating other living things. *Charnia* caught tiny plants in its 'feathers'.

◀ *Charnia* looked like a prehistoric plant, but it was actually an animal!

417 One of the first hunting animals was *Anomalocaris*. It lived 520 million years ago, swimming through the sea in search of prey. It caught smaller creatures in its pincers, then pushed them into its mouth. *Anomalocaris* was a cousin of crabs and insects. It was one of the biggest hunting animals of its time, even though it was only 60 centimetres long.

▲ The *Cooksonia* plant had forked stems that carried water. The earliest examples have been found in Ireland.

418 By 400 million years ago, plants on land were growing taller. They had stiff stems that held them upright and carried water to their topmost parts. An early upright plant was *Cooksonia*. It was the tallest living thing on land, yet it was only 5 centimetres high.

Very fishy

419 **The first fish could not bite – they were suckers!** About 500 million years ago, new animals appeared in the sea – the first fish. They had no jaws or teeth and probably sucked in worms and small pieces of food from the mud.

▲ *Hemicyclaspis* was an early jawless fish. It had eyes on top of its head and probably lived on the seabed. This way it could keep a look out for predators above.

420 **Some early fish wore suits of armour!** They had hard, curved plates of bone all over their bodies for protection. These fish were called placoderms and most were fierce hunters. Some had huge jaws with sharp sheets of bone for slicing up prey.

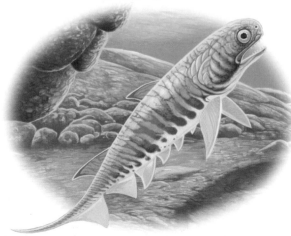

421 **Spiny sharks had spines, but they were not really sharks.** These fish were similar in shape to today's sharks, but they lived in rivers and lakes, not the sea, about 430 million years ago. *Climatius* was a spiny shark that looked fierce, but it was only as big as your finger!

◀ The fins on the back of *Climatius* were supported by needle-sharp spines. These helped to protect it from attacks by squid or other fish.

422 The first really big hunting fish was bigger than today's great white shark! *Dunkleosteus* grew to almost 10 metres long and swam in the oceans 360 million years ago. It sliced up prey, such as other fish, using its massive teeth made of narrow blades of bone, each one as big as this book.

423 Some early fish started to 'walk' out of water. Types of fish called lobefins appeared 390 million years ago. Their side fins each had a 'stump' at the base made of muscle. If the water in their pool dried up, lobefins could use their fins like stubby legs to waddle over land to another pool. *Eusthenopteron* was a lobefin fish about 1.2 metres long. Over millions of years, some lobefins evolved into four-legged animals called tetrapods.

VERY FISHY!

You will need:
waxed card (like the kind used to make milk cartons) crayons scissors piece of soap

Place the piece of waxed card face down. Fold the card up at the edges. Draw a fish on the card. Cut a small notch in the rear of the card and wedge the piece of soap in it. Put the 'fish' in a bath of cold water and watch it swim away.

◀ *Eusthenopteron* could clamber about on dry land when moving from one stretch of water to another.

Animals invade the land

424 The first land animals lived about 450 million years ago. These early creatures, which came from the sea, were arthropods – creatures with hard outer body casings and jointed legs. They included prehistoric insects, spiders and millipedes. *Arthropleura* was a millipede – it was 2 metres in length!

▶ *Arthropleura* was as long as a human and was the largest-ever land arthropod.

425 Some amphibians were fierce hunters. *Gerrothorax* was about one metre long and spent most of its time at the bottom of ponds or streams. Its eyes pointed upwards, to see fish swimming past, just above. *Gerrothorax* would then jump up to grab the fish in its wide jaws.

426 The first four-legged animal had eight toes on each front foot! *Acanthostega* used its toes to grip water plants as it swam. It lived about 380 million years ago and was one metre long. Creatures like it soon began to walk on land, too. They were called tetrapods, which means 'four legs'. They were a big advance in evolution – the first land animals with backbones.

◀ *Acanthostega* probably spent most of its time in water. It had gills for breathing underwater as well as lungs for breathing air.

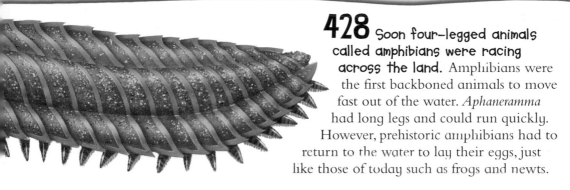

428 Soon four-legged animals called amphibians were racing across the land. Amphibians were the first backboned animals to move fast out of the water. *Aphaneramma* had long legs and could run quickly. However, prehistoric amphibians had to return to the water to lay their eggs, just like those of today such as frogs and newts.

427 Fins became legs for walking on land, and tails changed, too. As the fins of lobefin fish evolved into legs, their tails became longer and more muscular. *Ichthyostega* had a long tail with a fin along its upper side. This tail design was good for swimming in water, and also helpful when wriggling across a swamp.

429 Some amphibians grew as big as crocodiles! *Eogyrinus* was almost 5 metres long and had strong jaws and teeth, like a crocodile. However, it lived about 300 million years ago, long before any crocodiles appeared. Although *Eogyrinus* could walk on dry land, it spent most of its time in streams and swamps.

◄ *Ichthyostega* had short legs, so it could probably only move slowly on land.

Living with the dinosaurs

430 Some reptiles were as big and fierce as dinosaurs — but they lived in the sea. One of these was *Mosasaurus.* It grew up to 10 metres in length and may have weighed 10 tonnes, far bigger than today's great white shark.

431 One sea reptile had teeth the size of saucers! The huge, round, flat teeth of *Placodus* were more than 10 centimetres across. It used them to crush shellfish and sea urchins. *Placodus* was 2 metres long and lived at the same time as the first dinosaurs, about 230 million years ago.

I DON'T BELIEVE IT!

Fossils of *Mosasaurus* were found in the same place more than 200 years apart! The first was found in a quarry in the Netherlands in 1780. The second was found in the same place in 1998.

▼ *Mosasaurus* was a huge sea reptile. It had razor-sharp teeth and could swim with speed to catch its prey.

▼ *Archaeopteryx* had a long bony tail, unlike modern birds, which have no bones in their tails.

434 Fossils of the first bird were mistaken for a dinosaur. *Archaeopteryx* lived in Europe about 155 million years ago. Some of its fossils look very similar to the fossils of small dinosaurs. So *Archaeopteryx* was thought to be a dinosaur, until scientists saw the faint shape of its feathers and realized it was a bird.

432 Soon there were many kinds of bird flying above the dinosaurs. *Confuciusornis* was about 60 centimetres long and lived in what is now China, 120 million years ago. It had a backwards-pointing big toe on each foot, which suggests it climbed through the trees. It is also the earliest-known bird to have a true beak.

▲ Fossils of *Confuciusornis* have been found in China. It is named after the famous Chinese wise man, Confucius.

433 Mammals lived at the same time as dinosaurs. These animals have warm blood, and fur or hair, unlike a reptile's scaly skin. *Megazostrodon* was the earliest mammal known to scientists. It lived in southern Africa about 215 million years ago – only 15 million years or so after the dinosaurs began life on Earth. It was just 12 centimetres long, and probably hunted insects.

▼ *Megazostrodon* probably came out at night to hunt for its insect prey. It looked a little like a modern-day shrew.

The dinosaurs arrive!

435 **The earliest dinosaurs stalked the Earth almost 230 million years ago.** They lived in what is now Argentina, in South America. They included *Eoraptor* and *Herrerasaurus*. Both were slim, fast creatures.

436 *Eoraptor* and *Herrerasaurus* **could both stand almost upright and run on their two rear legs.** Few other animals of the time could run upright like this, on legs that were straight below their bodies. Most other animals had legs that stuck out sideways and then bent down, so they walked with a slow waddle.

▶ *Herrerasaurus* was about 3 metres long from nose to tail. It could run rapidly on its two rear legs, or walk slowly on all fours.

Legs were underneath the body, not sticking out to the sides as in other reptiles

437 These early dinosaurs were probably meat eaters. They hunted small animals such as lizards and other reptiles, insects and worms. They had lightweight bodies and long, strong legs to chase after prey. Their claws were long and sharp for grabbing victims. Their large mouths were filled with pointed teeth to tear up their food.

TWO LEGS GOOD!

You will need:

some stiff card   sticky tape
safe scissors   split pins

Cut out a model of Herrerasaurus; the head, body, arms and tail are one piece of card. Next, cut out each leg from another piece. Fix the legs on either side of the hip area of the body using a split pin. Adjust the angle of the head, body and tail to stand over the legs. This is how many dinosaurs stood and ran, well balanced over their rear legs and using little effort.

Long, pointed head and a long, bendy neck to look around and sniff for prey

Long tail to balance the head and body over the rear legs

Getting bigger

438 As the early dinosaurs spread over the land they began to change. This gradual and natural change in living things has happened since life began on Earth. New kinds of plants and animals appear, do well for a time, and then die out as yet more new kinds appear. The slow and gradual change of living things over time is called evolution.

Plateosaurus

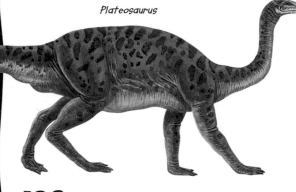

439 Some kinds of dinosaurs became larger and began to eat plants rather than animals. *Plateosaurus* was one of the first big plant-eating dinosaurs. It grew up to 8 metres long and lived 220 million years ago in what is now Europe. It could rear up on its back legs and use its long neck to reach food high off the ground.

440 *Riojasaurus* was an even larger plant eater. It lived 218 million years ago in what is now Argentina. *Riojasaurus* was 10 metres long and weighed about one tonne — as much as a large family car of today.

Riojasaurus

▼ *Rutiodon*, a crocodile-like meat eater, waits for *Riojasaurus*.

441 The early dinosaurs lived during the Triassic Period. This was the first period or part of the Age of Dinosaurs (the Mesozoic Era). The Triassic Period lasted from 251 to 200 million years ago.

442 The early plant-eating dinosaurs may have become larger so that they could reach up into trees for food. Their size would also have helped them fight enemies, as many big meat-eating reptiles were ready to make a meal of them. One was the crocodile *Rutiodon*, which was 3 metres long.

I DON'T BELIEVE IT!

Early plant-eating dinosaurs did not eat fruits or grasses — there weren't any. They hadn't appeared yet! Instead they ate plants called horsetails, ferns, cycads and conifer trees.

Claws for killing

443 **Nearly all dinosaurs had claws on their fingers and toes.** These claws were shaped for different jobs in different dinosaurs. They were made from a tough substance called keratin – the same as your fingernails and toenails.

Hypsilophodon

444 *Hypsilophodon* **had strong, sturdy claws.** This small plant eater, 2 metres long, probably used them to scrabble and dig in soil for seeds and roots.

445 *Deinonychus* **had long, sharp, hooked claws on its hands.** This meat eater, about 3 metres long, would grab a victim and tear at its skin and flesh. *Deinonychus* also had a huge hooked claw, as big as your hand, on the second toe of each foot. This claw could kick out and flick down like a pointed knife to slash pieces out of the prey.

Deinonychus

446 *Baryonyx* **also had a large claw but this was on the thumb of each hand.** It may have worked as a fish-hook to snatch fish from water. This is another clue that *Baryonyx* probably ate fish.

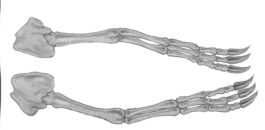

◀ These giant arms of the dinosaur *Deinocheirus* were found in Mongolia. Each one was bigger than a human, but nothing else of the skeleton has yet been found.

447 *Iguanodon* **had claws on its feet.** But these were rounded and blunt and looked more like hooves. *Iguanodon* also had stubby claws on its hands. However its thumb claw was longer and shaped like a spike, perhaps for stabbing enemies.

Iguanodon

QUIZ

Compare these modern animals' claws to the dinosaurs and their claws shown here. Which modern animal has claws with a similar shape and job to each dinosaur?

1. Lion – sharp, tearing claws
2. Deer – Rounded blunt hooves
3. Elephant – Flat, nail-like claws
4. Mole – Broad, strong digging claws

Answers:
1. Deinonychus 2. Iguanodon
3. Apatosaurus 4. Hypsilophodon

▼ Giant sauropod dinosaurs had almost flat claws. Dinosaurs like *Apatosaurus* looked like they had toenails on their huge feet!

Super-size dinosaurs

448 The true giants of the Age of Dinosaurs were the sauropods. These vast dinosaurs all had a small head, long neck, barrel-shaped body, long tapering tail and four pillar-like legs. The biggest sauropods included *Brachiosaurus*, *Mamenchisaurus*, *Barosaurus*, *Diplodocus* and *Argentinosaurus*.

▲ *Argentinosaurus* was up to 40 metres long, and weighed up to 100 tonnes.

449 Sauropod dinosaurs probably lived in groups or herds. We know this from their footprints, which have been preserved as fossils. Each foot left a print as large as a chair seat. Hundreds of footprints together showed many sauropods walked along with each other.

450 Sauropod dinosaurs may have swallowed pebbles – on purpose! Their peglike teeth could only rake in plant food, not chew it. Pebbles and stones gulped into the stomach helped to grind and crush the food. These pebbles, smooth and polished by the grinding, have been found with the fossil bones of sauropods.

451 The biggest sauropods like *Apatosaurus* were enormous beasts. They weighed up to ten times more than elephants of today. Yet their fossil footprints showed they could run quite fast – nearly as quickly as you!

Mamenchisaurus grew up to 26 metres long and weighed 30 tonnes. It lived in East Asia 160 million years ago

Barosaurus lived 150 million years ago in North America and Africa. It was 27 metres long and weighed 15 tonnes

Brachiosaurus grew up to 25 metres long and weighed up to 50 tonnes. It lived 150 million years ago in North America and Africa

Diplodocus lived in North America 150 million years ago. It grew to 27m long and weighed up to 12 tonnes

452 Sauropods probably had to eat most of the time, 20 hours out of every 24. They had enormous bodies, which would need great amounts of food, but only small mouths to gather the food.

This modern lorry is to the same scale as these huge dinosaurs!

I DON'T BELIEVE IT!

Diplodocus is also known as 'Old Whip-tail'! It could swish its long tail so hard and fast that it made an enormous CRACK like a whip. This leathery, scaly whip would scare away enemies or even rip off their skin.

195

Deadly meat eaters

453 The biggest meat–eating dinosaurs were the largest predators (hunters) ever to walk the Earth. Different types came and went during the Age of Dinosaurs. *Allosaurus* was from the middle of this time span. One of the last dinosaurs was also one of the largest predators – *Tyrannosaurus rex*, or *T rex*. An earlier hunting dinosaur from South America was bigger huge – *Giganotosaurus*.

I DON'T BELIEVE IT!

Some meat-eating dinosaurs not only bit their prey, but also each other! Fossils of several *T rex* had bite marks on the head. Perhaps they fought each other to become chief in the group, like wolves today.

454 These great predators were well equipped for hunting large prey – including other dinosaurs. They all had massive mouths armed with long, sharp teeth in powerful jaws. They had long, strong back legs for fast running, and enormous toe claws for kicking and holding down victims.

455 Meat-eating dinosaurs probably caught their food in various ways. They might lurk behind rocks or trees and rush out to surprise a victim. They might race as fast as possible after prey that ran away. They might plod steadily for a great time to tire out their meal. They might even scavenge - feast on the bodies of creatures that were dead or dying from old age or injury.

Carnotaurus from South America was 7.5 metres long and weighed one tonne

Allosaurus was 11 metres long and weighed 2 tonnes. It came from North America

Spinosaurus came from Africa. It was 14 metres long and weighed 4 tonnes

Albertosaurus was from North America. It was 9 metres long and weighed one tonne

The famous *T rex* was 13 metres long and weighed 6 tonnes. It lived in North America

The biggest carnivore was *Giganotosaurus*. It was a massive 15 metres long and weighed 7 tonnes

How deadly was T rex?

456 Was *T rex* a hunter that chased after its victims? Was it an ambush predator that hid in wait to rush out at prey? Was it a scavenger that ate any dead or dying dinosaurs it found? Or did it chase other dinosaurs from their kills and steal the meal for itself?

457 To be an active pursuit hunter, *T rex* must have been able to run fast. Scientists have tried to work out its running speed using models and computers, and by comparisons with other animals.

Who does what?

Research these animals living today and find out if they are mainly fast hunters, sneaky ambushers or scavengers.
Tiger Cheetah Hyaena
Crocodile Vulture
African wild dog

▶ *Tyrannosaurus rex* may have run down smaller dinosaurs such as these *Prenocephale*, perhaps rushing out from its hiding place in a clump of trees.

▲ When scavenging, *T rex* might sniff out a dinosaur that had died from illness or injury.

▲ When hunting, *T rex* would be at risk from injury, such as from the horns of *Triceratops*.

458 Some estimates for the running speed of *T rex* are as fast as 50 kilometres an hour, others as slow as 15 kilometres an hour. Most give a speed of between 20 and 30 kilometres an hour. This is slightly slower than a human sprinter, but probably faster than typical *T rex* prey such as *Triceratops*.

459 Evidence that *T rex* was a scavenger includes its very well-developed sense of smell for sniffing out dead, rotting bodies. Also, its powerful teeth could not chew food repeatedly like we do, but they could crush bones at first bite to get at the nutritious jelly-like marrow inside. Maybe a hungry *Tyrannosaurus rex* simply ate anything it could catch or find, so it was a hunter, ambusher and scavenger all in one.

460 Several *T rex* fossils show injuries to body parts such as shins, ribs, neck and jaws. These could have been made by victims fighting back, suggesting that *T rex* hunted live prey.

▶ *T rex* would tear and rip flesh from large prey, gulp in lumps and swallow them whole.

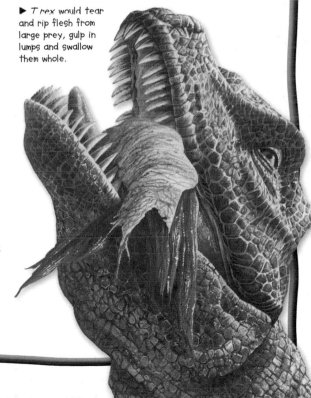

Profile of T rex

461 Fossil experts can work out what an extinct animal such a *Tyrannosaurus rex* looked like when it was alive. They study the size, shape, length, thickness and other details of its fossil bones, teeth, claws and other parts.

462 The tail of *T rex* was almost half its total length. It had a wide, muscular base and was thick and strong almost to the tip, quite unlike the long, thin, whiplike tails of other dinosaurs such as *Diplodocus*.

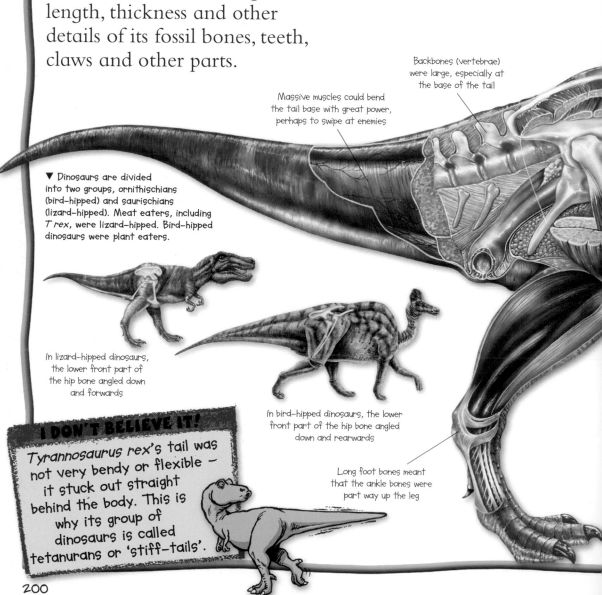

Backbones (vertebrae) were large, especially at the base of the tail

Massive muscles could bend the tail base with great power, perhaps to swipe at enemies

▼ Dinosaurs are divided into two groups, ornithischians (bird-hipped) and saurischians (lizard-hipped). Meat eaters, including *T rex*, were lizard-hipped. Bird-hipped dinosaurs were plant eaters.

In lizard-hipped dinosaurs, the lower front part of the hip bone angled down and forwards

In bird-hipped dinosaurs, the lower front part of the hip bone angled down and rearwards

Long foot bones meant that the ankle bones were part way up the leg

I DON'T BELIEVE IT!

Tyrannosaurus rex's tail was not very bendy or flexible — it stuck out straight behind the body. This is why its group of dinosaurs is called tetanurans or 'stiff-tails'.

463 The fossil bones of *T rex* show that it was a large, heavily built, powerful dinosaur. It had a huge skull, so its head and mouth were massive. There were holes in the skull for the eyes, ears and nasal openings or nostrils. There were also smaller holes in the bones for blood vessels and nerves.

▼ A cutaway *T rex* shows the thick, strong bones of its skeleton, which have been found preserved in many different fossil remains.

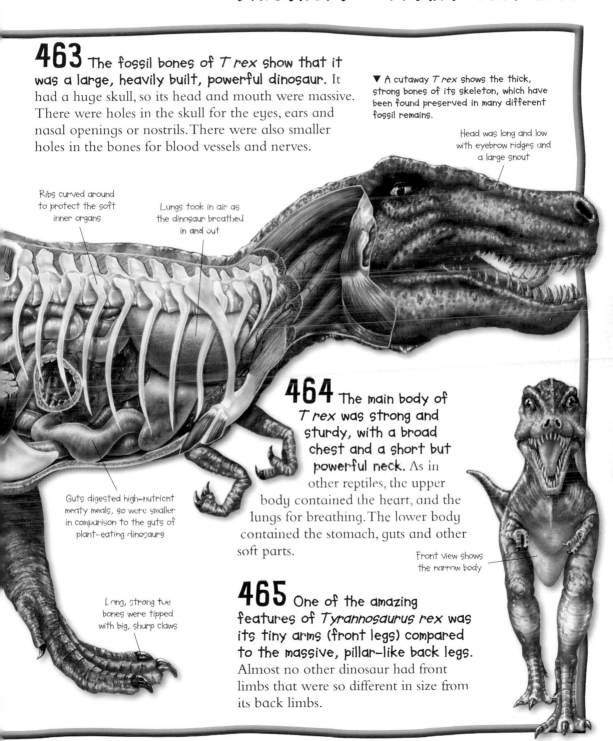

Head was long and low with eyebrow ridges and a large snout

Ribs curved around to protect the soft inner organs

Lungs took in air as the dinosaur breathed in and out

Guts digested high-nutrient meaty meals, so were smaller in comparison to the guts of plant-eating dinosaurs

Long, strong toe bones were tipped with big, sharp claws

464 The main body of *T rex* was strong and sturdy, with a broad chest and a short but powerful neck. As in other reptiles, the upper body contained the heart, and the lungs for breathing. The lower body contained the stomach, guts and other soft parts.

Front view shows the narrow body

465 One of the amazing features of *Tyrannosaurus rex* was its tiny arms (front legs) compared to the massive, pillar-like back legs. Almost no other dinosaur had front limbs that were so different in size from its back limbs.

Look! Listen! Sniff!

466 Like the reptiles of today, dinosaurs could see, hear and smell the world around them. We know this from fossils. The preserved fossil skulls had spaces for eyes, ears and nostrils.

467 Some dinosaurs like *Troodon* had very big eyes. There are large, bowl-shaped hollows in the fossil skull for them. Today's animals with big eyes can see well in the dark, such as mice, owls and night-time lizards. Perhaps *Troodon* prowled through the forest at night, peering in the gloom for small creatures to eat.

Ear

Eye

Nostril

468 There are also spaces on the sides of the head where *Troodon* had its ears. Dinosaur ears were round and flat, like the ears of other reptiles. *Troodon* could hear the tiny noises of little animals moving about in the dark.

◀ *Troodon* was about 2 metres long and lived in North America 70 million years ago.

469 The nostrils of *Troodon*, where it breathed in air and smelled scents, were two holes at the front of its snout. With its delicate sense of smell, *Troodon* could sniff out its prey of insects, worms, little reptiles such as lizards, and small shrew-like mammals.

▲ *Corythosaurus* has a bony plate on its head, instead of the tube like *Parasaurolophus*.

470 Dinosaurs used their eyes, ears and nose not only to find food, but also to detect enemies — and each other. *Parasaurolophus* had a long, hollow, tubelike crest on its head. Perhaps it blew air along this to make a noise like a trumpet, as an elephant does today with its trunk.

▶ *Parasaurolophus* was a 'duck-billed' dinosaur or hadrosaur. It was about 10 metres long and lived 80 million years ago in North America.

BIGGER EYES, BETTER SIGHT

Make a *Troodon* mask from card. Carefully cut out the shape as shown. Carefully cut out two small eye holes, each just one centimetre across. Attach elastic so you can wear the mask and find out how little you can see. Carefully make the eye holes as large as the eyes of the real *Troodon*. Now you can have a much bigger, clearer view of the world!

471 Dinosaurs like *Parasaurolophus* may have made noises to send messages to other members of their group or herd. Different messages could tell the others about finding food or warn them about enemies.

Dinosaur tanks

472 Some dinosaurs had body defences against predators. These might be large horns and spikes, or thick hard lumps of bone like armour-plating. Most armoured dinosaurs were plant eaters. They had to defend themselves against big meat-eating dinosaurs such as *Tyrannosaurus*.

473 *Triceratops* had three horns, one on its nose and two much longer ones above its eyes. It also has a wide shieldlike piece of bone over its neck and shoulders. The horns and neck frill made *Triceratops* look very fearsome. But most of the time it quietly ate plants. If it was attacked, *Triceratops* could charge at the enemy and jab with its horns, like a rhino does today.

▼ *Triceratops* was 9 metres long and weighed more than 5 tonnes. It lived 65 million years ago in North America.

474 *Euoplocephalus* was a well–armoured dinosaur. It had bands of thick, leathery skin across its back. Big, hard, pointed lumps of bone were set into this skin like studs on a leather belt. *Euoplocephalus* also had a great lump of bone on its tail. It measured almost one metre across and looked like a massive hammer or club. *Euoplocephalus* could swing it at predators to injure them or break their legs.

DESIGN A DINOSAUR!

Make an imaginary dinosaur! It might have the body armour and tail club of *Euoplocephalus*, or the head horns and neck frill of *Triceratops*. You can draw your dinosaur, or make it out of pieces of card or from modelling clay. You can give it a made-up name, like *Euoplo-ceratops* or *Tri-cephalus*. How well protected is your dinosaur? How does it compare to some well-armoured creatures of today, such as a tortoise, armadillo or porcupine?

Styracosaurus

Protoceratops

Euoplocephalus

In and over the sea

475 One prehistoric reptile had the bendiest neck ever! The sea reptile *Elasmosaurus* had a neck more than 5 metres long – the same as three people lying head-to-toe. Its neck was so bendy that *Elasmosaurus* could twist it around in a circle as it looked for fish and other creatures to eat.

476 The first big flying animals were not birds, but pterosaurs. They lived at the same time as the dinosaurs, and died out at the same time, too, about 65 million years ago. *Pteranodon* was one of the later pterosaurs and lived about 70 million years ago. It swooped over the sea to scoop up fish.

▼ *Pteranodon* scoops up prey while long-necked *Elasmosaurus* snaps its jaws in search of food.

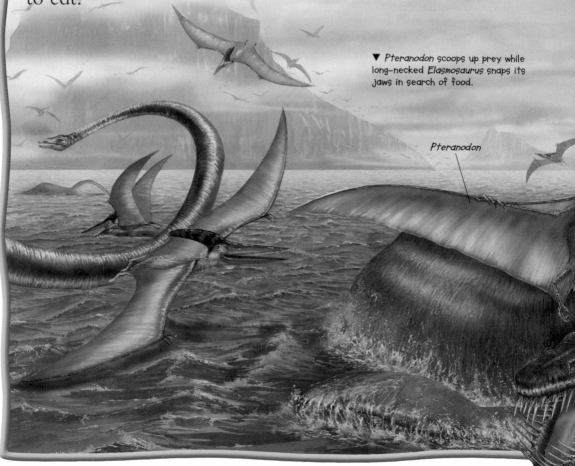

Pteranodon

477 The largest flying animal of all time was as big as a plane! With wings measuring up to 14 metres from tip to tip, the pterosaur *Quetzalcoatlus* was twice as big as any flying bird. It may have lived like a vulture, soaring high in the sky, and then landing to peck at a dead body of a dinosaur.

478 Some fossils of sea creatures are found thousands of kilometres from the sea. Around 100 to 70 million years ago, much of what is now North America was flooded. The shallow waters teemed with all kinds of fish, reptiles and other creatures. Today their fossils are found on dry land.

Elasmogaurus

After the dinosaurs

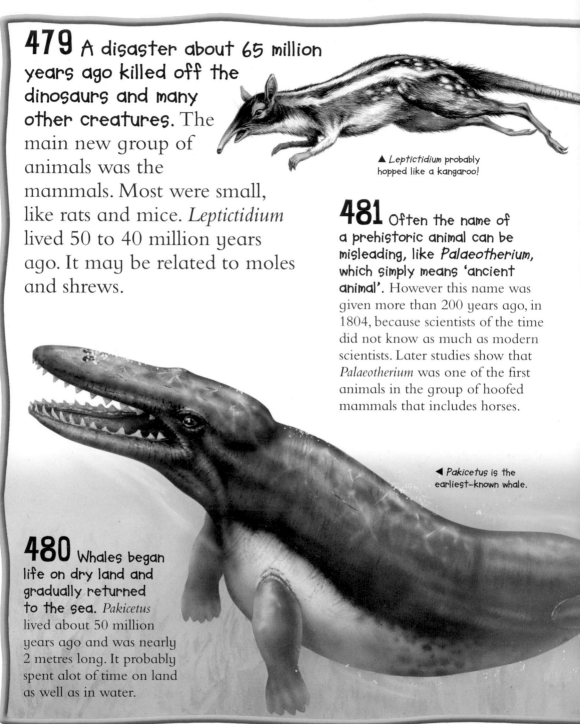

479 A disaster about 65 million years ago killed off the dinosaurs and many other creatures. The main new group of animals was the mammals. Most were small, like rats and mice. *Leptictidium* lived 50 to 40 million years ago. It may be related to moles and shrews.

▲ *Leptictidium* probably hopped like a kangaroo!

481 Often the name of a prehistoric animal can be misleading, like *Palaeotherium*, which simply means 'ancient animal'. However this name was given more than 200 years ago, in 1804, because scientists of the time did not know as much as modern scientists. Later studies show that *Palaeotherium* was one of the first animals in the group of hoofed mammals that includes horses.

◄ *Pakicetus* is the earliest-known whale.

480 Whales began life on dry land and gradually returned to the sea. *Pakicetus* lived about 50 million years ago and was nearly 2 metres long. It probably spent alot of time on land as well as in water.

▼ A mother *Uintatherium* and her baby. This strange-looking creature was the largest land animal of its time. Its head was covered in horns and it had small tusks.

482 Around 40 million years ago, the largest animal walking the Earth was *Uintatherium*. This plant eater was more than 3 metres long and nearly 2 metres tall at the shoulder – about the same size as a cow. Its fossils were found near the Uinta River in Colorado, USA. *Uintatherium* is thought to be a cousin of horses and elephants.

483 An animal's looks can be misleading. *Patriofelis* means 'father of the cats'. It lived 45 million years ago and was named because scientists thought it looked like an early cat. Later they realized that it merely looked like a cat and was really a member of an extinct group of hunting animals called creodonts.

QUIZ
1. What does the name *Patriofelis* mean?
2. How long was *Pakicetus*?
3. In what year were *Palaeotherium* fossils found?
4. How tall was *Uintatherium*?
5. When did dinosaurs die out and mammals start to take over?

Answers:
1. 'Father of the cats'
2. About 2 metres 3. 1804
4. Almost 2 metres tall at the shoulder
5. 65 million years ago

As the world cooled down

484 Before the world started to cool 30 million years ago, palm trees grew almost everywhere – but they became rare. These trees had thrived in warm, wet conditions. But as Earth cooled, other plants took over, such as magnolias, pines, oaks and birch. These changes meant that animals changed, too.

▼ *Brontotherium* was somewhere in size between a rhino and an elephant. Males used the Y-shaped horn on their snouts in fighting competitions.

485 *Pyrotherium* means 'fire beast', but not because this plant eater could walk through fire. Its fossils were found in layers of ash from an ancient volcano in Argentina, South America. The volcano probably erupted, and its fumes and ash suffocated and burned all the animals nearby. *Pyrotherium* was about as big as a cow and looked like a combination of a pig and a short-tusked elephant.

486 Many prehistoric animals have exciting names – *Brontotherium* means 'thunder beast'. Where the fossils of *Brontotherium* were found in North America, local people thought they were bones of the gods. They thought that these gods rode chariots across the sky and started thunderstorms, which led to the animal's name.

487 *Andrewsarchus was a real big-head!* At one metre long, it had the biggest head of any hunting mammal on land, and its strong jaws were filled with sharp, pointed teeth. Its whole body was bigger than a tiger of today. *Andrewsarchus* probably lived like a hyaena, crunching up bones and gristle from dead animals. Yet it belonged to a mammal group that was mostly plant eaters. It lived 30 million years ago in what is now the deserts of Mongolia, Asia.

▲ *Andrewsarchus* was the biggest meat-eating land animal ever to have lived.

▲ The horns on *Arsinoitherium's* head were hollow and may have been used to make mating calls.

QUIZ
1. What does *Brontotherium* mean?
2. What does *Pyrotherium* mean?
3. How long was the head of *Andrewsarchus*?
4. Where did *Arsinoitherium* live?

Answers:
1. Thunder beast 2. Fire beast 3. One metre 4. Northern Africa

488 *Some animals had horns as tall as people!* *Arsinoitherium's* two massive horns looked like powerful weapons – but they were light, fragile and made of very thin bone. This plant eater lived in northern Africa about 35 million years ago. It was almost as big as an elephant and may have been an ancient cousin of the elephant group.

Prehistoric prowlers

489 **Some animals probably ate just about anything.** Entelodonts were piglike animals that lived about 25 million years ago. *Dinohyus* was one of the largest entelodonts. Its teeth were sharp and strong, and it had powerful jaw muscles. It ate almost anything from leaves, roots and seeds, to small animals.

490 **Some predators (hunting animals) walked on tiptoe but others were flat-footed.** Most mammal predators, such as cats and dogs, walk on the ends of their toes. This helps them to run faster. *Daphoenodon* walked on flat feet, like a bear. It is often called a 'bear-dog' as it looked like a dog but walked like a bear.

▼ *Dinohyus* lived in North America and grew to be about 3 metres long. Its powerful neck muscles and large canine teeth suggest it could have broken bones and eaten flesh.

491 Fossils can show if predators hunted by day or at night. *Plesictis* was 75 centimetres long and its fossils show it had large sockets (spaces) for its eyes. This means that it probably hunted at night. It also had sharp claws and a long tail, so it probably scampered through trees hunting birds and insects, gripping with its claws and balancing with its tail.

492 Some predators have changed little over millions of years. *Potamotherium* was an early otter and lived in Europe, 23 million years ago. It looked almost like the otters of today. Its shape was so well-suited to hunting fish in streams that it has hardly changed.

QUIZ
1. Why is *Daphoenodon* sometimes called a 'bear–dog'?
2. Which hunter was active at night?
3. What prey did *Potamotherium* eat?
4. What do scientists think *Entelodon* ate?

Answers:
1. Because it looked like a dog, but walked like a bear 2. *Plesictis* 3. Fish 4. Almost anything

▲ *Potamotherium* had a bendy backbone to allow it to twist about in the water.

Amazing ancient elephants

493 **The first elephant had tiny tusks and almost no trunk.** *Moeritherium* lived in northern Africa about 36 million years ago. It stood just 60 centimetres tall and may have weighed around 20 kilograms – about the size of a large pet dog.

I DON'T BELIEVE IT!

The tusks of *Anancus* were more than 4 metres long – almost as long as the animal itself.

▶ Woolly mammoths had coats of shaggy hair. This hair kept their warm inner fur dry and waterproof in the freezing conditions of the Ice Age.

494 Some elephants were very hairy. The woolly mammoth was covered in thick, long dense hair to keep out the cold of the ice age. It was larger than a modern elephant and was probably hunted by early people. The last woolly mammoths may have died out less than 10,000 years ago.

495 One elephant had tusks like shovels. *Platybelodon* lived about nine million years ago in Europe, Asia and Africa. Its lower tusks were shaped like broad, flat shovels. Perhaps it used them to scoop up water plants to eat.

497 Some elephants had four tusks. *Tetralophodon* lived about eight million years ago and stood 3 metres tall. Its fossils have been found in Europe, Asia, Africa and America, so it was a very widespread and successful animal.

498 The biggest elephant was the Columbian mammoth. It stood 4 metres tall and may have weighed more than 10 tonnes – twice as much as most elephants today. It lived on the grasslands of southern North America.

▼ The Columbian mammoth had tusks that twisted into curved, spiral shapes.

496 Elephants were more varied and common long ago, than they are today. *Anancus* roamed Europe and Asia two million years ago. Like modern elephants, it used its trunk to pull leaves from branches and its tusks to dig up roots. However most kinds of prehistoric elephants died out. Only two kinds survive today, in Africa and Asia.

Our prehistoric relations

499 Monkeys, apes and humans first appeared over 50 million years ago – the first kinds looked like squirrels. This group is called the primates. *Plesiadapis* was one of the first primates. It lived 55 million years ago in Europe and North America.

◀ *Plesiadapis* had claws on its fingers and toes, unlike monkeys and apes, which had nails.

500 Early apes walked on all fours. About 20 million years ago, *Dryopithecus* lived in Europe and Asia. It used its arms and legs to climb trees. When it came down to the ground, it walked on all fours. It was 60 centimetres long and ate fruit and leaves.

I DON'T BELIEVE IT

The first fossils of the giant ape *Gigantopithecus* to be studied by scientists came from a second-hand shop in Hong Kong, more than 70 years ago.

▶ The early ape *Dryopithecus* walked flat on its feet, unlike other apes, which walked on their knuckles.

▼ The need to see longer distances on grasslands may have caused the first apes to walk on two legs.

502 Some kinds of ape may have walked on their two back legs, like us. About 4.5 million years ago *Ardipithecus* lived in Africa. Only a few of its fossils have been found. However, experts think it may have walked upright on its back legs. It could have made the first steps in the change, or evolution, from apes to humans.

503 One prehistoric ape was a real giant – over 3 metres tall! Its name, *Gigantopithecus*, means 'giant ape'. It was much larger than today's biggest ape, the gorilla, which grows to 2 metres tall. *Gigantopithecus* probably ate roots and seeds, and may have hunted small animals such as birds, rats and lizards.

▶ The enormous *Gigantopithecus* could probably stand on its hind legs to reach food.

501 Scientists work out which animals are our closest cousins partly from fossils – and also from chemicals. The chemical called DNA contains genes, which are instructions for how living things grow and work. The living animals with DNA most similar to ours are the great apes, chimpanzees and gorillas, both from Africa. So our ancient cousins were probably apes like them. The orang-utan, from Southeast Asia, is less similar.

What are fossils?

504 Fossils are the preserved remains of once-living things, such as bones, teeth and claws. Usually the remains were buried in sediments – layers of tiny particles such as sand, silt or mud. Very slowly, the layers and the remains inside them turned into solid rock.

505 In general it takes at least 10,000 years, but usually millions, for fossils to form. So the remains of living things that are a few hundred or thousand years old, such as the bandage-wrapped mummies of pharaohs in ancient Egypt, are not true fossils.

▲ A seed cone fossil of the extinct plant *Williamsonia*.

506 Many kinds of once-living things have formed fossils. They include all kinds of animals from enormous whales and dinosaurs to tiny flies and beetles. There are fossils of plants, too, from small mosses and flowers to immense trees. Even microscopic bacteria have been preserved.

◀ Teeth are very hard and so make excellent fossils – especially those from *Tyrannosaurus rex!*

▶ It is unusual for thin, delicate bones, such as those of the bat *Icaronycteris*, to fossilize.

507 In most cases, fossils formed from the hard parts of living things that did not rot away soon after death. As well as bones, teeth and claws these include shells, scales and the bark, roots, cones and seeds of plants.

508 Much more rarely, soft parts have been preserved as fossils, such as flower petals and worm bodies. Where this has happened, it gives a fascinating glimpse into how these ancient life-forms looked and lived.

▼ The tube worms' soft bodies soon decayed but their hard, coiled tubes were preserved in the seabed mud.

QUIZ

Which of these are true fossils?
A. A bird called the dodo, which died out over 300 years ago
B. Two thousand-year-old pots and vases from ancient Rome
C. The first shellfish that appeared in the sea over 500 million years ago

Answer:
C is a true fossil.
The others are much too recent.

How fossils form

▼ All living things die. Those living in water, such as this ichthyosaur, are more likely to leave fossils than those on land.

509 When a living thing dies, its flesh and other soft parts start to rot. Sometimes they are eaten by scavenging creatures such as worms and insects. The harder parts, such as teeth and bones, rot more slowly and last longer.

510 Fossil formation usually begins like this, and very often in water. Sediments tend to settle on dead animals and plants in ponds, lakes, rivers and seas. This is the main reason why most fossils are of plants and animals that lived in water or somehow got washed into water.

1. After death, the ichthyosaur sinks to the seabed. Worms, crabs and other scavengers eat its soft body parts.

START SOME FOSSILS

You will need:

small stones   glass mixing jug
sand   water

Imagine the stones are 'bones' of an ancient creature. They get washed into a river – put them in the jug and half-fill with water. Then the 'bones' are covered by sediment – sprinkle in the sand.

511 Over time, more sediment layers settle on top of the remains. As they are covered deeper, further rotting or scavenging is less likely.

512 Water trickles into the sediments and once-living remains. The water contains dissolved substances such as minerals and salts. Gradually, these replace the once-living parts and turn them and the sediments into solid rock. This is called permineralization.

513 Most living things rot away soon after death, so the chances of anything becoming a fossil are slim. Also, sedimentary rock layers change over time, becoming heated and bent, which can destroy fossils in them. The chances of anyone finding a fossil are even tinier. This is why the record of fossils in rocks represents only a tiny proportion of prehistoric life.

2. Sediments cover the hard body parts, such as bones and teeth, which gradually turn into solid rock.

3. Millions of years later the upper rock layers wear away and the fossil remains are exposed.

Fossils and time

514 Fossils are studied by many kinds of scientist. Palaeontologists are general experts on fossils and prehistoric life. Palaeozoologists specialize in prehistoric creatures, and palaeobotanists in prehistoric plants. Geologists study rocks, soil and other substances that make up the Earth. All of these sciences allow us to work out the immense prehistory of the Earth.

515 Earth's existence is divided into enormous lengths of time called eons, which are split into eras, then periods, epochs and finally, stages. Each of these time divisions is marked by changes in the rocks formed at the time – and if the rocks are sedimentary, by the fossils they contain. The whole time span, from the formation of the Earth 4600 million years ago to today, is known as the geological time scale.

▼ Starting with the Cambrian Period (far right), this timeline shows 11 major time periods in Earth's history. It gives examples of some of the fossil animals and plants that have been found for each period. 'MYA' stands for 'millions of years ago'.

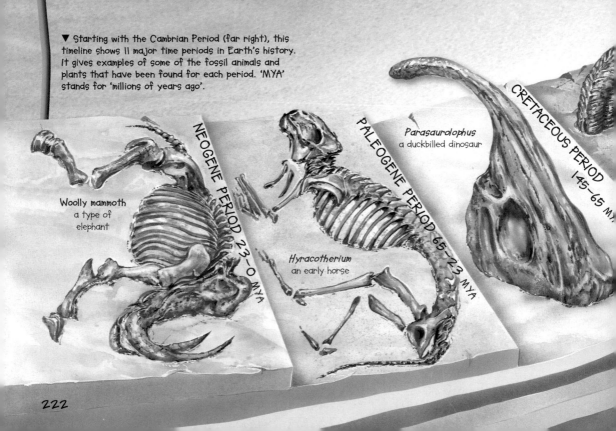

NEOGENE PERIOD 23–0 MYA

Woolly mammoth
a type of elephant

PALEOGENE PERIOD 65–23 MYA

Hyracotherium
an early horse

Parasaurolophus
a duckbilled dinosaur

CRETACEOUS PERIOD 145–65 MYA

CAMBRIAN PERIOD 542–488 MYA

Trilobite
a shelled marine creature

ORDOVICIAN PERIOD 488–444 MYA

SILURIAN PERIOD 444–416 MYA

DEVONIAN PERIOD 416–359 MYA

516 An example of a geological time division is the Cretaceous Period, from 145 to 65 million years ago. It is named after creta or *kreta*, a Latin word for chalk. Due to temperature, rainfall and other climate conditions, layers of chalk rocks formed. They contained fossils such as certain kinds of shellfish, the winged reptiles known as pterosaurs and many kinds of dinosaurs.

Graptolite
a simple marine animal

Birkenia
a type of fish

Crinoid
a simple marine animal

CARBONIFEROUS PERIOD 359–299 MYA

PERMIAN PERIOD 299–251 MYA

Lepidodendron
a primitive tree

TRIASSIC PERIOD 251–200 MYA

Diplocaulus
an early amphibian

JURASSIC PERIOD 200–145 MYA

Rhamphorhynchus
a winged reptile

Stephanoceras
a type of ammonite

MAKE CHALK FOSSILS

You will need:
chalk sticks   metal teaspoon

Chalk often contains fossil shellfish. Find pictures of long, thin examples, such as razorshells, mussels and belemnites. Use the spoon to scrape and carve the chalk sticks into shapes to make your own 'fossil' museum.

Fossil-hunting takes off

517 From the early 19th century, fossil-hunting became more popular. Towns and cities as well as rich individuals began to establish museums and collections of the 'wonders of nature' with displays of stuffed animals, pinned insects, pressed flowers – and lots of fossils.

FOSSIL MATCH

Match the scientific names of these fossils with the places they were found.

A. Argentinosaurus (dinosaur)
B. Toxorhynchites mexicanus (mosquito in amber)
C. Proconsul africanus (ape-monkey)

1 Mexico, Central America
2 Argentina, South America
3 Africa

Answers:
A2 B1 C3

518 People began to earn a living by finding and selling fossils. One of the first was Mary Anning (1799–1847) of Lyme Regis, southern England. For many years she collected fossils from the seashore, where waves and storms regularly cracked open boulders and cliffs to reveal new finds. Mary discovered fossil fish, ichthyosaurs, plesiosaurs, pterosaurs and many other animals.

▶ As in Mary Anning's time, fossils still appear from the rocks at Lyme Regis.

519 In 1881, the British Museum opened its display of natural history collections in London, which showed fossils and similar wonders from around the world. Other great cities had similar museums and sent fossil-hunters to remote places for the most spectacular finds.

▲ By the 1860s many museums had fossils on display, such as this 'sea serpent' or mosasaur.

▼ Cope and Marsh found and described about 130 new kinds of dinosaurs.

Othniel Charles Marsh

Edward Drinker Cope

521 Between the 1870s and 1890s, two of the leading fossil-hunters were Americans Othniel Charles Marsh and Edward Drinker Cope. Their teams tried to outdo each other to discover the most and best fossil dinosaurs, as well as other animals and plants, too.

▲ The first fossil stegosaur skulls were found in the 1870s.

▶ The dinosaur *Stegosaurus* was named by Marsh in 1877.

520 From the early 1900s, fossil-hunting spread to Africa and then in the 1920s to Mongolia and China. From the 1970s there were finds in South America and Australia. Today, fossil-hunters go all over the world in search of new discoveries.

At the dig

522 Some people look for fossils in their spare time and if they find one it's a bonus. At an important site, scientists such as palaeontologists organize an excavation or 'dig' that can last for many months.

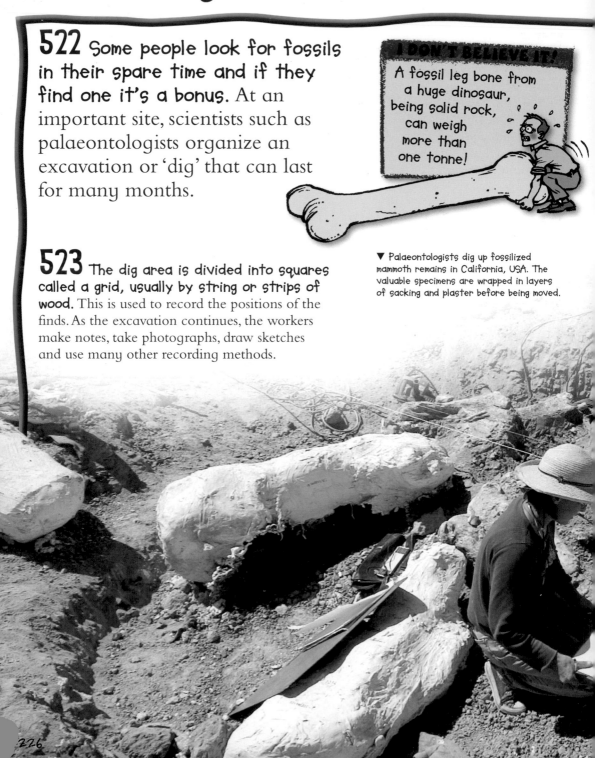

I DON'T BELIEVE IT!

A fossil leg bone from a huge dinosaur, being solid rock, can weigh more than one tonne!

523 The dig area is divided into squares called a grid, usually by string or strips of wood. This is used to record the positions of the finds. As the excavation continues, the workers make notes, take photographs, draw sketches and use many other recording methods.

▼ Palaeontologists dig up fossilized mammoth remains in California, USA. The valuable specimens are wrapped in layers of sacking and plaster before being moved.

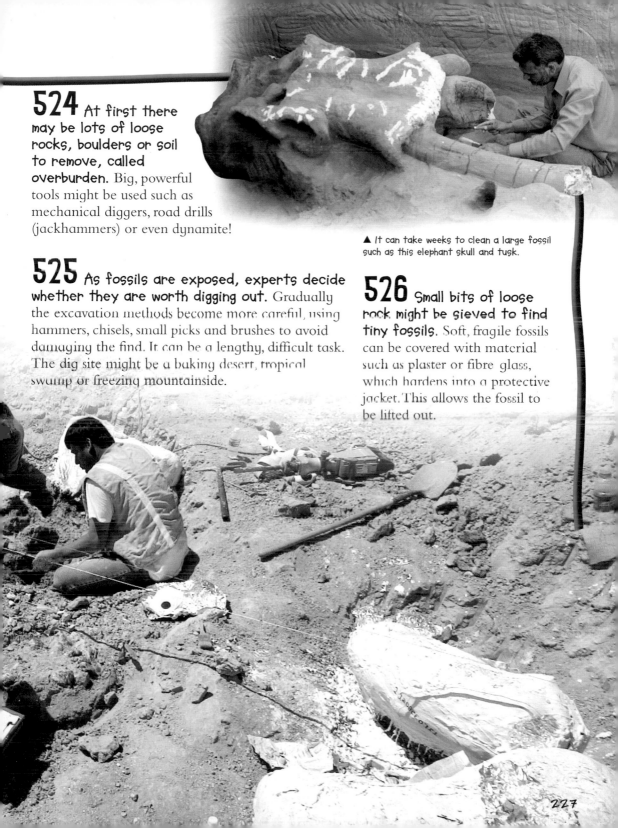

524 At first there may be lots of loose rocks, boulders or soil to remove, called overburden. Big, powerful tools might be used such as mechanical diggers, road drills (jackhammers) or even dynamite!

▲ It can take weeks to clean a large fossil such as this elephant skull and tusk.

525 As fossils are exposed, experts decide whether they are worth digging out. Gradually the excavation methods become more careful, using hammers, chisels, small picks and brushes to avoid damaging the find. It can be a lengthy, difficult task. The dig site might be a baking desert, tropical swamp or freezing mountainside.

526 Small bits of loose rock might be sieved to find tiny fossils. Soft, fragile fossils can be covered with material such as plaster or fibre glass, which hardens into a protective jacket. This allows the fossil to be lifted out.

Fossils come alive!

527 One of the most exciting parts of fossil study is to reconstruct (rebuild) the original plant or animal. This needs a detailed knowledge of anatomy, or body structure. For example, fossils of prehistoric birds are compared to the same body parts of similar birds alive today. This is called comparative anatomy.

528 Tiny marks or 'scars' on fossil bones show where the animal's muscles attached in real life. These help to reveal muscle shapes and arrangements so experts can gradually put the flesh on the (fossil) bones.

Fossil bones
Faint scars on fossil bones can help scientists work out how and where muscles were attached

▲ This reconstruction of an ankylosaur, an armoured dinosaur, is being done head-first. The tail is still bare fossils of the bones.

529 We can see how a living creature walks, runs and jumps using the joints between its bones. If fossil bones have their joints preserved, their detailed shapes and designs show the range of motion and how the animal moved.

MULTI-COLOURED BIRD

You will need:

pictures of *Archaeopteryx*   colour pens
tracing paper   white paper

No one knows what colour the first bird *Archaeopteryx* was. Look at pictures of it in books and on web sites. See how its feather colours and patterns differ. Trace an outline of *Archaeopteryx* from a book and colour it to your own amazing design.

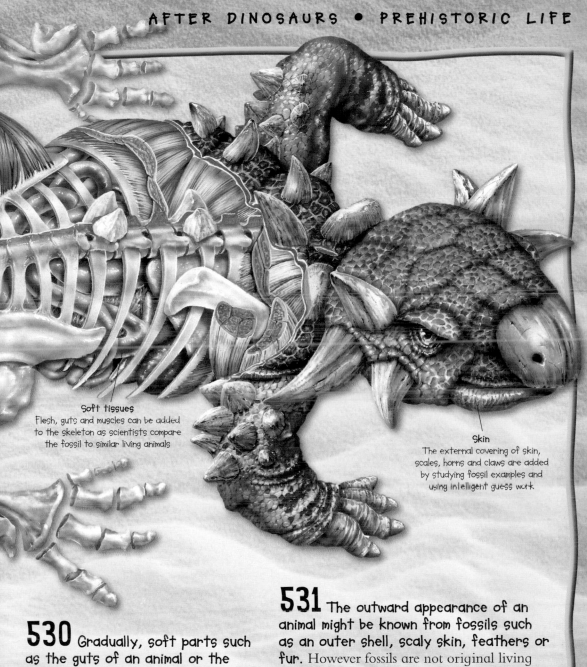

Soft tissues
Flesh, guts and muscles can be added to the skeleton as scientists compare the fossil to similar living animals

Skin
The external covering of skin, scales, horns and claws are added by studying fossil examples and using intelligent guess work

530 Gradually, soft parts such as the guts of an animal or the petals of a flower, can be guessed and added to the reconstruction. Again, experts use information from fossil relatives and living cousins.

531 The outward appearance of an animal might be known from fossils such as an outer shell, scaly skin, feathers or fur. However fossils are not original living parts – they have changed to rock. So the colour of fossil skin is the colour of the type of rock, not the animal. Experts guess at colours and patterns for their reconstructions.

THE ANIMAL WORLD

532 There are millions of animal species, or kinds, around the world. Some animals are large, such as elephants, and some are small, such as beetles. Animals live in nearly all habiats, from deserts to oceans. Scientists often discover new animals. At the same time, many animals are becoming endangered or extinct.

◄ Little is known about clouded leopards. They sleep all day and only hunt at night. Despite their length, these cats weigh only about 20 kilograms – roughly the same as a six-year-old child.

Mammals

533 There are nearly 4500 different types of mammal. Most have babies that grow inside the mother's body. While a baby mammal grows, a special organ called a placenta supplies it with food and oxygen from the mother's body. These mammals are called placental mammals.

▼ This echidna is part of a group of mammals called monotremes. They do not give birth to live young – they lay eggs instead.

535 Not all mammals' young develop inside the mother's body. Two smaller groups of mammals do things differently. Monotremes, like platypuses and echidnas or spiny anteaters, lay eggs. The platypus lays her eggs in a burrow, but the echidna keeps her single egg in a special dip in her belly until it is ready to hatch.

Duck-billed platypus

534 Mammal mothers feed their babies on milk from their own bodies. The baby sucks this milk from teats on special mammary glands, also called udders or breasts, on the mother's body. The milk contains all the food the young animal needs to help it grow.

▲ Olive baboons live in Africa in groups called troops of between 20 and 150 animals.

QUIZ

1. How many types of mammal are there?
2. Which types of mammal lay eggs?
3. How big is a baby kangaroo when it is born?
4. What supplies food and oxygen to a baby mammal in the womb?

Answers:
1. nearly 4500 2. Platypus and echidnas 3. 2 centimetres 4. The placenta

536 Marsupials give birth to tiny young that finish developing in a pouch. A baby kangaroo is only 2 centimetres long when it is born. Tiny, blind and hairless, it makes its own way to the safety of its mother's pouch. Once there, it latches onto a teat in the pouch and begins to feed.

▲ The baby kangaroo stays in the pouch for about six months while it grows.

▲ Fallow deer have a good sense of smell, and excellent sight.

537 Most mammals have good senses of sight, smell and hearing. Their senses help them watch out for enemies, find food and keep in touch with each other. For many mammals, smell is their most important sense. Plant eaters such as rabbits and deer sniff the air for signs of danger such as the scent of a predator.

Midnight marsupials

538 Kangaroos and koalas are marsupials, or pouched mammals, and most members of this group are nocturnal. There are about 196 types of marsupial living in and around Australia and about 85 types that live on the American continent. They are a strange group of animals that give birth to tiny youngsters that grow in a pouch on their mother's belly.

539 Red kangaroos live in the great heat of the Australian outback where it's too hot for most animals to be active during the day. The red kangaroo is the world's largest marsupial. Its body reaches 1.6 metres in length and its tail is another 1.2 metres. It forages at night, nibbling at shoots, tender plants and leaves.

540 Marsupials that spend all day sleeping and all night eating. They eat and sleep up in the trees, and eucalyptus leaves are their main food. With stocky bodies, short limbs and leathery noses, koalas are easy to recognize.

▼ Red kangaroos have a good sense of smell and they use it to find water in the Australian deserts.

I DON'T BELIEVE IT!

Quolls are cat-like marsupials of Australia. They spend the night hunting, but during the day they like to sleep. Quolls find it difficult to nap if there's too much noise, so these clever creatures can fold their ears down to block out sound!

541 Virginia opossums forage at night and survive on all sorts of food, including grubs, fruit, eggs and scraps they scavenge from bins. They live in North and Central America and shelter in piles of vegetation or under buildings. Opossums have an unusual skill – if they are scared they drop down and act dead, with their eyes and mouths open. They do this for up to six hours at a time – long enough for a predator to get bored and wander off!

▲ A Tasmanian devil gorges on its meal alone, but other devils may soon come to join in, drawn by the smell of fresh meat.

▼ A female Virginia opossum has up to 18 young in her litter, but she only has teats to feed 13 of them. She protects her young until they are old enough to fend for themselves.

542 In Australia's southern island of Tasmania, a terrible screeching and barking may be heard in the night – a Tasmanian devil. These marsupials are known for their noisy, aggressive behaviour and if they are alarmed, devils screech and bark. They can smell dead animals from far away and have such powerful jaws they can grind and chew bones and gristle.

Beautiful bats

543 A flutter of wings and the glimpse of a swooping body in the night sky are often the only clues you'll get that a bat is nearby. Bats are the nocturnal masters of the sky. They are small, furry mammals that are so well adapted to life on the wing that they can pass by almost unnoticed by humans and animals alike.

◄ During the day, bats hang upside down and rest – this is called roosting.

544 Except for the polar regions, bats can be found all over the world. They roost in caves, trees, under logs and in buildings. There are nearly 1000 different types, or species, of bat – the smallest have wingspans of 15 centimetres, and the biggest have wingspans of 1.5 metres or more!

545 Bats are the only mammals that have wings. Their wings have developed from forelimbs and have a thin membrane of skin that stretches over long, bony digits, or fingers. Bats can change direction easily in flight, which helps them chase and catch insects.

546 Although bats have good eyesight, they depend more on their senses of smell and hearing to find their prey at night. Most types of bat have a special sense called echolocation. They produce very high-pitched sounds – too high for most people to hear – that bounce off objects in front of them. When the sound comes back to a bat's ears, like an echo, they can tell by the way it has changed, how far away the object is and its size.

I DON'T BELIEVE IT!

Bats can live for a long time – often for 10 to 25 years. Some wild bats have been known to live to the age of 30! This is partly because bats are able to avoid being eaten as few animals can catch them when they dash and dart between trees.

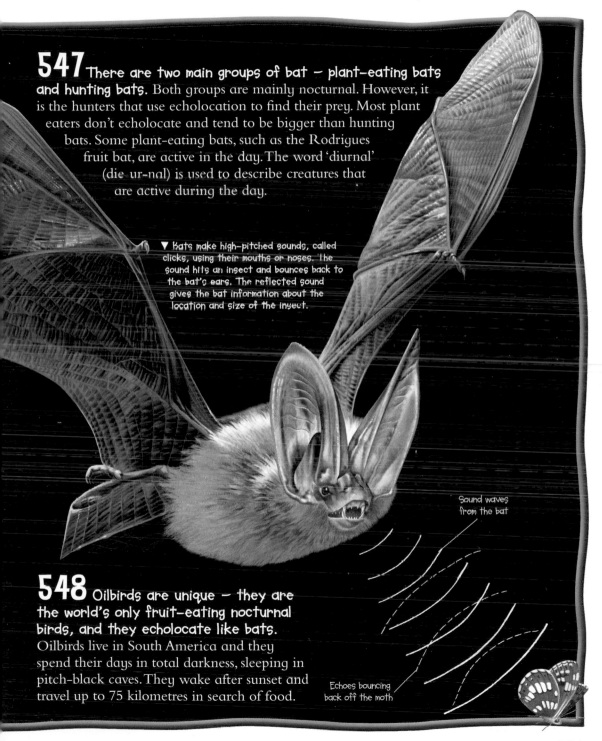

547 There are two main groups of bat — plant-eating bats and hunting bats. Both groups are mainly nocturnal. However, it is the hunters that use echolocation to find their prey. Most plant eaters don't echolocate and tend to be bigger than hunting bats. Some plant-eating bats, such as the Rodrigues fruit bat, are active in the day. The word 'diurnal' (die-ur-nal) is used to describe creatures that are active during the day.

▼ Bats make high-pitched sounds, called clicks, using their mouths or noses. The sound hits an insect and bounces back to the bat's ears. The reflected sound gives the bat information about the location and size of the insect.

Sound waves from the bat

548 Oilbirds are unique — they are the world's only fruit-eating nocturnal birds, and they echolocate like bats. Oilbirds live in South America and they spend their days in total darkness, sleeping in pitch-black caves. They wake after sunset and travel up to 75 kilometres in search of food.

Echoes bouncing back off the moth

Insect eaters

549 Since many insects, grubs and worms are active at night, so are the mammals that hunt them. Aardvarks are unusual ant-eating animals of Africa that snuffle and snort in the darkness. Their name means 'earth-pig' in Afrikaans, one of many languages spoken in South Africa, and they do look quite like long-nosed pigs with their big, fleshy snouts.

◄ Hedgehogs sleep during the day. At night, they come out to search for insects and worms to eat.

551 If they are scared, hedgehogs roll themselves into a tight ball with only their sharp spines showing. They may be able to defend themselves against foxes, but hedgehogs are no match for a car – thousands of these European mammals are killed on roads every year.

► Aardvarks live alone and come out at sunset to forage for food. These long-snouted animals can eat up to 50,000 insects in one night!

550 At night, aardvarks search for termites and ants using their good sense of smell as their eyesight is poor. They rip open nests and lick up the insects with their long tongues. Aardvarks also have large front claws, which they use for digging their burrows where they sleep during the day. They can close their ears and nostrils to stop dirt from getting in them as they dig.

552 Few people ever see pangolins as they are shy and secretive nocturnal creatures. Pangolins are armoured animals that live in Africa and Asia. Their bodies are covered in thick, overlapping scales, which are formed from layers of hardened skin. Pangolins don't have teeth, but lick up ants and termites with their long, sticky tongues.

I DON'T BELIEVE IT!

Armadillos are nocturnal, armour-plated relatives of anteaters. Their eyesight is so poor, they have been known to walk into the legs of people standing in their way! Armadillos eat almost anything they can find and have been known to dig into graves and munch on dead bodies!

▲ Pangolins have short legs and bodies measuring up to one metre in length. They can climb trees or dig burrows underground using their long, sharp claws.

553 Shrews are active by night as well as day, since they must eat every few hours to survive. They are mouse-like, furry creatures with long snouts and are some of the smallest mammals in the world. They rely mostly on their sense of smell to find food, but some of them use echolocation – a way of locating objects using sound that is used by bats and oilbirds.

◀ The pygmy shrew is only 5 centimetres in length and weighs up to 6 grams. It is one of the smallest mammals in the world.

Chisellers and chewers

554 Some of the world's commonest mammals are nocturnal rodents such as mice, rats and beavers. This group of animals can exist in almost any habitat all over the world, except the Antarctic. They have big eyes to see in the dark, furry bodies, and teeth that are perfect for gnawing and chewing.

ODD ONE OUT

Mammals have hair or fur, and feed their young with milk. Which one of these animals is not a mammal?

Wolf   Bat   Squirrel
Alligator   Dolphin

Answer:
Alligators are reptiles, not mammals

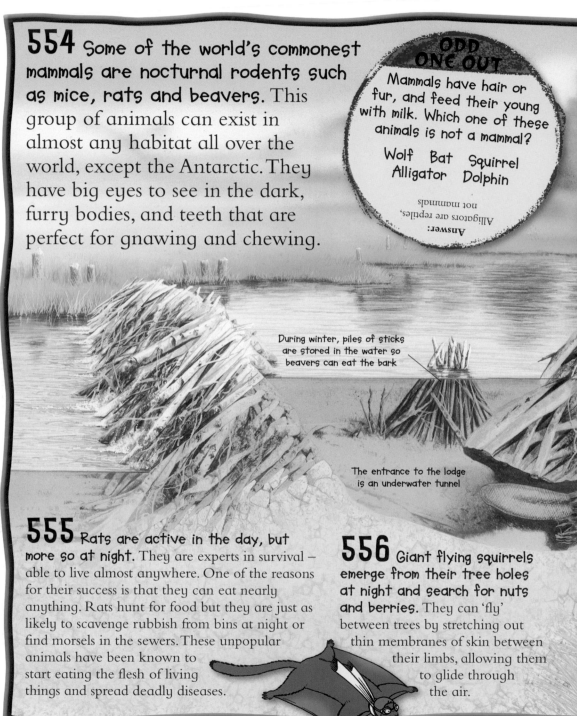

During winter, piles of sticks are stored in the water so beavers can eat the bark

The entrance to the lodge is an underwater tunnel

555 Rats are active in the day, but more so at night. They are experts in survival – able to live almost anywhere. One of the reasons for their success is that they can eat nearly anything. Rats hunt for food but they are just as likely to scavenge rubbish from bins at night or find morsels in the sewers. These unpopular animals have been known to start eating the flesh of living things and spread deadly diseases.

556 Giant flying squirrels emerge from their tree holes at night and search for nuts and berries. They can 'fly' between trees by stretching out thin membranes of skin between their limbs, allowing them to glide through the air.

The lodge is hollow inside. The floor is above water so the beavers can eat and rest in the dry

Chewing through trees wears down a beaver's teeth, but the teeth never stop growing

557 American beavers are large rodents, often measuring more than one metre in length from nose to tail-tip. They spend the day resting in a lodge, which is a nest made from mud and sticks with underwater entrances. Beavers leave their nests as the sun begins to set and they remain busy through much of the night, feeding on plants.

▲ Beavers chisel at trees and branches, cutting them up for use in the dams they build on rivers and streams. These dams create wetlands where many types of animal and plant thrive.

What is a primate?

558 Primates such as monkeys and apes are covered in fur or hair and the young feed on their mothers' milk. They have big brains and can work out solutions to difficult problems. Primates have been known to learn new skills and teach them to their young.

▶ A gorilla's bones are strong but lightweight. They support the muscles, hold the body upright and allow movement.

559 Primates are mammals. This means that they have back bones and warm-blooded bodies. They are divided into three groups — prosimians such as bushbabies, monkeys such as baboons, and apes such as gorillas.

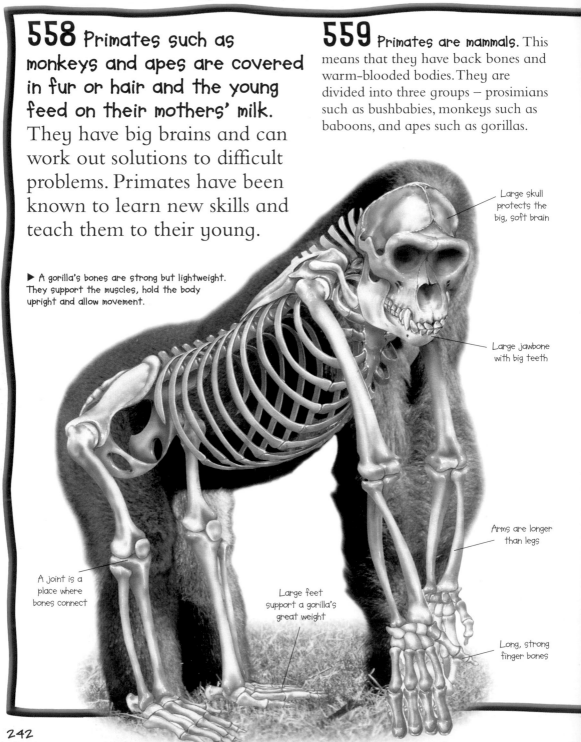

Large skull protects the big, soft brain

Large jawbone with big teeth

Arms are longer than legs

A joint is a place where bones connect

Large feet support a gorilla's great weight

Long, strong finger bones

560
Unlike many other animals, primates have large eyes at the front of their head. This allows them to focus clearly on objects in front of them. Since most primates live in trees and leap between branches, this is a very useful feature. Unlike most other creatures, primates can see in colour.

▼ Primates' hands and feet can grab, hold, pinch and probe. Most primates can grip objects and tools precisely in their hands.

Tarsier hand

Tarsier foot

Spider monkey hand

Spider monkey foot

Chimpanzee hand   Chimpanzee foot

561
Primates prefer to live in groups. They often live with their families, or large groups of related families. Primates communicate with one another in many ways – using sound, scent, touch and movement. Young primates usually stay with their families for years while they learn how to survive.

▶ In many primate groups, such as the baboons shown here, adults help the mother by finding food and helping to look after the baby. Males will also gather food and play with the young.

562
Primates have hands that are very similar to ours. Instead of paws and claws, they have fingers and flat fingernails. They can bring their forefingers and thumbs together in a delicate pinching movement.

Leaping lemurs

563 Lemurs are long-legged primates that live in just one place on Earth – Madagascar. This large island in the Indian Ocean is home to lots of animals that aren't found anywhere else. Many of them, including lemurs, are dying out – partly because their forest homes are being cut down.

QUIZ

Most lemurs live in trees. What word is used to describe the place where an animal lives?

1. Halibut   2. Habit   3. Habitat

Answer:
3. Habitat

▶ An aye-aye uses its long middle finger to probe into cracks in a tree and pick out tasty grubs to eat.

564 Ring-tailed lemurs are elegant, curious creatures. Unlike most other lemurs, they spend a lot of time on the ground and as they walk they hold their boldly-patterned tails high in the air. These primates rub their tails with smelly substances from under their arms. When two rival lemurs meet they wave their stinky tails at one another!

▼ As well as being agile tree climbers, ring-tailed lemurs can move swiftly on the ground.

565 Newborn lemurs are soon strong enough to grasp onto their mothers' fur. As a female travels around between trees, her infant holds on tight, safe from predators. However the youngster is always at risk of falling to its death should it let go for a second.

566 The aye-aye is probably the ugliest primate. This shaggy-haired lemur builds its nest in the forks of trees and emerges at night to eat insects and fruit. Using its large ears, the aye-aye can hear beetles as they scratch around on the forest floor. An aye-aye's middle finger is unusually long – ideal for digging into wood and pulling out grubs to eat.

▶ Sifakas can stand upright and run on their hind feet. They can leap 10 metres between branches.

567 Indris and sifakas are types of large lemur that are very close to extinction. They are gentle, plant-eating animals with loud voices, and can be heard calling from several kilometres away. Farmers and loggers are cutting down the forests where they live, and they are also hunted for meat.

Spider monkeys

568 If you are a monkey, it's a good idea to spend most of your time up in the trees. Hidden amongst the leaves and branches, it's easier to stay out of the reach of other animals that may want to eat you. Although big cats such as jaguars can climb trees, they can't chase monkeys onto the thinnest branches.

569 Spider monkeys are some of the fastest, most nimble of the primate climbers. Their arms, legs and tails are extremely long, and they can hang from a tree by a single limb or tail. They usually run along a tree's branches with their tails curled over their backs, and it's rare for them to walk around on the ground.

570 Spider monkeys can travel up to 5 kilometres a day browsing for their favourite food of ripe fruit. During the dry season, from July to September, there is less food around, so the monkeys spend most of their day resting and saving energy.

246

THAT'S HANDY!

Find out just how useful your hands are!
You will need:
big bowl of cold water   apples
Put the apples in the bowl and place it
on the floor. Keep your hands behind
your back and grab an apple out of
the bowl, using just your mouth.
It's not easy!

◀ High up in the forest canopy,
black-handed spider monkeys hang
by a hand, foot or tail and swing
at speed between branches.

571 Spider monkeys are noisy
animals and make loud barking calls if
they're scared. This warns the rest of
the troop to beware, because a predator,
such as a wild cat or snake, may be
around. If some members of the family
are separated, they make whinnying
noises until they find one another.

572 While many primates use
their thumbs to grip, some spider
monkeys don't even have any!
Despite being thumbless, these agile
animals can hold onto branches by
using a hand and four long fingers
like a hook.

247

Clever chimps

573 **Chimpanzees are our closest living relatives, yet they are in danger of extinction.** It seems strange that humans don't do everything in their power to save the lives of their animal cousins, but chimps – the best known of all the great apes – are fighting a tough battle for survival.

574 **These apes live in the rainforests of western and central Africa.** They spend much of their time in trees, and they can swing from branches like gibbons, but not so well. When they are on the ground, chimps walk on all four limbs, and even run in this position. They can also stand up on their legs and can walk for up to one kilometre. Walking upright leaves their hands free for throwing stones at enemies, which they sometimes do!

◀ Not many animals are clever enough to use tools. This chimp is using a leaf to collect water.

575 Like most monkeys and apes, chimps eat plants and insects. They visit trees laden with fruit, when it's in season, but otherwise they eat flowers, seeds, nuts, eggs and honey. Unlike most other primates, chimps hunt other animals to eat. They also eat termites – small ant-like insects.

▲ Chimps are 60 to 90 centimetres tall and weigh up to 60 kilograms. They spend a lot of time in trees, looking for food.

576 Termites live in large nests, so they can be difficult to reach. Chimps have worked out a way to get to the termites by using sticks. They poke the sticks into the termite nest and, once the bugs have swarmed all over the sticks, they pull them out and eat the termites.

577 Chimps don't just use sticks to catch termites, they use them to pull down fruit from trees. They've also learnt how to use leaves to wipe down their bodies or to scoop up water to drink. Young chimps don't know how to do these things naturally – they only find out by watching adults and copying them.

◄ Chimps insert sticks into termite mounds to catch and eat the termites. Scientists have discovered that it is much harder than it looks!

QUIZ

Newborn apes are called 'babies' or 'young'. Can you match these animals to their young, which are given special names?

goat calf elephant caterpillar butterfly foal horse kid

Answers:
goat – kid elephant – calf
butterfly – caterpillar horse – foal

249

Gentle giants

578 There are three types of gorilla — western, eastern and mountain — but they all look alike. These apes are the largest of all primates, and a mature adult male — called a silverback — can reach nearly 2 metres in height and weigh 200 kilograms.

579 Although there are three different types of gorilla, they all lead very similar lives. Gorillas live in forests — either tropical rainforests or rainforests in mountainous areas that can become cold. Mountain gorillas have longer, thicker fur to keep them warm. Gorillas eat plants and spend much of their day chewing leaves, shoots and stems.

580 At night, gorillas make themselves nests to sleep in. It only takes an adult about five minutes to break and bend twigs to create a good sleeping place. They never sleep in the same nest twice.

581 Gorillas are more likely to walk away from trouble than fight. If a family can't escape an intruder, the oldest male stares at the stranger, or barks. If this doesn't work, he stands up tall, hoots and beats his chest. He only runs at the intruder as a last resort but he may use his huge fangs and considerable strength to kill his enemy.

◀ Gorillas live in groups. The silverback is the leader and protector of the group. He makes all of the day-to-day decisions.

▲ Gorillas like to rest after every meal and at night. They make nests to sleep in up in trees. Large males make nests on the ground.

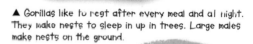

QUIZ

1. What is the largest primate?
2. What is an adult male called?
3. How many types of gorilla are there?

Answers:
1. Gorilla 2. Silverback 3. Three

582 About two out of every five gorillas die before they reach their first birthday. Some are killed by silverbacks from other families, but scientists don't know the reason for most of the deaths. It's most likely that the babies simply become ill.

Whales and dolphins

583 The mammal group of cetaceans is made up of about 80 kinds of whale, dolphin and porpoise. The whale group is divided into two main types – baleen whales and toothed whales.

584 Baleen whales are the largest members of the cetacean group and are often called great whales. They catch food with long strips in their mouths called baleen or whalebone. One example is the sei whale, which is about 16 metres in length and can reach a weight of 25 tonnes.

▲ The sperm whale is the biggest toothed whale. It only seems to have teeth in its lower jaw because those in its upper jaw can barely be seen.

CREATE A DOLPHIN!

You will need:
paper   coloured pens or pencils

Draw a dolphin outline and colour it any pattern you wish. You can name it after its colour, such as the pink-spotted dolphin. Or use your own name, like Amanda's dolphin.

585 Toothed whales catch prey with their sharp teeth. This subgroup includes sperm whales, beaked whales and pilot whales. One example is the beluga, also known as the white whale. It lives in the cold waters of the Arctic and can grow up to 5 metres in length. It is one of the noisiest whales, making clicks, squeaks and trills.

▼ The finless porpoise, with its blunt 'beak' and bulging forehead, is one of the smallest cetaceans at about 1.5 metres in length.

587 Another group is made up of beaked whales. These are medium-sized whales with long, beak-shaped mouths. There are about 20 kinds, but some are very rare and hardly ever seen. The shepherd's beaked whale, which is about 7 metres in length, has been seen fewer than 20 times.

586 There are six species of porpoise. They are usually quite small, at 2 metres or less in length. They have blunter, more rounded heads than dolphins. The finless porpoise, as its name suggests, has a smooth back with no fin

▼ The dusky dolphin is very inquisitive and likes to swim and leap near boats, perhaps in the hope of being fed.

588 There are more than 35 kinds of dolphin. Most of them are 2 to 3 metres in length. They are fast swimmers and can often be seen leaping above the waves. The dusky dolphin is one of the highest leapers, twisting and somersaulting before it splashes back into the sea.

Gigantic whales

589 **Whales are the biggest kind of animal in the world today.** Some are longer and heavier than the largest trucks. They need a lot of muscle power and energy to move such large bodies. As they live in the ocean, the water helps to support their enormous bulk.

591 **The blue whale is the largest animal ever to have lived.** It can grow up to 30 metres in length, which is as long as seven cars placed end to end. It reaches up to 150 tonnes in weight – that's as heavy as 2000 adults or 35 elephants.

590 **On land, bears and tigers are the biggest hunting animals.** However, the sperm whale is more than 100 times larger, and easily the biggest predator (active hunter) on Earth. It grows up to 20 metres in length and 50 tonnes in weight.

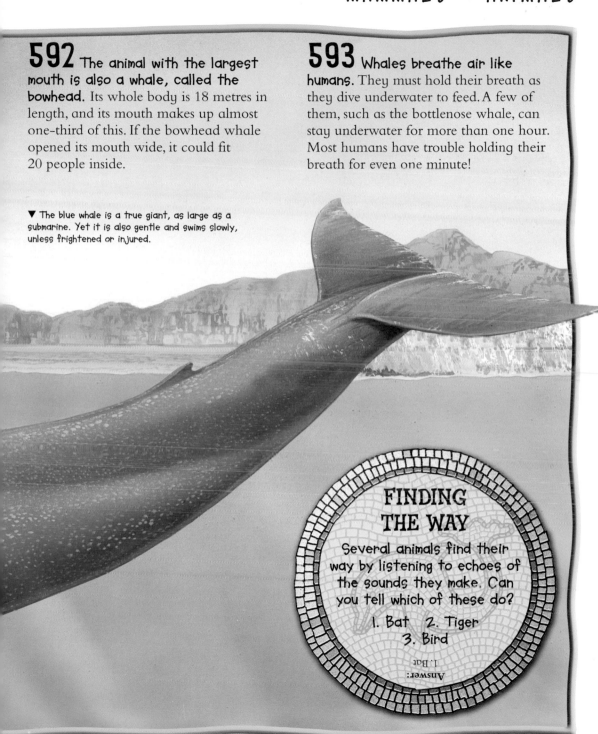

592 The animal with the largest mouth is also a whale, called the bowhead. Its whole body is 18 metres in length, and its mouth makes up almost one-third of this. If the bowhead whale opened its mouth wide, it could fit 20 people inside.

593 Whales breathe air like humans. They must hold their breath as they dive underwater to feed. A few of them, such as the bottlenose whale, can stay underwater for more than one hour. Most humans have trouble holding their breath for even one minute!

▼ The blue whale is a true giant, as large as a submarine. Yet it is also gentle and swims slowly, unless frightened or injured.

FINDING THE WAY

Several animals find their way by listening to echoes of the sounds they make. Can you tell which of these do?

1. Bat   2. Tiger
3. Bird

Answer:
1. Bat

Inside whales and dolphins

594 Whales, dolphins and porpoises are mammals, like humans. They have the same parts inside their bodies as humans. These include bones to make up the skeleton, lots of muscles, a stomach to hold food, a heart to pump blood, and lungs to breathe air.

595 Most mammals have hair or fur, including humans. Whales, dolphins and porpoises are unusual because they have smooth, hairless skin to help them slip easily through the water. Only a few hairs, mainly bristles, can be found around the eyes, nose and mouth.

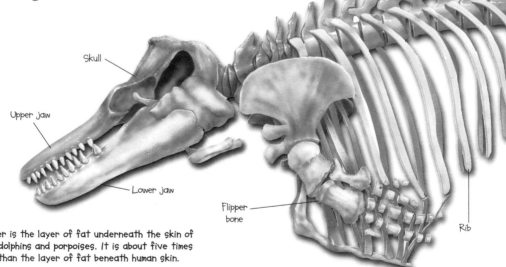

Skull

Upper jaw

Lower jaw

Flipper bone

Rib

▼ Blubber is the layer of fat underneath the skin of whales, dolphins and porpoises. It is about five times thicker than the layer of fat beneath human skin.

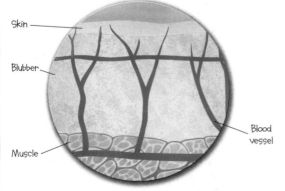

Skin

Blubber

Muscle

Blood vessel

596 On land, fur keeps mammals warm in cold places. The sea can be cold, too. Cetaceans have a different way of keeping in their body heat. They have a thick layer of fat just under the skin called blubber. In large whales, the blubber can be more than 50 centimetres thick!

597 Cetaceans often have small animals growing inside their bodies called parasites, such as lice. Parasites aren't needed for survival – the whale or dolphin provides them with food. Some baleen whales have their heads covered with barnacles (shellfish), which normally grow on seaside rocks.

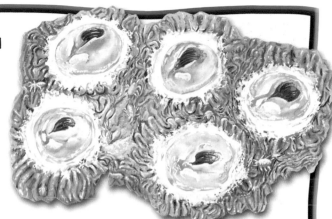

▲ Barnacles are a type of shellfish. They stick firmly to large whales and cannot be rubbed off!

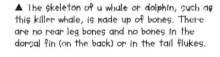

Backbone
(vertebra)

▲ The skeleton of a whale or dolphin, such as this killer whale, is made up of bones. There are no rear leg bones and no bones in the dorsal fin (on the back) or in the tail flukes.

I DON'T BELIEVE IT!

The sperm whale has the biggest brain in the world. It weighs about 8 kilograms – that's over five times the size of a human brain. As far as scientists know, the sperm whale is not the cleverest animal.

598 Compared to most animals, whales, dolphins and porpoises have large brains for their size. Dolphins are clever creatures, able to learn tricks and solve simple puzzles. Some scientists believe that dolphins have even developed their own language.

Flippers, flukes and fins

599 **Most mammals have four legs and a tail.** Whales, dolphins and porpoises don't. They have flippers, a fin and a tail. Flippers are their front limbs, similar to human arms. In fact, flipper bones and human arm and hand bones are alike. Flippers are mainly used for swimming, scratching and waving to send messages to others in the group.

600 The tail of a cetacean is in two almost identical parts. Each part is called a fluke. Unlike the flippers, flukes have no bones. They are used for swimming as the body arches powerfully to swish them up and down. They can also be slapped onto the water's surface to send messages to other whales. This is called lobtailing.

▼ Whales can often be seen splashing backwards into the water. This is known as breaching. Even the massive humpback whale can breach – and it weighs more than 30 tonnes!

▼ The humpback whale waves its flippers in the air and splashes them onto the surface. This is called flipper-slapping.

601 The fin on the back of many whales, dolphins and porpoises is known as a dorsal fin. In some, such as the killer whale, it is tall and narrow. In others, such as the bottlenose dolphin, it is shaped like a swept-back triangle. The blue whale has a tiny dorsal fin near its tail. Right whales, the bowhead, beluga and narwhal have no dorsal fin at all.

MAKE A WHALE!

You will need:
long balloon newspaper strips
paints papier-mâché paste

Paste three layers of newspaper onto the balloon. Let it dry, then paint the whale and stick on paper fins and a tail.

602 Many whales, dolphins and porpoises jump out of the water and crash back down with a big splash. This is called breaching. It may be done to send a loud message to others in the group, or to try and get rid of skin pests, such as barnacles and whale lice.

Sieving the sea

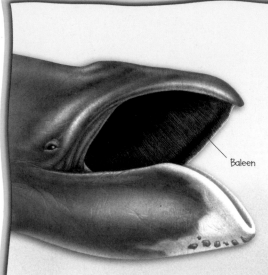

Baleen

▲ The bowhead whale's baleen hangs like a huge curtain, big enough for ten people to hide behind.

603 Great whales are also called baleen whales because of the baleen in their mouths. Baleen is sometimes called whalebone, but it is not bone. It's light, tough and springy, almost like plastic. It hangs down in long strips from the whale's upper jaw. The size and shape of the strips vary from one kind of whale to another.

604 Most baleen whales, such as the blue, fin and sei whales, cruise-feed. This means that they feed by swimming slowly through a swarm of shrimp-like creatures called krill with their mouths open.

605 As a baleen whale feeds, it takes in a huge mouthful of water — enough to fill more than 100 bathtubs. This makes the skin around its throat expand like a balloon. The whale's food, such as krill, is in the water. The whale pushes the water out between the baleen plates. The baleen's bristles catch the krill like a giant filter. Then the whale licks off the krill and swallows them.

606 The humpback whale makes a 'bubble curtain'. It dives down, then swims up slowly in small circles as it breathes out. The bubbles created rise quickly and form a tube-shaped 'curtain' that keeps the krill or other food close together in one place as a 'bait-ball'. Then the humpback lunges into the bait-ball with its mouth wide open.

I DON'T BELIEVE IT!

In summer, the blue whale eats 4 tonnes of food in one day! That's about four million krill. In winter, it eats hardly anything for many weeks because food is scarce.

607 The grey whale often feeds on the shallow seabed. It swims on one side and drags its mouth through the mud. Then it pushes the water and mud out of its mouth. This traps food in its baleen, such as shellfish and shrimps. Its feeding method leaves deep grooves in the seabed, like a ploughed field.

◄ Humpback whales feed by rising up through shoals of fish with their mouths open and throat skin bulging. They scoop up water, push it out through the baleen and eat the food left inside their mouths.

261

Fierce hunters

608 Dolphins, porpoises and toothed whales are active hunting carnivores. They eat meat – the flesh of sea creatures, especially fish and squid. Some of them crunch up hard-shelled crabs, shrimps and prawns, or shellfish, such as oysters and whelks.

► Bottlenose dolphins swim around small fish that gather into a tight group called a 'bait-ball'. Then the dolphins dash into the bait-ball and try to grab the fish.

609 A typical dolphin has 60 to 100 teeth. They are in pairs, left and right, in the upper and lower jaws. These teeth are not usually thin and sharp like fangs, but wide and cone-shaped. The teeth are the same shape all along the jaw, unlike the teeth of a cat, dog or human. This is the best design for catching their slippery food.

610 Beaked whales mainly eat squid. In some species, males have just two or four teeth, which look like tusks. Females have none at all. These whales suck in their prey and swallow it whole.

611 The sperm whale has about 50 teeth in its lower jaw, which are about 20 centimetres in length. The teeth in its upper jaw are so tiny, they can barely be seen.

612 Most dolphins and porpoises must chase their speedy prey, quickly twisting and turning in the water, snapping at victims. Once a dolphin catches its prey, it flicks the fish back into its mouth, and swallows it whole. With a larger victim, the dolphin bites off a big chunk and swallows it. Whales, dolphins and porpoises hardly ever chew their food.

Dogs and wolves

613 Wolves, coyotes and African hunting dogs belong to the dog family. Most live and hunt in groups, or packs. By working together, a pack can attack and kill large prey, such as deer and bison.

◀ When a wolf feels threatened, the fur on its back, called its hackles, stands on end. This makes it look bigger and fiercer.

614 Wolves have excellent senses of sight, hearing and smell to help them to find their prey. These strong, agile creatures have been known to travel a distance of 100 kilometres in just one night in search of food.

615 Coyotes are wild dogs that live in North America. They normally hunt in pairs or on their own, although they may join together as a group to chase large prey, such as deer.

616 Like wild cats, coyotes hunt by keeping still and watching an animal nearby. They wait for the right moment, then creep towards their prey and pounce, landing on top of the startled victim. Coyotes are swift runners and often chase jackrabbits across rocks and up hills.

BE A WOLF!

1. One person is Mr Wolf and stands with their back to the other players.
2. The players stand 10 paces away and shout, "What's the time, Mr Wolf?".
3. If Mr Wolf shouts, "It's 10 o'clock", the players take 10 steps towards Mr Wolf.
4. Watch out because when Mr Wolf shouts "Dinnertime", he chases the other players and whoever he catches is out of the game!

▶ When African hunting dogs pursue their prey, such as the wildebeest, the chase may go on for several kilometres, but the dogs rarely give up. They wait until their prey tires, then leap in for the kill.

617 African wild dogs are deadly pack hunters. They work as a team to chase and torment their prey. The whole pack shares the meal, tearing at the meat with their sharp teeth.

What is a bear?

618 There are eight types, or species, of bear including polar bears, grizzly bears and giant pandas. All have large, heavy bodies, big heads and short, powerful legs.

619 Most bears are brown in colour. Polar bears have white, or yellow-white coats, which help them blend into their snowy Arctic habitat. Pandas have striking black-and-white markings. Bears have thick fur, which helps to keep them warm – and makes them look even bigger than they actually are.

620 When they show their teeth and growl, bears are a scary sight. They belong to a group of meat-eating creatures called carnivores. The large, sharp teeth at the front of their mouths are called canines, and they use them for stabbing and tearing at meat. These teeth may measure between 5 and 8 centimetres in length.

621 A close look at a bear reveals that its eyes are actually quite small compared to the size of its head. Bears have good eyesight, but their sense of smell is much stronger. They can even smell food hidden in a glove compartment, inside a locked car!

◄ An angry bear may roar, opening its powerful jaw to reveal massive teeth.

▶ A bear's paws and claws are fearsome weapons, but they are most often used for digging up food such as roots. The Malayan sun bear's long, curved claws make it an excellent climber.

I DON'T BELIEVE IT!

Bears may look like they rely on strength rather than speed to survive, but don't be fooled. Brown bears can run at nearly 50 kilometres an hour — much faster than most humans.

622 Bears use their teeth to defend themselves in fights and to hunt other animals. They have powerful paws to swipe at their attackers, and one blow can knock another animal to the ground. Their claws are long, knife-like, and reach up to 15 centimetres in length.

▼ A bear's skeleton helps to support its weight. The large skull protects the brain and the ribcage protects the internal organs.

Pelvis

Ribcage

Spine

Shoulder

Skull

Black bears

623 Areas of North America and Canada are home to black bears. They live in mountains and forests, and despite being very shy, they sometimes stray into towns. They avoid brown bears, which also live in the American continent.

624 Most black bears are black, but some have brown or even white fur. Dark-furred black bears sometimes have lighter fur on their muzzles (noses) and chests. Their long, curved claws help them grip tree trunks when climbing trees.

TRUE OR FALSE?

1. A muzzle is the name given to some animals' long noses.
2. Black bears live in Europe.
3. 'Scavenge' means finding scraps and waste food.
4. A carnivore eats meat.

Answers:
1. True 2. False 3. True 4. True

625 These big bears need to eat plenty of food to keep their energy levels high. During the summer they mostly eat plants, but the actual food they eat depends on where they live, the time of the year and what is available. Black bears rarely hunt other animals, although they eat insects such as beetles, and love honey

626 Black bears are regarded as the most intelligent of all bears. Those that live near humans often use their sense of smell to locate rubbish bins. They find ways to break into the bins and rifle through piles of garbage. Black bears are often found in national parks where they wander into campsites in search of food, particularly at night.

627 Thousands of black bears are killed by humans every year. Only one out of every ten black bears dies naturally. The others are all killed by hunters, or after being hit by cars. Yet black bears manage to survive and are not in danger of becoming extinct.

◄ Black bears avoid humans, and if they see people they are much more likely to run away or climb up a tree than attack.

Polar bears

628 The polar bear is the biggest type of bear, and the largest meat-eating animal on Earth. These huge beasts have to fight to survive in one of the planet's bleakest places.

629 The Arctic is a snow-and-ice-covered region around the North Pole. Temperatures are record-breaking, dropping to an incredible -70°C and, unsurprisingly, very few living things are found there. Polar bears, however, manage to cope with howling winds, freezing snow blizzards and long winters.

I DON'T BELIEVE IT!

The word 'Arctic' comes from the Greek word 'Arkitos', which means country of the Great Bear. This doesn't refer to polar bears though, but to the Great Bear constellation, or pattern of stars, in the sky.

630 Polar bears are covered in a thick layer of white fur. This helps them to stay warm because it keeps in their body heat, and even absorbs some of the Sun's warming energy. Each hair is a colourless hollow tube, which appears white when it reflects light. Some bears have yellow fur, especially in the summer when they spend less time in water and their coats get dirty.

631 Polar bears also have a layer of fat called blubber beneath the skin, which traps in heat. This is where the bears store energy for the months when they may not be able to find food. The blubber may be up to 12 centimetres thick and is so effective at helping the bear stay warm that polar bears are more likely to get too hot than too cold!

632 Female polar bears spend the winter months in dens so their cubs can be born safely. A mother spends five or six months in the snug den with her cubs, while the bad winter weather rages outside. She doesn't eat or drink during all of this time, but survives on her body fat.

◀ The Arctic summer is short, so polar bears like to soak up the sunshine in between hunting trips. Young cubs stay close to their mother at all times.

271

Brown bears

633 The mighty brown bear is a massive, shaggy-haired beast that lives in the northern parts of the world. Long ago, brown bears were spread far and wide across the world, but now they are finding it difficult to survive in places where they come into contact with humans.

634 Brown bears are now mostly found in forests, mountains and scrubland, in remote places where few people roam. There are brown bears in Northern Europe, Siberia, Asia, Alaska, Canada and parts of the United States. Bears from different areas can look quite different from one another. They vary in colour from yellowish to almost black.

▲ In the far north, where winters are long and cold, the brown bear sleeps for weeks on end. In warmer southern areas, it sleeps much less.

635 Kodiak bears are the largest of all brown bears and can weigh up to 800 kilograms. They stand almost twice as high as a human. Their size is due to their diet – these big animals eat lots of fish, which is packed with healthy fats and proteins. Kodiak bears live on Kodiak Island, in Alaska, North America.

I DON'T BELIEVE IT!

In Siberia, tigers and bears occasionally attack one another. However, a fight between the two animals is so evenly matched that they usually avoid one another!

637 Brown bears may be huge animals, but they can run with speed if they need to. Their walking looks slow and lumbering, but a scared bear can change pace very quickly – and run faster than most other animals.

636 Brown bears live in northern areas where it is very cold in winter, so they usually hibernate. Some types spend up to seven months in a den, but all bears wake up occasionally. When they wake they rearrange their bedding, clean themselves and return to sleep.

▶ Male bears are called boars and may sometimes fight one another using jaws, paws and claws.

638 Grizzlies are the famous brown bears of North America. They get their name from the white hairs that grow in their brown coats, giving them a grizzled appearance.

Giant pandas

639 With its distinctive white face and black eye patches there are few animals that are as easy to recognize as the giant panda. These large bears have been brought to the brink of extinction, partly by human actions.

I DON'T BELIEVE IT!

Pandas use all four limbs to grip onto tree trunks as they climb up or down. Sometimes they lose their hold and fall, but their thick fur helps to cushion them as they land.

640 Pandas spend a lot of time on the ground, but they climb trees to rest or sleep. Youngsters first start climbing when they are just six months old and use their claws to help them grip onto the trees. Pandas like to rest in forked branches, and watch the world beneath them. They often come down from trees head first!

▼ Giant pandas only live in the cool bamboo woodlands and forests in China, South Asia. These areas are often covered in snow.

641 Pandas rarely eat meat, and spend around 16 hours a day chewing bamboo. This is a tough grass-like plant that grows very tall. Pandas also eat honey, eggs, fish, and occasionally mice.

▶ When they feed, giant pandas sit with their legs outstretched in front of them.

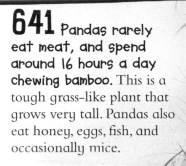

642 Pandas have a special bone on their wrists, which grows rather like a thumb. This bone enables pandas to grab hold of clumps of bamboo in their paws, making it easier for them to collect and eat their food. Pandas have to drink fresh water regularly, so they visit streams or rivers almost every day.

▶ Pandas' forepaws are bigger than their hind paws. The forepaw has a special pad of tough skin over an extra bone, which it uses like a thumb to help it grip bamboo.

643 Pandas are not ready to mate until they are about five years old. During the mating season males sometimes fight. Females usually give birth to one or two tiny cubs that are entirely helpless. Usually, a mother only feeds the first cub that is born and leaves the other one to die.

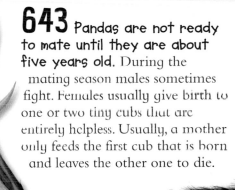

King of the jungle

► Lions are often incorrectly referred to as 'Kings of the Jungle'. However, it is tigers, not lions, that are at home in this environment. Tigers are endangered, which means that if we do not do enough to save them, they may soon become extinct.

644 The tiger is the largest of all the cats and also one of the hardest to find. Tigers live deep in the jungle where huge trees block out the sunlight, helping them to blend into the murky darkness. Their stripes camouflage them as they tread silently through the dappled shadows. This coat is also perfect for hiding the tiger in long grass.

645 Tigers hunt by stealth. They hunt at night, when they can creep up on their prey. Tigers may travel several kilometres each night, roaming along tracks, searching for their victims. Tigers hunt for deer, wild pigs, cattle, monkeys and reptiles. They will even kill young elephants or rhinoceroses.

646 Tigers love swimming. When it is hot they may take a dip in lakes and rivers to cool down. They are good swimmers and can make their way across large stretches of water.

647 Although they are powerful hunters, tigers may have to stalk 20 animals before they manage to catch just one. They normally kill once every five to six days and eat up to 40 kilograms of meat in one go! Tigers often return to a kill for several days until they have finished it, or scavengers have carried it away.

▼ People who need to go into the tigers' forest in Sundarban in east India and Bangladesh, wear masks on the back of their heads. This confuses the tigers into leaving them alone.

QUIZ
1. Why do tigers have stripes?
2. What name is given to animals that eat food that's been left by others?
3. If you were walking in a tiger's forest, how could you try to keep yourself safe?

Answers:
1. A stripy coat helps to camouflage them in the forest 2. Scavengers, e.g. hyaena and vultures 3. You could wear a mask on the back of your head

649 No two tigers have the same pattern on their coats. White tigers with black stripes are occasionally seen in the wild and are bred in zoos because they are very popular with visitors. Although they don't look like their parents, these tigers are not different in any other way.

▼ White tigers are rare in the wild. This white tiger cub is less likely to survive because its coat does not provide good camouflage.

648 Bengal tigers have a reputation as 'man-eaters'. Tigers don't usually eat people unless they are too sick or old to find other prey, but some tigers prefer the taste of human flesh. Between 1956 and 1983, more than 1500 people were killed by tigers in one region alone.

Spotted sprinter

650 Cheetahs are the world's fastest land animals and can run as fast as a car. Within two seconds of starting a chase, a cheetah can reach speeds of 75 kilometres an hour, and it soon reaches a top speed of about 105 kilometres an hour. Cheetahs run out of energy after only 30 seconds of sprinting, so if its prey can keep out of the cheetah's jaws for this amount of time, it may escape capture.

651 This big cat lives in the grasslands and deserts of Africa and Middle East and Western Asia. Cheetahs do not often climb trees, as they have difficulty in getting down again. Cubs often hide in bushes so that they can surprise their prey. The word 'cheetah' means 'spotted wind' – the perfect name for this speedy sprinter.

▼ Cheetahs prefer wide open spaces where they can easily spot prey such as gazelles.

652 Like most of the big cats, cheetahs often live alone. Females live in an area called their 'home range', only leaving if food is scarce. When cubs leave their mothers they often stay together in small groups. Eventually the females go off to find their own home ranges, but the cubs may stay together and attack other cheetahs that come too close.

▶ Cheetah mothers keep their cubs hidden until they are old enough to start learning how to hunt.

653 There are usually between four and six cubs in one litter. Sadly, only one cub in every 20 lives to be an adult cheetah. The others are usually killed by lions or hyenas.

654 Cubs have thick tufts of long, white fur on their heads, necks and shoulders. No one knows why they have this hair, but it might make them look bigger and stronger than they really are.

655 Cheetahs kill antelopes by biting their throats, stopping them from getting any air. Cheetahs can spend a whole day eating if they are undisturbed by vultures or lions, which will steal the food if they can.

How fast are these animals?

Put them in order of fastest to slowest:
1. Cheetah 2. Kangaroo
3. Spur-winged goose
4. Thompson's gazelle

Answer: 1 3 4 2

Sociable Simba

656 Lions are sociable animals. They live in family groups called prides that normally include between four and six adults, all related, and their cubs. Large prides of perhaps 30 animals develop where there is plenty of food.

▶ Lionesses give birth to a litter of between one and six cubs. The cubs stay with their mother for over two years.

657 Unlike other big cats, male and female lions look very different. They both have sandy-coloured fur that blends into sun-scorched grasslands, but the males have manes of darker hair on their heads and shoulders that make them look powerful and threatening.

658 The best time to hunt is early morning or evening. The lionesses prepare an ambush by spreading out and circling their prey. They hunt zebra, wildebeest, impala and buffalo. A group of lionesses has been known to bring down an adult giraffe that was 6 metres tall!

659 Although it is unusual, lions do sometimes attack and eat humans. In the 1930s and 1940s, a family of lions in Tanzania preferred human flesh to the normal lion diet of antelope. They killed nearly 1500 people in just 15 years.

I DON'T BELIEVE IT!

Every cat's favourite pastime is napping. Lions spend almost 80 percent of their time sleeping, lying down or sitting doing nothing!

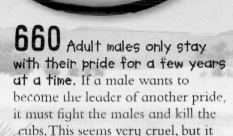

660 Adult males only stay with their pride for a few years at a time. If a male wants to become the leader of another pride, it must fight the males and kill the cubs. This seems very cruel, but it does this to make the lionesses ready to have more cubs before it mates with them. The new leader then knows that all the cubs in the pride will be their own.

661 Few animals would dare to attack a healthy lion. When a lion has become old and weak, however, it may be easy prey for a band of hyenas. It is said that lions only fear hyaenas – this is because they know they could end up in the bellies of several of them!

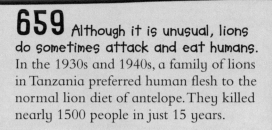

Athletic puma

▲ Pumas live in the New World, from the southern tip of South America all the way to Alaska.

662 The puma is a great athlete. Pumas have long hind legs packed with muscles – ideal for jumping, running and climbing. Of all the big cats, these are the most graceful. They can spring 2 metres into a tree then bound up a further 18 metres before leaping down to the ground.

663 Pumas are known by a variety of names including cougar, panther, red jaguar, mountain screamer, catamount, deer tiger and mountain lion. People from Central and South America call them *chimblea*, *miztil*, *pagi* or *leopardo*.

I DON'T BELIEVE IT!

Though large in size, the puma is not one of the seven species of 'big cats', so it cannot roar. Instead, it makes an ear-piercing scream, which scares both humans and animals alike!

664 When you live in a hot climate and are covered in a coat of fur, it can be difficult to keep cool. Pumas, like other cats, pant to lose heat. When an animal pants, it opens its mouth and lets its tongue hang out. This means that water can evaporate off the surface of the tongue, lowering the animal's body temperature.

665 Rabbits, mice, rats and hares are popular prey for pumas. They will also attack larger mammals, including deer, cattle and elks. In some places, humans have built houses in or near the pumas' natural habitat. This has resulted in people being attacked – even killed – by these wild animals. Now, people are beginning to realize that they have to respect the pumas' natural instincts and stay away from their territory.

667 These big cats are highly skilled killers. They hunt by slowly creeping up on an unsuspecting victim. When ready, they pounce, knocking their prey to the ground in one sudden hit. A single, swift bite kills the puma's victim immediately.

▼ Pumas often hunt small animals, such as hares, squirrels, beavers and turkeys.

666 Although pumas can kill porcupines, it is not an easy task. They need to flip the prickly creature onto its back before biting its soft belly. If the porcupine manages to spear the puma with one of its many spines, the wound may prove fatal.

◄ The North American porcupine can climb trees and has a crest of long spines, or quills, on its head and back.

A coat to die for

668 The jaguar is the owner of a beautiful fur coat – so beautiful that many people want to own it, too. Although it is against the law to capture a jaguar for its skin, they are still hunted. Jaguars live in rainforests, often in areas where farmers are cutting back trees to grow crops. As jaguars' habitats continue to shrink, so will their numbers.

669 At first glance a jaguar looks like a leopard, but it is possible to tell them apart by a few tell-tale differences. A jaguar's head is bigger and rounder than a leopard's, with round ears instead of pointed ones. Its tail is quite a bit shorter than the leopard's and its shoulders are broad and packed with muscle.

670 Of all the big cats jaguars are the most water-loving. They like swampy areas, or places that flood during wet seasons. Jaguars are strong swimmers and seem to enjoy bathing in rivers. They live in Central and South America but less than a hundred years ago, they were living as far north as California and Texas.

▼ Jaguars are similar to leopards but they have broader shoulders, shorter legs and larger heads. All jaguars love water.

671 Young jaguars climb trees where they hunt for birds and small mammals. As they grow bigger, they become too heavy for the branches. Adults tend to stay on the ground, or in water, to hunt.

▲ A capybara's eyes, ears and nose are on the top of its head so that it can spot a lurking predator as it wallows in water.

672 Jaguars hunt a wide range of animals including deer, tapirs, birds, fish and capybaras. Capybaras are the world's heaviest rodent and can measure up to 130 centimetres in length.

▶ Jaguars can feed on turtles because they have large, strong teeth and immensely powerful jaws.

I DON'T BELIEVE IT!

In one year alone, at least 13,500 jaguars were killed for their coats. Today, the future of the jaguar is most at risk from the destruction of its rainforest habitat.

673 Jaguars' powerful jaws are so strong that they can crack open the hard shells of turtles and tortoises. These cats will even kill large animals, such as cattle and horses. It is their habit of killing cows that upsets many people who share the jaguars' territory. Cattle are very important to the farmers, who may poison or shoot jaguars that are killing their livestock.

Super leopard

▲ There are probably more leopards in the wild than all the other big cats put together. This success has earned leopards the nickname 'supercat'.

674 Leopards can live close to humans but never be seen by them. They live in Africa and as far east as Malaysia, China and Korea. Leopards hunt by night and sleep in the day. They are possibly the most common of all the big cats, but are rarely seen in the wild.

675 Leopards may sit in the branches of a tree, waiting patiently for their meal to come to them. As their prey strolls past, the leopard drops from the branches and silently, quickly, kills its victim.

676 Leopards nearly always hunt at night. A leopard approaches its prey in absolute silence, making sure that it does not snap a twig or rustle leaves. With incredible control, it places its hind paws onto the exact places where its forepaws had safely rested. When it is within striking distance of its victim it will attack.

677 Leopards are not fussy eaters. They will eat dung beetles, frogs or birds if nothing better comes along. They prefer to hunt monkeys, pigs and antelopes.

◄ Dung beetles feed on dung and lay their eggs in it. They make a crunchy snack for hungry leopards.

678 Once a leopard has caught its meal, it does not want to lose it to passing scavengers such as hyaenas or jackals. The leopard might climb up a tree, hauling its prey with it. It may choose to eat immediately or store the animal for later. Hiding food like this is called 'caching' (known as 'cashing').

679 Although the name 'panther' is usually given to pumas, it is also used for leopards that have black fur. Black panthers are not a different type of leopard – some cubs are simply born with black fur rather than the normal tawny-brown hide.

◄ If you could get close enough to a black panther you would see that its fur is spotted.

Polar seals

680 Many kinds of seal live in the Arctic region. These include ringed seals, bearded seals, harp seals, spotted seals, ribbon seals and hooded seals. Most feed on fish, squid and small shrimp-like creatures called krill, which are also eaten by whales.

TRUE OR FALSE?

1. Seals are the only animals that eat krill.
2. Seals have a layer of blubber.
3. Walruses sunbathe in summer.
4. Seals usually give birth to three pups.
5. Polar bears prey on seals.

Answers:
1. False 2. True 3. True 4. False 5. True

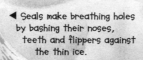

◀ Seals make breathing holes by bashing their noses, teeth and flippers against the thin ice.

681 Seals have very thick fur to keep out the cold water. Like their main enemy, the polar bear, they also have a layer of fatty blubber under the skin to keep them warm. They swim well but have to come up to breathe every few minutes. Sometimes they use breathing holes they make in the ice.

682 In spring, mother seals come onto the ice to give birth. Their babies, or pups, have very thick, fluffy fur to keep them warm. Each mother seal usually has only one pup. She feeds it on very rich milk, and it grows very quickly.

▼ In the snow, the pup lies perfectly still. Its thick, white fur keeps it warm and hides it in its snowy surroundings. The pup's fur is yellow at birth, but it soon turns white. The pup then grows a new, darker fur coat.

683 Mother seals have to return to the water to feed, leaving their pups alone on the ice. At this time pups are in danger from polar bears, wolves and other predators. Within a couple of weeks the young seal is big enough to look after itself.

▶ Walruses show off their tusks at breeding time to impress a mate. Tusks are used in feeding, to lever shellfish off the seabed.

684 The walrus is a huge seal with two long upper teeth, called tusks. A big walrus can grow to 3 metres in length and weigh 1.5 tonnes! Walruses often use their flippers and tusks to haul themselves out of the water onto rocky shores, to sunbathe during the brief summer.

Enormous elephants

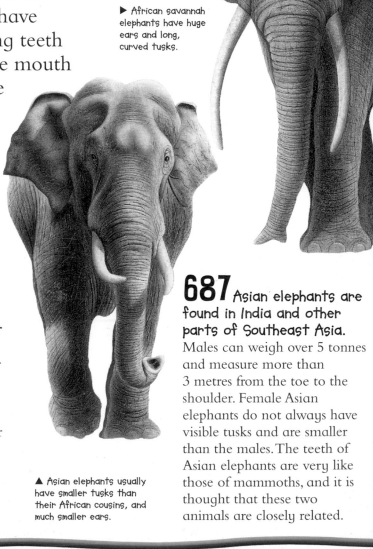

685 There are three main types of elephant — two African and one Asian. African elephants are larger and they can measure up to 5 metres in length. Both males and females have tusks, which are long teeth that grow out of the mouth on either side of the trunk. They only live in Africa, but they are found in many types of habitat.

▶ African savannah elephants have huge ears and long, curved tusks.

686 There are two types of African elephant — forest and savannah. Forest elephants have darker skin than those that live on the savannah. They also have yellow-brown tusks that point downwards rather than curve upwards, and their trunks can be quite hairy. Forest elephants live in areas where there is a lot of thick vegetation.

▲ Asian elephants usually have smaller tusks than their African cousins, and much smaller ears.

687 Asian elephants are found in India and other parts of Southeast Asia. Males can weigh over 5 tonnes and measure more than 3 metres from the toe to the shoulder. Female Asian elephants do not always have visible tusks and are smaller than the males. The teeth of Asian elephants are very like those of mammoths, and it is thought that these two animals are closely related.

688 Mammoths are extinct relatives of modern elephants. Their remains have been found in many places in the world, as far south as Mexico and as far north as Alaska. The best remains of mammoths have been found in Siberia, where the bodies have stayed frozen for thousands of years. Mammoths that lived in North America had huge, spiralling tusks that measured nearly 5 metres!

▼ Asian elephants have been used for farming and carrying loads for centuries. Like all elephants, they enjoy soaking in water.

▼ Most African elephants live on the savannah (huge grasslands) although they can also survive in mountains, deserts and forests.

ASIA

AFRICA

◄ The ears of a forest elephant are slightly smaller and more rounded than those of a savannah elephant.

Fun at the waterhole

689 Elephants enjoy splashing in water, and a waterhole is a perfect place to cool down, drink, play and rest. Elephants live in hot places, and when they are feeling uncomfortable in the heat, they make their way to a waterhole or river to paddle, wallow and swim.

690 All elephants are excellent swimmers. They often dip below the water's surface using their trunks as snorkels to breathe. Some have even been seen to roll right over, so only the soles of their feet can be seen poking above the water!

691 Elephants are mammals. This means they have warm blood and give birth to live babies. Most mammals have fur to protect their skin from the sun and wind, but elephants have little body hair. This means that their skin can get dry and damaged. At a waterhole, elephants coat their skin in mud to cool and protect it.

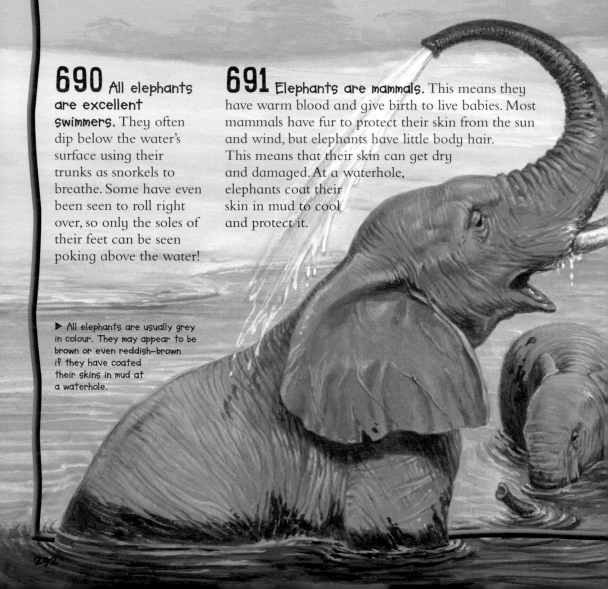

▶ All elephants are usually grey in colour. They may appear to be brown or even reddish-brown if they have coated their skins in mud at a waterhole.

692 Elephants can use their ears like giant fans to cool down their whole bodies. The huge ears are full of blood vessels, and when an elephant flaps them, air moves all around, cooling the blood inside. The blood travels to other parts of the body, helping the elephant to control its temperature.

I DON'T BELIEVE IT!

Baby elephants can swim almost as soon as they can walk, and can even suckle (drink their mother's milk) while underwater.

Teeth and tusks

693 Elephants have unusual teeth that are ideal for chewing and grinding tough plants, such as bark and grass. They only have two front teeth – these are the tusks that grow long and curved. The other teeth are huge molars that are covered with ridges that help to mash food, breaking it into smaller pieces that can be swallowed.

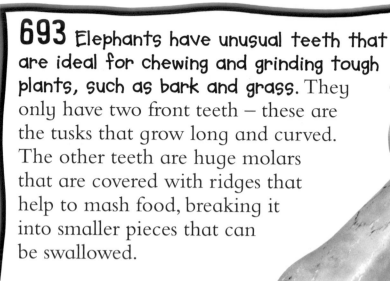

694 Humans have two sets of teeth in their lifetime, but elephants have six. This is because their teeth wear out quickly due to all the chewing they have to do. Baby elephants are born with their first set of four molar teeth in their mouths. These have usually fallen out by the time the elephant is two years old, and a new set grows in their place.

▲ Elephants have sturdy bones to help support their bodies. This elephant skull is filled with air bubbles, which prevent the head from being too heavy.

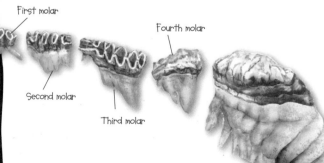

First molar

Second molar

Third molar

Fourth molar

Fifth molar

Sixth molar

▲ It is possible to work out how old an elephant is by looking at its teeth. By the time an elephant has its sixth molar, it is about 40 years old.

695 Tusks are enormous upper front teeth that keep growing throughout an elephant's life. They grow faster in males than in females, and can grow 17 centimetres in just one year. The longest tusks ever recorded measured nearly 3.5 metres in length! African elephants usually have bigger tusks than Asian elephants, whose tusks may not grow beyond the lips and out of the mouth.

Asian male

African female

African male

Mammoth

696 The tusks have roots that fit into the skull. The inside of the tooth contains blood, pulp and nerves. When tusks grow, they have enamel on them, but this soon wears away, leaving a creamy-white substance called ivory.

▲ The biggest tusks belonged to mammoths. Today, the African male elephant has the biggest tusks.

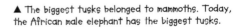

I DON'T BELIEVE IT!

Older elephants may die because the ridges on their teeth have worn away, causing the elephants to starve.

697 Tusks are not used as teeth, but as tools and weapons. They are used to dig in the dry soil for tasty roots to eat. Male elephants use their tusks to fight one another, and when elephants get tired, they often rest their heavy trunks on their tusks for a while!

Horses, zebras and asses

698 Horses, ponies, zebras and asses all belong to the same animal family – the equids. All members of this family have a single toe on each foot and are called 'odd-toed' animals (unlike cows and deer, which have two toes on each foot). Like other animals with fur, horses are mammals and they give birth to live young, which they feed with milk.

▲ Zebras are easily recognized by their stripy coats. These wild equids live in Africa.

699 Ponies are smaller than horses. Although horses and ponies are the same type of animal, they are different sizes. Horses are measured in 'hands', not centimetres, and a pony is a horse that is less than 14.2 hands (or 148 centimetres) tall. Ponies also have wider bodies and shorter legs than horses.

▶ A horse's height is measured from its feet to the top of its shoulders, which are known as 'withers'.

700 Equids live all over the world. Wild equids, such as zebras, live on grasslands where they can graze all day on plants. Horses that live and work with humans can be found almost everywhere across the world, and these are known as domestic horses.

701 Equids have manes of long hair on their heads and necks and thick, tufted tails. Their long legs, deep chests and powerful muscles allow them to run a long way at great speed without getting tired.

MEASURE IN HANDS

Normally we use centimetres and metres as units of measurement, but you can use anything you like – even your hands.

Measure the height of a table using your hands. Then ask an adult to measure it as well. Did you get the same measurement? If not, why not?

702 Wild horses live in large groups called herds. All horses, wild or domestic (tame), are very loyal to one another and can form close bonds with other animals, including humans.

703 Horses are intelligent animals. They can communicate with each other by whinnying or braying, but, like many other animals, horses also sniff and smell one another to communicate. They also enjoy nuzzling and grooming each other's fur.

▼ In a herd, horses who get on well with each other will groom and nuzzle one another.

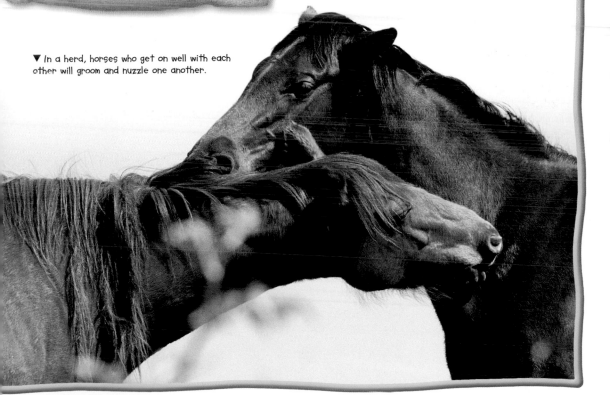

Mighty monsters

704 Not all deadly creatures kill for food. Many of them only attack when they are frightened. Some plant-eating animals fight to protect their young, or when they feel scared.

705 Hippos may appear calm when they are wallowing at the edge of a waterhole, but they kill more people in Africa than any other large animal. These huge creatures fiercely protect their own stretch of water, and females are extremely aggressive when they have calves and feel threatened.

706 African buffaloes can be very aggressive towards other animals and humans. If they become scared, they move quickly and attack with their huge horns. Groups of buffaloes surround a calf or ill member of the herd to protect it. They face outwards to prevent predators getting too close.

707 With huge bodies and massive horns, rhinos look like fearsome predators. They are actually related to horses and eat a diet of leaves, grass and fruit. Rhinos can become aggressive, however, when they are scared. They have poor eyesight, which may be why they can easily feel confused or threatened, and attack without warning.

◀ Male hippos fight one another using their massive teeth as weapons. Severe injuries can occur, leading to the death of at least one of the hippos

I DON'T BELIEVE IT!

Adult male elephants are called bulls, and they can become killers. A single stab from an elephant's tusk is enough to cause a fatal wound, and one elephant is strong enough to flip a car over onto its side!

The bird world

708 There are more than 9000 different types, or species, of bird. These have been organized by scientists into groups called orders which contain many different species. The largest order is called the passerines, also known as perching or songbirds. These include common birds such as robins.

Crown

Bill (beak)

Throat

Lung

Heart

Liver

Toes

Stomach

Flight feathers

Light, hollow bones, or skeleton

Kidney

Tail feathers

▲ Most doves and pigeons are hunted by predators. Strong wing muscles, that make up a third of their weight, help them to take off rapidly and accelerate to 80 kilometres an hour.

709 Birds are the only creatures that have feathers. The feathers are made of keratin – the same material as our hair and nails. Feathers keep a bird warm and protect it from the wind and rain. Its wing and tail feathers allow a bird to fly. Some birds also have very colourful feathers, which help them to attract mates or blend in with their surroundings. This is called camouflage.

▶ The bird with the most feathers is thought to be the whistling swan, with more than 25,000 feathers.

710 All birds have wings. These are the bird's front limbs. There are many different wing shapes. Birds that soar in the sky for hours, such as hawks and eagles, have long broad wings. These allow them to make the best use of air currents. Small fast-flying birds such as swifts have slim, pointed wings.

► The egg protects the growing young and provides it with food. While the young develops the parent birds, such as this song thrush, keep the egg safe and warm.

711 **All birds lay eggs.** It would be impossible for birds to carry their developing young inside their bodies like mammals do – they would become too heavy to fly.

712 **All birds have a beak for eating.** The beak is made of bone and is covered with a hard material called horn. Birds have different kinds of beak for different types of food. Insect-eating birds tend to have thin, sharp beaks for picking up their tiny prey. The short, strong parrot's beak is ideal for cracking hard-shelled nuts.

QUIZ

1. How many types of bird are there?
2. How many feathers does the whistling swan have?
3. What are feathers made of?
4. What is the largest order of birds called?
5. What sort of beaks do hunting birds have?

Answers:
1. More than 9000
2. More than 25,000 3. Keratin
4 The passerines 5. Powerful hooked beaks

◄ Hunting birds, such as this goshawk, have powerful hooked beaks for tearing flesh.

Fast fliers

713 **The fastest flying bird is the peregrine falcon.** It hunts other birds in the air and makes spectacular high-speed dives to catch its prey. During a hunting dive, a peregrine may move as fast as 180 kilometres an hour. In normal level flight, it flies at about 95 kilometres an hour. Peregrine falcons live almost all over the world.

▲ The peregrine falcon does not just fold its wings and fall like many birds, it actually pushes itself down towards the ground. This powered dive is called a stoop.

▼ When this hummingbird lands, it has to tilt its head right back to support the weight of its huge bill.

714 **Ducks and geese are also fast fliers.** Many of them can fly at speeds of more than 65 kilometres an hour. The red-breasted merganser and the common eider duck can fly at up to 100 kilometres an hour.

715 **A hummingbird's wings beat 50 or more times a second as it hovers in the air.** The tiny bee hummingbird may beat its wings at an amazing 200 times a second. When hovering, the hummingbird holds its body upright and beats its wings backwards and forwards, not up and down, to keep itself in one place in the air. The fast-beating wings make a low buzzing or humming sound that gives these birds their name.

Tail feathers spread for landing

FEED THE BIRDS!

In winter, food can be scarce for birds. You can make your own food cake to help them.

You will need:
225g of suet, lard or dripping
500g of seeds, nuts, biscuit crumbs, cake and other scraps

Ask an adult for help. First melt the fat, and mix it thoroughly with the seed and scraps. Pour it into an old yogurt pot or similar container, and leave it to cool and harden. Remove the cake from the container. Make a hole through the cake, put a string through the hole and hang it from a tree outside.

716 The swift spends nearly all its life in the air and rarely comes to land. It can catch prey, eat, drink and mate on the wing. After leaving its nest, a young swift may not come to land again for two years, and may fly as far as 500,000 kilometres.

717 The greater roadrunner is a fast mover on land. It runs at speeds of 20 kilometres an hour as it hunts for insects, lizards and birds' eggs to eat. It can fly but seems generally to prefer running.

◄ The spine-tailed swift is thought to fly at speeds of up to 160 kilometres an hour.

Swifts have long, slim wings that are perfect for their life in the air

303

River birds

718 The jacana can walk on water! It has amazingly long toes that spread the bird's weight over a large area and allow it to walk on floating lily pads as it hunts for food such as insects and seeds. Jacanas can also swim and dive. There are eight different types of jacana, also called lilytrotters. They live in parts of North and South America, Africa and Asia.

719 The kingfisher makes its nest in a tunnel in a riverbank. Using their strong beaks, a male and female pair dig a tunnel up to 60 centimetres long and make a nesting chamber at the end. The female lays up to eight eggs which both parents take turns to look after.

720 The heron catches fish and other water creatures. This long-legged bird stands on the shore or in shallow water and reaches forwards to grab its prey with a swift thrust of its dagger-like beak.

721 The pelican collects fish in the big pouch that hangs beneath its long beak. When the pelican pushes its beak into the water the pouch stretches and fills with water – and fish. When the pelican then lifts its head up, the water drains out of the pouch leaving any food behind.

The pelican uses its pouch like a net to catch fish

QUIZ

1. How long is a kingfisher's nest burrow?
2. How many types of jacana are there?
3. What do pelicans eat?

Answers:
1. About 60 centimetres 2. Eight 3. Fish

▼ The dipper can walk along the bottom of a stream, snapping up prey such as insects and other small creatures.

722 A small bird called the dipper is well-adapted to river life. It usually lives around fast-flowing streams and can swim and dive well. There are five different types of dipper and they live in North and South America, Asia and Europe.

Desert dwellers

723 **Many desert birds have sandy-brown feathers to blend with their surroundings.** This helps them hide from their enemies. The cream-coloured courser lives in desert lands in Africa and parts of Asia. It is hard to see on the ground, but when it flies, the black and white pattern on its wings makes it more obvious. So the courser runs around rather than fly. It feeds on insects and other creatures it digs from the desert sands.

▶ The elf owl is able to catch prey in its feet as it flies.

Cream-coloured courser

724 **Birds may have to travel long distances to find water in the desert.** But this is not always possible for little chicks. To solve this problem, the male sandgrouse has special feathers on his tummy which act like sponges to hold water. He flies off to find water and thoroughly soaks his feathers. He then returns home where his young thirstily gulp down the water that he's brought.

▶ The sandgrouse lives throughout Asia, often in semi-desert areas.

725 **The elf owl makes its nest in a hole in a desert cactus.** This prickly, uncomfortable home helps to keep the owl's eggs safe from enemies, who do not want to struggle through the cactus' spines. The elf owl is one of the smallest owls in the world and is only about 14 centimetres long. It lives in desert areas in the southwest of the USA.

726 The cactus wren eats cactus fruits and berries.
This little bird hops about among the spines of cactus plants and takes any juicy morsels it can find. It also catches insects, small lizards and frogs on the ground. Cactus wrens live in the southwestern USA.

I DON'T BELIEVE IT!

The lammergeier vulture drops bones onto rocks to smash them into pieces. It then swallows the soft marrow and even splinters of bone, bit by bit. Powerful acids in the bird's stomach allow the bone to be digested.

727 The lappet-faced vulture scavenges for its food.
It glides over the deserts of Africa and the Middle East, searching for dead animals or the left-overs of hunters such as lions. When it spots something, the vulture swoops down and attacks the carcass with its strong hooked bill. Its head and neck are bare so it does not have to spend time cleaning its feathers after feeding from a messy carcass.

▼ The lappet-faced vulture has very broad wings. These are ideal for soaring high above the plains of its African home, searching for food.

What is a penguin?

728 **Like all birds, penguins are covered in feathers and lay eggs.** Most birds have bodies that help them fly, but penguins' bodies are perfectly suited to swimming. There are 17 types of penguin, all quite similar in appearance.

729 **Penguins have stout, upright bodies covered in black-and-white feathers.** Their black backs and white bellies help to camouflage the birds as they swim. When seen from below penguins appear white, blending into the light sky, but when seen from above they blend into the dark sea water.

▶ Birds, like this Chinstrap penguin, are vertebrates — just like reptiles, amphibians and mammals. This means that they have bony skeletons that support their bodies.

Skull

Bill (beak)

Spine

The bones in a penguin's flipper are similar to those in other birds' wings, and a human's arm

Ribcage

Hip bone

Penguins have sharp-clawed toes on their feet

I DON'T BELIEVE IT!

No one knows for sure where penguins got their strange name from, but it may come from the Latin word for 'fat', which is 'pinguis'.

◀ Penguins evolved (gradually changed over millions of years) from flying birds into flightless birds, so their flippers look quite similar to wings.

732 All birds have wings, but not all of them can fly. Wings are limbs, just like arms and legs, but they are mostly used for flying. The wings of penguins are too small and stumpy to be used for flight, but they have evolved for moving through water.

Flipper of a Magellanic penguin

Wing of a herring gull

▼ The long-extinct *Waimanu* had bird-like wings, rather than flippers, but probably could not fly.

730 The largest penguin that ever lived was almost as tall as a human. Scientists know this from studying fossil bones of penguins that lived millions of years ago. These bones give us clues about how prehistoric penguins looked and behaved. *Waimanu*, for example, was a small penguin-like bird that lived around 60 million years ago.

731 Male and female penguins usually look alike. It is very difficult to tell them apart, but the males are often taller and slightly heavier. Most penguins build nests or dig burrows where they lay their eggs, and both parents help to take care of the eggs and chicks.

On the ice

733 **Penguins live in the Southern Hemisphere.** This is the half of the Earth below the Equator (the imaginary line that runs through the middle of the Earth). Antarctica and the South Pole are found here, and many types of penguin make this icy habitat their home.

734 **In the Antarctic, winter temperatures drop as low as –70°C.** The land is covered in ice, and penguins that live here battle against the worst weather on Earth.

735 **It is easier to stay warm if you have a bigger body.** For this reason, the biggest penguins normally live in the coldest regions, and the smallest penguins live in warmer places.

▼ These eight species (types) of penguin live in or around the freezing Antarctic – the coldest, driest and windiest place on Earth.

King

Adelie

Rockhopper

736 **The largest penguins are Emperor penguins.** They measure just over one metre in height, and weigh up to 40 kilograms. Their bulk helps them to keep warm in temperatures that reach far below zero.

Emperor

▶ The shaded areas on the map show where these penguins may be found.

SOUTH AMERICA

ATLANTIC OCEAN

AFRICA

INDIAN OCEAN

PACIFIC OCEAN

ANTARCTICA

NEW ZEALAND

AUSTRALIA

737 **There is a layer of ice 4 kilometres deep covering the Antarctic, and it is so cold even the sea freezes over.** During the winter there may only be sunlight for an hour a day, but in the middle of summer daylight lasts for nearly 24 hours.

Gentoo

Royal

Chinstrap

Macaroni

Getting warmer

738 Not all penguins are found in cold places — some live in areas where the weather can be very hot. These birds are found in places, such as South America, Australia, New Zealand and South Africa, or even on islands at the Equator, where the temperatures can soar.

739 Penguins that live in warm places often get too hot. Some of them have patches of bare skin on their faces to help them stay cool. If they get too hot, they may rest in burrows, or leap into the sea.

740 The air may be warm, but the sea is still cold. Currents from the Antarctic bring chilly water to the coastal areas where these penguins hunt for fish and other food. They have to be able to survive both hot and cold temperatures.

Peruvian

Snares

Little

Fjordland

Magellanic

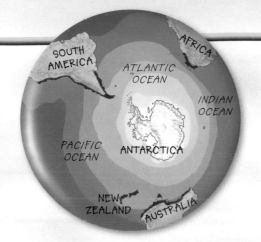

These nine species of penguin, live in the Southern Hemisphere, some distance from the ice-covered South Pole. The shaded areas on the map show where these penguins live.

741 Most penguins live in remote places where there are few other animals. They are not used to defending themselves against predators, such as wild dogs and cats, so they find it difficult to survive where these animals live.

742 Little penguins of Australia and New Zealand often live near people's homes along the shore. They are shy birds, but often build their nests beneath beach houses. These are the smallest penguins, measuring only 35 centimetres in height.

313

Ravenous raptors

743 Eagles, hawks, kites, owls and falcons are fearsome predators called birds of prey. Equipped with incredible eyesight, powerful legs, and sharp claws and bills, they hunt during the day, soaring high in the sky as they look for food.

▶ The Philippine eagle has a wingspan of more than 2 metres and is a formidable predator, catching prey such as flying lemurs in mid-flight. It is in danger of extinction because more than 90 percent of its Philippine forest home has been cut down.

744 Birds of prey are also known as raptors, which comes from the Latin word 'rapere', meaning 'to seize'. Once they have captured their prey, such as a mouse, bird or frog, a raptor usually takes it to its nest to start pulling off fur and feathers. Bones are also thrown away, and the ground near a raptor's nest may be strewn with animal remains.

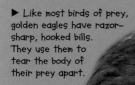

▶ Like most birds of prey, golden eagles have razor-sharp, hooked bills. They use them to tear the body of their prey apart.

745 Birds do not have teeth. They have bills, or beaks, instead. Tearing large pieces of meat is a difficult job using just a bill. Birds of prey use their curved claws, called talons, to hold or rip their food apart, or they just swallow it whole.

QUIZ

The names of raptors have been jumbled up. Can you work out what they are?

1. GELEA
2. ITKE
3. CFALNO
4. LOW
5. PRYESO
6. KAWH

Answers:
1. Eagle 2. Kite 3. Falcon 4. Owl 5. Osprey 6. Hawk

746 Known as the lord of the jungle, the Philippine eagle soars over Asian rainforests, hunting monkeys and squirrels. It is one of the world's biggest raptors (birds of prey), but also one of the most endangered. There are now probably no more than 500 alive.

747 Ospreys dive, feet-first, into the water from a great height in pursuit of their prey. Fish may be slippery, but ospreys have spiky scales on the underside of the feet so they can grip more easily. Once ospreys have a fish firmly in their grasp, they fly away to find a safe place to eat.

◀ Like ospreys, bald eagles live on a diet of fish, which they swipe out of the water using their talons.

315

Night hunter

748 Owls are nocturnal birds of prey with superb vision and excellent hearing. Their eyes are large and face forwards, which helps them to judge distance. Their hearing is so good, they can locate their prey in total darkness just by listening!

749 The heart-shaped face of a barn owl works like a pair of ears! It helps to direct sound towards the sides of the owl's head, where the ears are situated at different heights. This helps them to pinpoint exactly where a sound is coming from. As they hover in the sky, barn owls can hear the tiny, high-pitched sounds made by small animals hidden in the vegetation below. Barn owls are able to fly almost silently towards their prey.

I DON'T BELIEVE IT!

Barn owls have white undersides, which may not appear to be the best camouflage for a nocturnal animal. This actually helps them to disappear against the sky when seen from below, allowing them to stalk and attack their prey more easily.

750 Barn owls are the most widespread land birds in the world and live on every continent, except Antarctica. They spend the day roosting (resting) in barns, buildings or trees and at night they come out to hunt. They catch rodents, such as rats, voles and mice.

▲ Barn owls have special adaptations that help them to hunt in the dark. Their soft feathers deaden the noise of flapping wings as they descend towards their unsuspecting prey.

751 Barn owls can see twice as well as humans by day and many times better at night. If an owl and a human were looking at the same image at night, the owl would see the image much more brightly. It would also be able to detect the smallest movement, which would be invisible to the human eye.

752 If they feel threatened or scared, owls slap their beaks together loudly making a clapping noise – this can sometimes be heard after dark. Barn owls shriek and hiss, but tawny owls are much more vocal. Their range of different calls can often be heard in the forests of Europe and Asia where they live. Male tawny owls make a loud 'hu-hooo' sound, which carries far in the still darkness. Females make a 'ke-wick' sound in reply. These noisy birds also make soft warbles and ear-piercing screeches!

Reptiles and amphibians

753 **Reptiles and amphibians can be divided into smaller groups.** There are four kinds of reptiles – snakes and lizards, the crocodile family, tortoises and turtles, and the tuatara. Amphibians are split into frogs and toads, newts and salamanders, and caecilians.

▼ Crocodiles are the largest reptiles in the world. Their eyes and nostrils are placed high on their heads so that they can stay mostly under water while approaching their prey.

754 **Reptiles do a lot of sunbathing!** They do this, called basking, to get themselves warm with the heat from the sun so that they can move about. When it gets cold, at night or during a cold season, they might sleep or hibernate, which means that they go into a very deep sleep.

755 **Most reptiles have dry, scaly, waterproof skin.** This stops their bodies from drying out. The scales are made of keratin and may form very thick, tough plates. Human nails are also made of the same sort of material.

756 The average amphibian has skin that is moist, fairly smooth and soft. Oxygen can pass easily through their skin, which is important because most adult amphibians breathe through their skin as well as with their lungs. Reptiles breathe only through their lungs.

757 Amphibians' skin is kept moist by special glands just under the surface. These glands produce a sticky substance called mucus. Many amphibians also keep their skin moist by making sure that they are never far away from water.

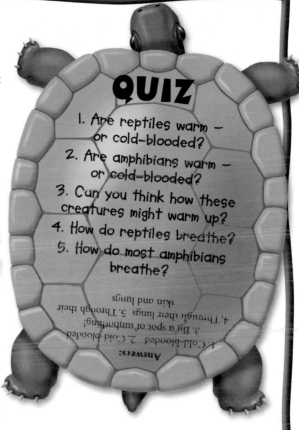

QUIZ
1. Are reptiles warm — or cold-blooded?
2. Are amphibians warm — or cold-blooded?
3. Can you think how these creatures might warm up?
4. How do reptiles breathe?
5. How do most amphibians breathe?

Answers:
1. Cold-blooded 2. Cold-blooded
3. By a spot of sunbathing!
4. Through their lungs 5. Through their skin and lungs

758 Some amphibians have no lungs. Humans breathe with their lungs to get oxygen from the air and breathe out carbon dioxide. Most amphibians breathe through their skin and lungs, but lungless salamanders breathe only through their skin and the lining of the mouth.

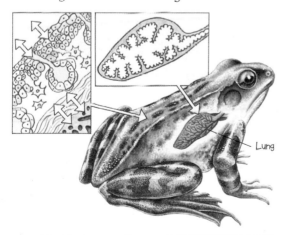

Lung

◀ Oxygen passes in through the skin and into the blood, while carbon dioxide passes out.

319

In the water

759 Amphibians are well known for their links with water, but some types of reptile are also aquatic (live in the water). Different types of amphibian and reptile have developed all kinds of ways of tackling watery lifestyles.

Hellbender

Rough-skinned newt

Eastern newt

760 Newts and salamanders swim rather like fish. They make an 'S'-shape as they move. Many have flat tails that help to propel them along in the water.

761 Toads and frogs propel themselves by kicking back with their hind legs. They use their front legs as a brake for landing when they dive into the water. Large, webbed feet act like flippers, helping them to push through the water.

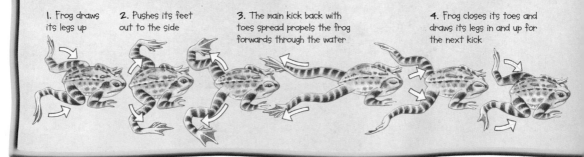

1. Frog draws its legs up

2. Pushes its feet out to the side

3. The main kick back with toes spread propels the frog forwards through the water

4. Frog closes its toes and draws its legs in and up for the next kick

762 A swimming snake may seem unlikely, but most snakes are experts in the water. Sea snakes can stay submerged for five hours and move rapidly through the depths. European grass snakes are also good swimmers. They have to be because they eat animals that live around water.

I DON'T BELIEVE IT!

Floating sea snakes often find themselves surrounded by fish who gather at the snake's tail to avoid being eaten. When the snake fancies a snack, it swims backwards, fooling the unlucky fish into thinking its head is its tail!

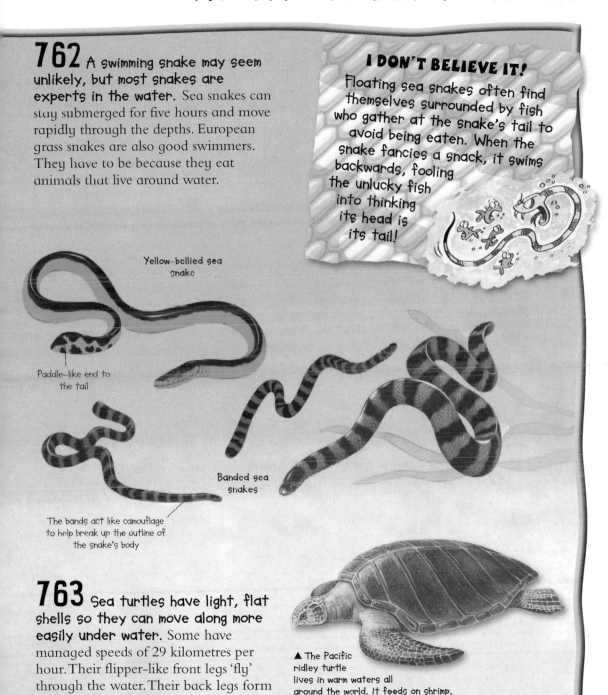

Yellow-bellied sea snake

Paddle-like end to the tail

Banded sea snakes

The bands act like camouflage to help break up the outline of the snake's body

763 Sea turtles have light, flat shells so they can move along more easily under water. Some have managed speeds of 29 kilometres per hour. Their flipper-like front legs 'fly' through the water. Their back legs form mini-rudders for steering.

▲ The Pacific ridley turtle lives in warm waters all around the world. It feeds on shrimp, jellyfish, crabs, sea-snails and fish.

Restless reptiles

◄ Tokay geckos are one of the largest geckos and they can be aggressive. They will attack other lizards and even bite humans who try to handle them. Tokay geckos can reach up to 35 centimetres in length and are usually brightly patterned.

764 Most reptiles live in hot countries and many wait until the coolness of night to become active. Geckos are small lizards that can climb walls and even walk upside down on ceilings. They have large eyes to help them see in the dark and thick toe pads that stick to surfaces.

765 Snakes are superb hunters because their senses are so well adapted to detecting prey even in the dark. Some snakes have an extra skill – they can feel the heat from another animal's body. Snakes, such as the western diamond rattlesnake, do this using special heat-detecting pits between their eyes and nostrils. Using this extra sense, the snake can find its prey in the dark and strike with deadly accuracy.

Heat-sensing pit

Body heat emitted from prey

The snake moves its head from side to side to locate its prey

▲ A western diamondback rattlesnake uses its heat-detecting pits to work out the distance and direction of its prey.

766 Some reptiles are huge and fearsome hunters. Black caimans, which are members of the crocodile family, can reach 6 metres in length. They live in South America in freshwater rivers and lakes and at night they come to shallow water or land to hunt. Their dark skin colour means they can creep up on prey, such as deer or large rodents, unnoticed.

▼ During the day, common kraits are placid snakes and will rarely bite, even if disturbed. However at night they are more likely to be aggressive.

QUIZ

Unlike reptiles, amphibians have moist skins and usually lay their eggs in water. Sort these animals into the two groups:

TURTLE FROG CROCODILE GECKO TOAD NEWT SNAKE

Answers:
Reptiles: turtle crocodile gecko snake
Amphibians: toad frog newt

767 Common kraits are one of the deadliest snakes of Pakistan, India and Sri Lanka, and they are nocturnal. They prey on other snakes and rodents, sometimes straying into buildings to find them. Once they have found their prey, kraits lunge their fangs into it, injecting a lethal venom.

Scary snakes

► Venomous snakes, such as the rattlesnake, inject venom using their large fangs. Snakes use their venom to paralyze (stop all movement) or kill their prey.

Venom runs down the groove on the outside of the fangs and is then injected into the victim's body

769 Cobras kill more than 10,000 people in India every year. As a warning sign, cobras spread their neck ribs, or hoods, to make them look more fearsome. Then they quickly lunge forwards and sink their fangs into their prey.

768 With unblinking eyes, sharp fangs and flickering tongues, snakes look like menacing killers. Despite their fearsome reputation, snakes only attack people when they feel threatened.

770 The taipan is one of Australia's most venomous snakes. When this snake attacks, it injects large amounts of venom that can kill a person in less than an hour.

771 Carpet vipers are small snakes found throughout many parts of Africa and Asia. They are responsible for hundreds, maybe thousands, of human deaths every year. Carpet viper venom affects the nervous system and the blood, causing the victim to bleed to death.

I DON'T BELIEVE IT!

Snakes can open their jaws so wide that they can swallow their prey whole. Large snakes, such as constrictors, can even swallow antelopes or pigs!

◀ Primitive snakes have a heavy skull with a short lower jaw and few teeth.

Short jaw that cannot open very wide

◀ Rear-fanged snakes have fangs in the roof of their mouths.

Fangs are towards the rear of the mouth, below the eye

772 Gaboon vipers have the longest fangs of any snake, reaching 5 centimetres in length. They produce large amounts of venom, which they inject deeply into the flesh with dagger-like teeth. Although slow and calm by nature, Gaboon vipers attack with great speed and a single bite can kill a human in less than two hours.

◀ Some snakes have fangs at the front of their mouths.

The fangs are hollow, and positioned at the front of the mouth

▶ Snakes kill their prey with a lethal bite. Then they swallow the victim, such as a rodent, whole.

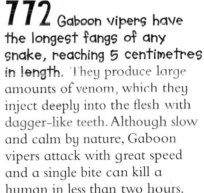

Dragons and monsters

▼ Komodo dragons use their powerful jaws to tear the flesh of their victim, and then eat everything, including bones and fur.

773 Komodo dragons are not really dragons, but lizards. They can reach 3 metres in length and up to 100 kilograms in weight, making them the largest lizards in the world. They hunt their prey using their sensitive sense of smell.

774 Once the Komodo has caught its prey, it sinks its sharp teeth into the victim's flesh. With a mouth full of poisonous bacteria, one bite is enough to kill an animal with an infection, even if it escapes the Komodo's clutches.

QUIZ

1. What colour is the Gila monster?
2. Why does the fire salamander have bold patterns on its skin?
3. How does the Komodo dragon hunt its prey?

Answers:
1. Black, pink and yellow 2. To warn predators that it is poisonous 3. Using its sensitive sense of smell

775 There are only two truly poisonous lizards — the Gila monster and the Mexican beaded lizard. Gila monsters live in North America and they have bands of black, pink and yellow on their scaly skin to warn predators to stay away.

▶ Gila monsters use their sense of smell to hunt small animals and find reptile eggs. They can kill their prey with a single bite.

▼ Fire salamanders are amphibians, like frogs. They hunt insects and earthworms, mainly at night.

776 Fire salamanders look like a cross between a lizard and a frog. They have bold patterns on their skin to warn predators that they are poisonous. The poison, or toxin, is on their skin and tastes foul. They squirt the toxin at predators, irritating or even killing them.

327

Ambush and attack

777 Lurking beneath the surface of the water, a deadly hunter waits, ready to pounce. Lying absolutely still, only its eyes and nostrils are visible. With one swift movement, the victim is dragged underwater. This killer is the crocodile, a relative of the dinosaurs.

▲ Crocodiles and alligators are well-suited to their aquatic lifestyle. They spend much of their day in water, keeping cool and hidden from view.

Only teeth in the upper jaw are visible

Alligator

▲▼ When a crocodile's mouth is closed, some of the teeth on its lower jaw can be seen. Alligators have wide u-shaped jaws, but the jaws of crocodiles are narrow and v-shaped.

Teeth in the lower jaw can be seen

Crocodile

778 When a crocodile has its prey in sight, it moves at lightning speed. The prey has little chance to escape as the crocodile pulls it underwater. Gripping the victim in its mighty jaws, the crocodile twists and turns in a 'deathspin' until its victim has drowned.

779 The largest crocodiles in the world live in estuaries, where rivers meet the oceans. They are called estuarine crocodiles and can reach a staggering 7 metres in length. These giant predators are often known as man-eating crocodiles, although they are most likely to catch turtles, snakes, monkeys, cows and pigs.

780 Alligators are very strong reptiles with wide jaws and thick, scaly skin on their backs. They live in marshes, ponds and rivers, often close to where people live. Like all crocodiles and alligators, the American alligator will catch and eat anything. They have even been known to attack humans.

▼ Crocodiles and alligators have huge jaws, full of teeth. As well as being used for grabbing and holding prey, they use their teeth to slice pieces from the body of the victim.

I DON'T BELIEVE IT!

Crocodiles and alligators store their uneaten food underwater for several weeks. The remains rot, making it easier for the reptiles to swallow. Yum!

Cooler customers

781 Many amphibians are common in cooler, damper parts of the world. Amphibians like wet places. Most mate and lay their eggs in water.

782 As spring arrives, amphibians come out of hiding. The warmer weather sees many amphibians returning to the pond or stream where they were born. This may mean a very long journey through towns or over busy roads.

I DON'T BELIEVE IT!

Look out — frog crossing the road! In some countries, signs warn drivers of a very unusual 'hazard' ahead — frogs or toads travelling along the roads to return to breeding grounds.

783 When the weather turns especially cold, amphibians often hide away. They simply hibernate in the mud at the bottom of ponds or under stones and logs. This means that they go to sleep in the autumn, and don't wake up until spring!

► This aquatic, or water-living, salamander is called a mudpuppy. It lives in freshwater lakes, rivers and streams in North America.

▲ The marbled newt of France and Italy is more colourful than most of its European relatives. Only juveniles and females have the vivid orange stripe along the spine. This species sometimes interbreeds with the great crested newt to produce hybrids.

784 Journeys to breeding grounds may be up to 5 kilometres long, a long way for an animal only a few centimetres in length! This is like a man walking to a pond 90 kilometres away without a map! The animals find their way by scent, landmarks, the Earth's magnetic field and the Sun's position.

Water babies

785 **Amphibians live in water and on land.** Most are born and grow up in fresh water such as ponds, pools, streams and rivers. They move onto dry land when they are adults and return to water to breed.

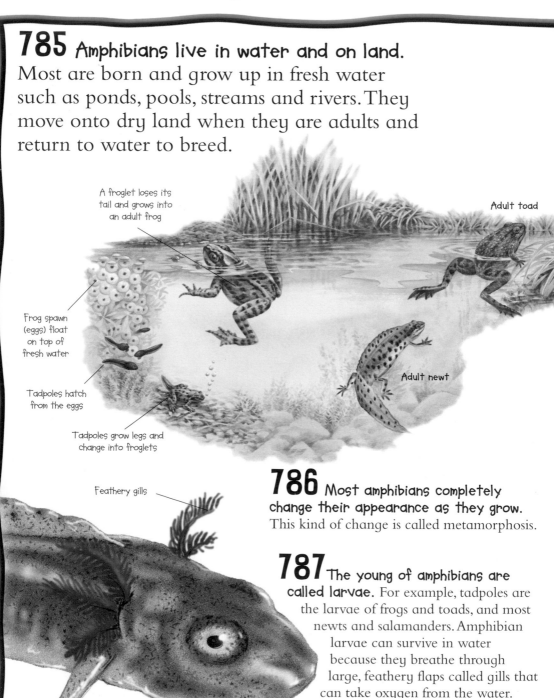

A froglet loses its tail and grows into an adult frog

Adult toad

Frog spawn (eggs) float on top of fresh water

Tadpoles hatch from the eggs

Tadpoles grow legs and change into froglets

Adult newt

Feathery gills

786 **Most amphibians completely change their appearance as they grow.** This kind of change is called metamorphosis.

787 **The young of amphibians are called larvae.** For example, tadpoles are the larvae of frogs and toads, and most newts and salamanders. Amphibian larvae can survive in water because they breathe through large, feathery flaps called gills that can take oxygen from the water.

▼ The axolotl lives only in Mexico, in the southern part of North America.

I DON'T BELIEVE IT!

The male South American Surinam toad is quite an acrobat. When mating underwater, he has to press the eggs onto his mate's back. The eggs remain there until they hatch.

788 The axolotl is an amphibian that has never grown up. This type of water-living salamander has never developed beyond the larval stage. It does, however, develop far enough to be able to breed.

789 The majority of amphibians lay soft eggs. These may be in a jelly-like string or clump of tiny eggs called spawn, as with frogs and toads. Newts lay their eggs singly.

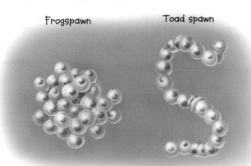

Frogspawn   Toad spawn

▲ Most amphibians lay their eggs in clumps or strings like these.

790 A few amphibians give birth to live young instead of laying eggs. The eggs of the fire salamander, for example, stay inside their mother, where the young hatch out and develop. She then gives birth to young that are like miniature adults.

Fearsome frogs and toads

791 **At first glance, few frogs appear fearsome.** They may not have teeth or claws, but frogs and toads produce a deadly substance in their moist skin. This substance may taste foul or even be poisonous. The most poisonous frogs live in the forests of Central and South America. They are called poison-dart frogs.

792 **One of the deadliest frogs is the golden poison-dart frog.** It lives in rainforests in western Colombia, and its skin produces a very powerful poison – one of the deadliest known substances. A single touch is enough to cause almost instant death.

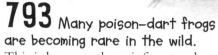

▼ The strawberry poison-dart frog is also known as the 'blue jeans' frog because of its blue legs.

793 **Many poison-dart frogs are becoming rare in the wild.** This is because the rainforests where they live are being cut down. Some poison-dart frogs can be kept in captivity, where they gradually become less poisonous. When they are raised in captivity, these frogs are not poisonous at all.

◄ The male green poison–dart frog carries tadpoles on his back. He takes them to a safe place in water where they will grow into adults.

I DON'T BELIEVE IT!

Poison–dart frogs are brightly coloured or boldly patterned. Their jewel-like appearance warns predators to stay away. This means that these frogs can hunt for bugs during the day, without fear of being eaten.

794 Looking after eggs is the job of male green poison–dart frogs. The female lays her eggs amongst the leaf litter on the forest floor. The male guards them until they hatch into tadpoles, then carries them to water, where they will grow into frogs.

795 The marine toad produces venom from special areas, called glands, behind its eyes. The venom is not used to kill prey, but to protect the toad from being eaten by other animals because it is extremely poisonous if swallowed.

▶ Marine toads are the largest toads in the world. When they are threatened, venom oozes from the glands in the toad's skin. This poison could kill a small animal in minutes.

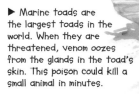

Speedy sharks

796 **Sharks are meat-eating fish, and nearly all of them live in the sea.** Every kind of shark is a meat-eater or carnivore. Many are active hunters and chase after their prey. Some lie in wait to grab victims. Others are scavengers, feasting on the dying and dead bodies of animals, such as whales and seals.

▼ The mako shark is slim and speedy, and races after prey, such as mackerel, tuna and squid. It can leap more than 10 metres out of the water.

NAME THE FINS...

3

1   4   5   2

Answers:
1. Caudal fin (tail)
2. Pectoral fin
3. Dorsal fin
4. Anal fin
5. Pelvic fin

797 **Sharks have several fins that help them to swim and cut through the water.** On the back are the dorsal fins. Pectoral fins are on the lower sides near the front, and pelvic fins on the lower sides near the tail. The anal fin is on the underside just in front of the tail. The tail itself is called the caudal fin.

▼ A shark's dorsal (back) fin stops its whole body swinging from side to side while swimming.

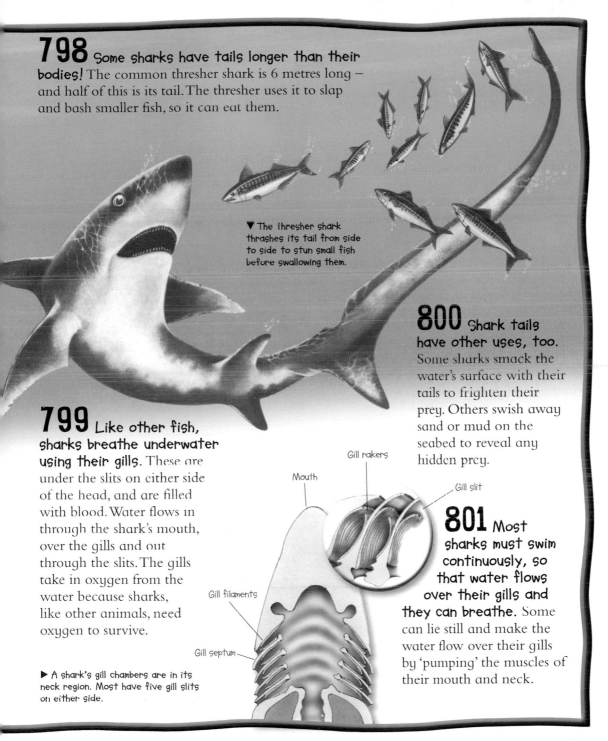

798 Some sharks have tails longer than their bodies! The common thresher shark is 6 metres long – and half of this is its tail. The thresher uses it to slap and bash smaller fish, so it can eat them.

▼ The thresher shark thrashes its tail from side to side to stun small fish before swallowing them.

800 Shark tails have other uses, too. Some sharks smack the water's surface with their tails to frighten their prey. Others swish away sand or mud on the seabed to reveal any hidden prey.

799 Like other fish, sharks breathe underwater using their gills. These are under the slits on either side of the head, and are filled with blood. Water flows in through the shark's mouth, over the gills and out through the slits. The gills take in oxygen from the water because sharks, like other animals, need oxygen to survive.

Gill rakers

Mouth

Gill slit

Gill filaments

Gill septum

801 Most sharks must swim continuously, so that water flows over their gills and they can breathe. Some can lie still and make the water flow over their gills by 'pumping' the muscles of their mouth and neck.

▶ A shark's gill chambers are in its neck region. Most have five gill slits on either side.

Some sharks are giants

802 **The biggest fish in the world is a type of shark called the whale shark.** It grows to 12 metres long, about the same as three family cars end-to-end. It can weigh more than 12 tonnes, which is three times heavier than three family cars put together!

803 **Despite the whale shark's huge size, it mostly eats tiny prey.** It opens its enormous mouth, takes in a great gulp of water and squeezes it out through the gill slits on either side of its neck. Inside the gills, small animals such as shrimp-like krill, little fish and baby squid are trapped and swallowed.

▶ Krill look like small shrimps and are usually 2 to 3 centimetres long. Millions of them, along with other small creatures, make up plankton.

804 **Whale sharks like cruising across the warm oceans, swimming up to 5000 kilometres in one year.** They wander far and wide, but tend to visit the same areas at certain times of year, when their food is plentiful.

▲ The whale shark swims with its mouth wide open to filter krill from the water. It sometimes swallows larger animals, such as penguins, smaller sharks and tuna fish.

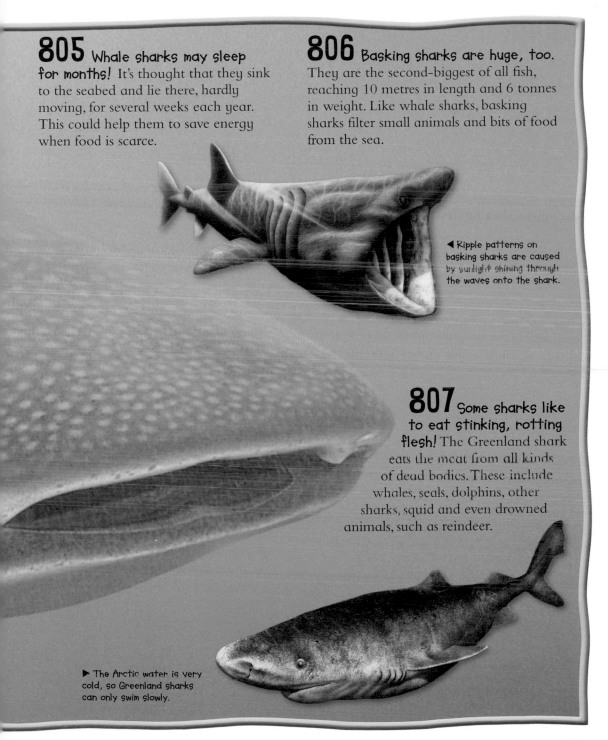

805 Whale sharks may sleep for months! It's thought that they sink to the seabed and lie there, hardly moving, for several weeks each year. This could help them to save energy when food is scarce.

806 Basking sharks are huge, too. They are the second-biggest of all fish, reaching 10 metres in length and 6 tonnes in weight. Like whale sharks, basking sharks filter small animals and bits of food from the sea.

◄ Ripple patterns on basking sharks are caused by sunlight shining through the waves onto the shark.

807 Some sharks like to eat stinking, rotting flesh! The Greenland shark eats the meat from all kinds of dead bodies. These include whales, seals, dolphins, other sharks, squid and even drowned animals, such as reindeer.

► The Arctic water is very cold, so Greenland sharks can only swim slowly.

Hammers for heads

▲ The hammerhead's eyes, nostrils and electricity-sensing organs are at each end of the wing-shaped head.

808 **The hammerhead shark really does have a hammer-like head.** Experts suggest several reasons for this strange shape. One is that the head is shaped like the wings of a plane. As the shark swims, water flowing over its head helps to keep its front end lifted up, rather than nose-diving – just as wings keep a plane in the air.

809 **The hammer-shaped head may improve the shark's senses.** The nostrils are at each end of the 'hammer'. Smells drifting from the side reach one nostril well before the other. By swinging its head from side to side, the hammerhead can pinpoint the direction of a smell more quickly.

▼ Hammerheads often swim close to the seabed, searching for buried fish and shellfish.

810 Most sharks live alone, but hammerheads like a crowd. They gather together in huge groups called schools at certain times of the year, probably to breed.

◄ A bonnet head shark swallows a ray it has just found part-buried in seabed sand.

811 The great hammerhead is one of the biggest predatory sharks, growing to 6 metres long. There are another eight kinds of hammerhead shark, including the scalloped hammerhead and the bonnet head.

Why does the hammerhead have a hammer-shaped head?

1. To break apart rocks to get at prey behind them
2. To help sense the direction of smells in the water
3. To smash open windows in shipwrecks.

812 Hammerheads are among the most dangerous sharks. They have been known to attack people, although their usual food includes fish, squid, crabs and shellfish. They also eat stingrays and don't seem to be affected by the painful sting. However, hammerheads are themselves eaten – by people. They are caught and cut up for their tasty meat and for the thick oil from their livers.

Answer: 2

341

Ultimate killer

813 The world's biggest predatory, or hunting, fish is the great white shark. In real life it is certainly large – at 6 metres in length and weighing more than one tonne. Great whites live around the world, mainly in warmer seas. They have a fearsome reputation.

▼ Great whites are curious about unfamiliar items in the sea. They often come very close to investigate anti-shark cages and the divers protected inside. This is partly because great whites are always on the lookout for food.

I DON'T BELIEVE IT!

The risk of being struck by lightning is 20 times greater than the risk of being attacked by a shark.

814 Great whites get hot! This is because they can make their bodies warmer than the surrounding water. This allows their muscles to work more quickly, so they can swim faster and more powerfully. It means the great white is partly 'warm-blooded' like you.

815 The great white has 50 or more teeth and each one is up to 6 centimetres long. The teeth are razor-sharp but slim, like blades, and they sometimes snap off. But new teeth are always growing just behind, ready to move forwards and replace the snapped-off teeth.

817 The great white 'saws' lumps of food from its victim. Each tooth has tiny sharp points along its edges. As the shark starts to feed, it bites hard and then shakes its head from side to side. The teeth work like rows of small saws to slice off a mouthful.

816 Great whites let their victims bleed to death. They bite on their first charge then move off, leaving the victim with terrible wounds. When the injured prey is weak, the great white comes back to devour its meal.

Insects everywhere!

818 The housefly is one of the most common, widespread and annoying insects. There are many other members of the fly group, such as bluebottles, horseflies, craneflies ('daddy longlegs') and fruitflies. They all have two wings. Most other kinds of insects have four wings.

Housefly

819 The ladybird is a noticeable insect with its bright red or yellow body and black spots. It is a member of the beetle group. This is the biggest of all insect groups, with more than half a million kinds, from massive goliath and rhinoceros beetles to tiny flea-beetles and weevil-beetles.

Ladybird

820 The white butterfly is not usually welcome in the garden. Their young, known as caterpillars, eat the leaves of the gardener's precious flowers and vegetables. There are thousands of kinds of butterflies and even more kinds of their night-time cousins, the moths.

▼ Insects like these white butterflies do not have a bony skeleton inside their bodies like we do. Their bodies are covered by a series of horny plates. This is called an exoskeleton.

White butterfly feeding from a flower

▶ This earwig is being threatened, so it raises its tail to try to make itself look bigger.

821 The earwig is a familiar insect in the park, garden, garage, shed – and sometimes house. Despite their name, earwigs do not crawl into ears or hide in wigs. But they do like dark, damp corners. Earwigs form one of the smaller insect groups, with only 1300 different kinds.

▼ Ants use their antennae and sense of touch as a means of communication.

SPOT THE INSECTS!

Have you seen any insects so far today? Maybe a fly whizzing around the house or a butterfly flitting among the flowers? On a warm summer's day you probably see many kinds of insects. On a cold winter's day there are fewer insects about. Most are hiding away or have not yet hatched out of their eggs.

822 Ants are fine in the garden or wood, but are pests in the house. Ants, bees and wasps make up a large insect group with some 300,000 different kinds. Most can sting, although many are too small to hurt people. However, some, such as bulldog ants, have a painful bite.

How insects grow

823 **All insects begin life inside an egg.** The female insect usually lays her eggs in an out-of-the-way place, such as under a stone, leaf or bark, or in the soil.

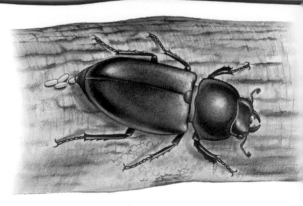

▲ The female stag beetle lays her eggs in rotting wood. Larvae hatch and feed on wood for up to six years before they pupate.

824 **When some types of insect hatch, they do not look like their parents.** A young beetle, butterfly or fly is very different from a grown-up beetle, butterfly or fly. It is soft-bodied, wriggly and wormlike. This young stage is called a larva. There are different names for various kinds of larvae. A fly larva is called a maggot, a beetle larva is a grub and a butterfly larva is a caterpillar.

825 **A female insect mates with a male insect before she can lay her eggs.** The female and male come together to check that they are both the same kind of insect, and they are both healthy and ready to mate. This is known as courtship. Butterflies often flit through the air together in a 'courtship dance'.

◀ Large caterpillars always eat into the centre of the leaf from the edge. Caterpillars grasp the leaf with their legs, while their specially developed front jaws chew at their food.

◀ This butterfly is emerging from its pupal case and is stretching its wings for the first time.

828
Some kinds of insect change shape less as they grow up. When a young cricket or grasshopper hatches from its egg, it looks similar to its parents. However, it may not have any wings yet.

826
The larva eats and eats. It sheds its skin several times so it can grow. Then it changes into the next stage of its life, called a pupa. The pupa has a hard outer case, which stays still and inactive. Inside, the larva is changing body shape again. This change of shape is known as metamorphosis.

827
At last the pupa's case splits open and the adult insect crawls out. Its body, legs and wings spread out and harden. Now the insect is ready to find food and also find a mate.

829
The young cricket eats and eats, and sheds or moults its skin several times as it grows. Each time it looks more like its parent. A young insect that resembles the fully grown adult like this is called a nymph. At the last moult it becomes a fully formed adult, ready to feed and breed.

I DON'T BELIEVE IT!
Courtship is a dangerous time for the male praying mantis. The female is much bigger than the male, and as soon as they have mated, she may eat him!

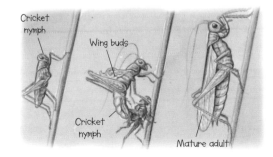

Cricket nymph

Wing buds

Cricket nymph

Mature adult

Air aces

830 Most kinds of insect have two pairs of wings and use them to fly from place to place. One of the strongest fliers is the Apollo butterfly of Europe and Asia. It flaps high over hills and mountains, then rests on a rock or flower in the sunshine.

Apollo butterfly

831 A fast and fierce flying hunter is the dragonfly. Its huge eyes spot tiny prey such as midges and mayflies. The dragonfly dashes through the air, turns in a flash, grabs the victim in its legs and whirrs back to a perch to eat its meal.

832 Some insects flash bright lights as they fly. The firefly is not a fly but a type of beetle. Male fireflies 'dance' in the air at dusk, the rear parts of their bodies glowing on and off about once each second. Female fireflies stay on twigs and leaves and glow in reply as part of their courtship.

833 The smallest fliers include gnats, midges and mosquitoes. These are all true flies, with one pair of wings. Some are almost too tiny for us to see. Certain types bite animals and people, sucking their blood as food.

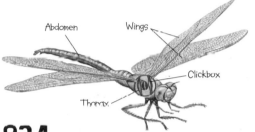

Abdomen
Wings
Clickbox
Thorax

834 An insect's wings are attached to the middle part of its body, the thorax. This is like a box with strong walls, called a clickbox. Muscles inside the thorax pull to make the walls click in and out, which makes the wings flick up and down. A large butterfly flaps its wings once or twice each second. Some tiny flies flap almost 1000 times each second.

MAKE A FLAPPING FLY

You will need:

stiff card   tissue paper
round-ended scissors   sticky tape

1. Ask an adult for help. Carefully cut out the card to make a box with two open ends as shown.

2. Use strips of stiff card to make struts for the wings and attach these to the side walls of the box. Make the rest of the wings from tissue paper.

3. Hold the box as shown. Move the top and bottom walls in, then out. This bends the side walls and makes the wings flap, just like a real insect.

835 A few insects lack wings. They are mostly very small and live in the soil, such as bristletails and springtails. One kind of bristletail is the silverfish — a small, shiny, fast-running insect.

Super sprinters

836 Some insects rarely fly or leap. They prefer to run, and run, and run… all day, and even all night, too. Among the champion insect runners are cockroaches. They are tough and adaptable, with about 3600 different kinds.

837 A few cockroaches burrow in soil or live in caves. But most scurry speedily across the ground on their long legs. They have low, flat bodies and can dart into narrow crevices, under logs and stones and bricks, and into cupboards, furniture — and beds!

▲ Cockroaches are not dirty creatures. They work hard to keep themselves clean in order to preserve a coating of wax and oils that prevents them from drying out.

▼ Tiger beetles have huge eyes. They use their massive biting jaws to catch and cut up their food.

838 The green tiger beetle is an active hunter that races over open ground almost too fast for our eyes to follow. It chases smaller creatures such as ants, woodlice, worms and little spiders. It has huge jaws for its size and soon rips apart any victim.

I DON'T BELIEVE IT!

For its size, a green tiger beetle runs ten times as fast as a person! It is 12–15 millimetres long and runs at about 60–70 centimetres per second. That is like a human sprinter running 100 metres in one second!

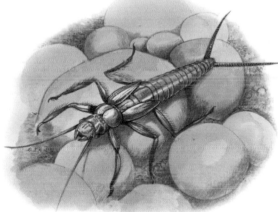

▲ The stonefly nymph, the larva of the stonefly, runs around on the bed of its river home searching for food.

839 One of the busiest insect walkers is the devil's coach-horse, a type of beetle with a long body that resembles an earwig. It belongs to the group known as rove beetles which walk huge distances to find food. The devil's coach-horse has powerful mouthparts and tears apart dead and dying small caterpillars, grubs and worms.

Devil's coach-horse

840 Some insects walk not only across the ground, but also up smooth, shiny surfaces such as walls and even windows. They have wide feet with many tiny hooks or sticky pads. These grip bumps that are too small to see in substances such as glossy, wet leaves or window glass.

Stunning swimmers

841 Many kinds of insect live underwater in ponds, streams, rivers and lakes. Some walk about on the bottom, such as the young forms or nymphs of dragonflies and damselflies. Others swim strongly using their legs as oars to row through the water.

842 The great diving beetle hunts small water creatures such as tadpoles and baby fish. It can give a person a painful bite in self-defence.

843 Some water insects, such as the great silver water beetle, breathe air. So they must come to the surface for fresh supplies. The hairs on the beetle's body trap tiny bubbles of air for breathing below.

Mayfly nymphs

Damselfly nymph

844
Some insects even walk on water. The pond skater has a slim, light body with long, wide-splayed legs. It glides across the surface 'skin' or film caused by the feature of water known as surface tension. It is a member of the bug group of insects and eats tiny animals that fall into the pond.

845
The nymphs of dragonflies, damselflies, stoneflies and mayflies have tails with feathery gills. These work like the gills of a fish, for breathing underwater. These young insects never need to go to the surface until they change into adults.

MAKE AN INSECT DIVING SUIT

Young caddisflies, called nymphs, make tube-shaped cases, called caddis cases. These protect the nymph's body underwater. They are made using small bits that the nymph collects from its surroundings. Each caddis uses different bits to make its case. You can make your own caddis case, and you can even choose what sort of caddis you want to be!

With the help of an adult, roll up some pieces of cardboard to make tubes to wear on your forearm. Stick bits on to build giant caddis cases. Make a great red sedge caddis of leaves or a silver-horn caddis of pebbles and pieces of grit. Put your arm through a tube and wiggle your fingers like the caddis's head!

Pond skater

Great diving beetle

Dragonfly nymph

Brilliant burrowers

846 Soil teems with millions of creatures — and many are insects. Some are the worm-like young forms of insects, called larvae or grubs, as shown below. Others are fully grown insects, such as burrowing beetles, ants, termites, springtails and earwigs. These soil insects are a vital source of food for all kinds of larger animals. Many animals from spiders and shrews to moles and birds prey on these small insects.

848 The larva of the click beetle is shiny orange, up to 25 millimetres long and called a wireworm. It stays undergound, feeding on plant parts, for up to five years. Then it changes into an adult and leaves the soil. Wireworms can be serious pests of cereal crops such as barley, oats and wheat. They also eat beet and potatoes that you would find underground.

◀ The European mole burrows and feeds on the insects and worms that live in the soil.

Cranefly

Cranefly larva, leatherjacket

847 However, insects in the soil can also cause great damage to plants, especially farm crops. They eat roots and other underground parts, especially crops such as potatoes and carrots.

▶ Many insects pose a threat to farmers' crops. Farmers can use pesticides, chemicals to kill the insects, but many people think that this harms other plants and animals.

849 The larva of the cranefly ('daddy long-legs') is called a leatherjacket after its tough, leathery skin. Leatherjackets eat the roots of grasses, including cereal crops such as wheat. They hatch from their eggs in late summer, feed in the soil through autumn and winter and spring, and change into pupae and then adults the next summer.

QUIZ

Sort out the following items into three groups:

A Larger animals which eat insect larvae
B Insect larvae
C Plants eaten by larvae

1. Crow
2. Potato
3. Wireworm
4. Mole
5. Cicada grub
6. Carrot

Answers:
A. 1 and 4, B. 3 and 5,
C. 2 and 6.

Click beetle

Click beetle larva, wireworm

Cicada

850 The larva of the cicada may live underground for more than ten years. Different types of cicadas stay in the soil for different periods of time. The American periodic cicada is probably the record-holder, taking 17 years to change into a pupa and then an adult. Cicada larvae suck juices from plant roots. Grown-up cicadas make loud chirping or buzzing sounds.

Cicada larva

Veggie bugs

851 About nine out of ten kinds of insects eat some kind of plant food. Many feed on soft, rich, nutritious substances. These include the sap in stems and leaves, the mineral-rich liquid in roots, the nectar in flowers and the soft flesh of squashy fruits and berries.

852 Solid wood may not seem very tasty, but many kinds of insect eat it. They usually consume the wood when they are larvae or grubs, making tunnels as they eat their way through trees, logs, and timber structures such as bridges, fences, houses and furniture.

Elm beetle

Elm beetle larva

Furniture beetle

Flowerbug

Mealy-bug

Woodworm (Furniture beetle larva)

I DON'T BELIEVE IT!

Animal droppings are delicious and tasty to many kinds of insect. Various types of beetles lay their eggs in warm and steamy piles of droppings. The larvae soon hatch out and eat the dung!

Capsid bug

Shield bug

Fly

Lacebug

853 Insects even feed on old bits of damp and crumbling wood, dying trees, brown and decaying leaves and smelly, rotting fruit. They are not fussy eaters! This is nature's way of recycling goodness and nutrients in old plant parts, and returning them to the soil so new trees and other plants can grow.

Towns for termites

854 Some insects live together in huge groups called colonies — which are like insect cities. There are four main types of insects which form colonies. One is the termites. The other three are all in the same insect subgroup and are bees, wasps and ants.

855 Some kinds of termite make their nests inside a huge pile of mud and earth called a termite mound. The termites build the mound from wet mud, which goes hard in the hot sun. The main part of the nest is below ground level. It has hundreds of tunnels and chambers where the termites live, feed and breed.

856 Inside the termite 'city' there are various groups of termites, with different kinds of work to do. Some tunnel into the soil and collect food such as tiny bits of plants. Others guard the entrance to the nest and bite any animals that try to enter. Some look after the eggs and young forms, or larvae.

▶ Termites mounds are incredibly complex constructions. They can reach 10 metres tall, and have air conditioning shafts built into them. These enable the termites to control the temperature of the nest to within one degree.

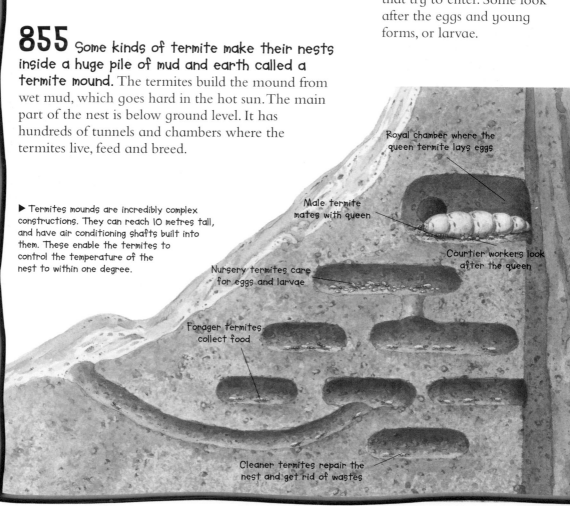

Royal chamber where the queen termite lays eggs

Male termite mates with queen

Courtier workers look after the queen

Nursery termites care for eggs and larvae

Forager termites collect food

Cleaner termites repair the nest and get rid of wastes

859 A wasp nest will have about 2000 wasps in it, but these are small builders in the insect world! A termite colony may have more than 5,000,000 inhabitants! Other insect colonies are smaller, although most have a similar set-up with one queen and various kinds of workers. Wood ants form nests of up to 300,000 and honeybees around 50,000. Some bumblebees live in colonies numbering only 10 or 20.

857 The queen termite is up to 100 times bigger than the workers. She is the only one in the nest who lays eggs – thousands every day

858 Leafcutter ants grow their own food! They harvest leaves which they use at the nest to grow fungus, which they eat.

▼ When the sections of leaf are taken back to the nest, other ants cut them up into smaller sections. They are then used in gardens to grow the ants' food.

I DON'T BELIEVE IT!

Ants get milk from green cows! The 'cows' are really aphids. Ants look after the aphids. In return, when an ant strokes an aphid, the aphid oozes a drop of 'milk', a sugary liquid called honeydew, which the ant sips to get energy.

Camouflage

860 Insects have some of the best types of camouflage in the whole world of animals. Camouflage is when a living thing is coloured and patterned to blend in with its surroundings, so it is difficult to notice. This makes it hard for predators to see or find it. Or, if the insect is a predator itself, camouflage helps it to creep up unnoticed on prey.

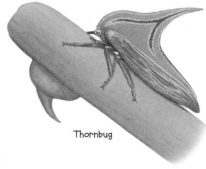
Thornbug

862 The thornbug has a hard, pointed body casing. It sits still on a twig pretending to be a real thorn. It moves about and feeds at night.

861 Stick and leaf insects look exactly like sticks and leaves. The body and legs of a stick insect are long and twiglike. The body of a leaf insect has wide, flat parts, which are coloured to resemble leaves. Both these types of insects eat plants. When the wind blows they rock and sway in the breeze, just like the real twigs and leaves around them.

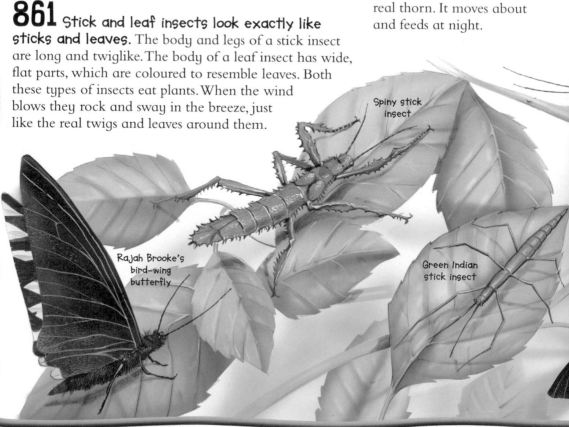
Spiny stick insect
Rajah Brooke's bird-wing butterfly
Green Indian stick insect

863 Shieldbugs have broad, flat bodies that look like the leaves around them. The body is shaped like the shield carried by a medieval knight in armour.

Shieldbug

864 Many butterflies seem too brightly coloured to blend in with their surroundings. But when the wings are held together over the butterfly's back, the undersides show. These are usually brown or green – dark colours like the leaves.

Green Indian stick insect

Rajah Brooke's bird-wing butterfly

MAKE A CAMOUFLAGE SCENE

1. Carefully cut out a butterfly shape from stiff card. Colour it brightly with a bold pattern, such as yellow and brown spots on an orange background, or orange stripes on a blue background.

2. Cut out 10–20 leaf shapes from card. Colour them like your butterfly. Stick the leaves on a cardboard branch.

3. Your butterfly may seem far too bright and bold to be camouflaged. But put the butterfly on your branch. See how well its camouflage works now!

865 The bird-dropping caterpillar looks just like – a pile of bird's droppings! Not many animals would want to eat it, so it survives longer.

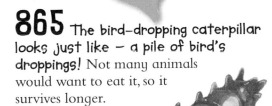

Night-time bugs

866 Insects and other bugs are amongst the noisiest nocturnal animals, especially in hot countries. An evening walk in a rainforest is accompanied by a chorus of clicks, buzzing, humming and chattering. These are some of the sounds made by millions of insects, which are invertebrates – animals without backbones.

▲ Common earwigs are insects that measure 8 to 18 millimetres in length. They are native to Europe, but are found in many countries.

867 Just like bigger creatures, insects and bugs use sound to communicate with each other at night. Cockroaches are leathery-skinned insects that are common throughout the world. Most spend their time scuttling silently through the leaf litter and twigs on the forest floor. However, the Madagascan hissing cockraoch can hiss if it's disturbed by pushing air out through its abdomen.

868 They may look menacing, but earwigs are completely harmless. By day they hide under leaves or in cracks and crevices. At night they come out to eat rotting plant and animal matter. They have pincers on the ends of their tails, which they use to scare predators away.

◄ Cockroaches can feel movement through their feet, which warns them to dash under cover to avoid predators.

▲ Feathery moth antennae can detect tiny scent particles.

869 Moths have special organs on the front of their heads called antennae. These long, slender or feathery structures detect smells and moths use them to find food and mates. These sensitive organs also help moths find their way in the dark. Moths with damaged antennae can't fly in straight lines – they crash into walls or fly backwards!

▲ Female moon moths produce a chemical that tells males they are ready to mate. Males use their antennae to pick up the scent of the female moths from several hundred metres away.

870 Moths are some of the most elegant and beautiful nocturnal insects. They have decorative patterns that help to camouflage, or hide, them. Members of the tiger moth family are often brightly coloured to tell predators that they are poisonous. Tiger moths also make high-pitched clicks to deter bats, which hunt by sound not sight. Once a bat has tried to eat one nasty-tasting tiger moth, it knows to avoid all clicking moths!

◄ There are many different types of tiger moth but most of them have fat bodies and brightly coloured wings. These warn predators that they are poisonous.

BED-SHEET BUGS!

Find out what nocturnal insects share your habitat.

You will need:
large white sheet   torch
notebook and pencil or camera

On a warm evening, hang up a sheet outside and shine a torch onto it. Wait patiently nearby and soon insects will be attracted to the sheet. Take photos or make sketches of all the bugs you see so you can identify them later. Be careful not to touch them though!

Silky spiders

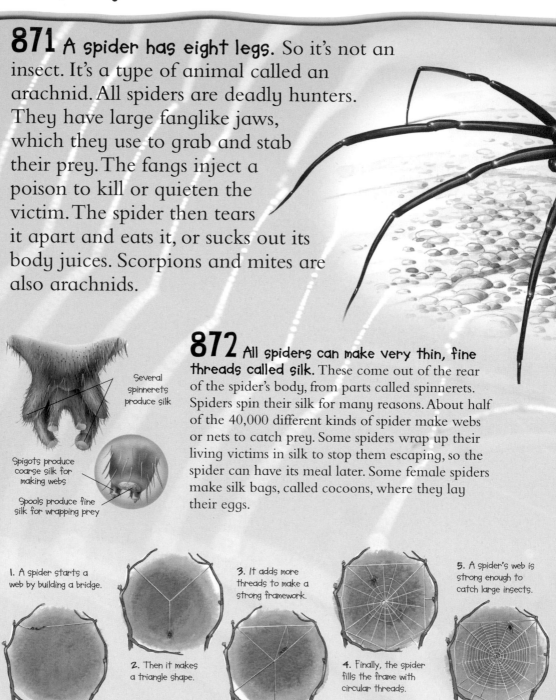

871 **A spider has eight legs.** So it's not an insect. It's a type of animal called an arachnid. All spiders are deadly hunters. They have large fanglike jaws, which they use to grab and stab their prey. The fangs inject a poison to kill or quieten the victim. The spider then tears it apart and eats it, or sucks out its body juices. Scorpions and mites are also arachnids.

Several spinnerets produce silk

Spigots produce coarse silk for making webs

Spools produce fine silk for wrapping prey

872 **All spiders can make very thin, fine threads called silk.** These come out of the rear of the spider's body, from parts called spinnerets. Spiders spin their silk for many reasons. About half of the 40,000 different kinds of spider make webs or nets to catch prey. Some spiders wrap up their living victims in silk to stop them escaping, so the spider can have its meal later. Some female spiders make silk bags, called cocoons, where they lay their eggs.

1. A spider starts a web by building a bridge.

2. Then it makes a triangle shape.

3. It adds more threads to make a strong framework.

4. Finally, the spider fills the frame with circular threads.

5. A spider's web is strong enough to catch large insects.

◄ The Australian redback spider is one of the most deadly of a group called widow spiders. These spiders get their name because, once they have mated, the female may well eat the male!

873 Some spiders have very strange ways of using their silk threads. The spitting spider squirts sticky silk at its victim, like throwing tiny ropes over it. The bolas spider catches moths and other insects flying past with its own kind of fishing line. The water spider makes a criss-cross sheet of silk that holds bubbles of air. It brings the air down from the surface, so the spider can breathe underwater.

MAKE A SPIDER'S WEB

You will need:
piece of card   reel of cotton
round-ended scissors   glue or sticky tape

1. Ask an adult for help. Cut a large hole out of the card. Stretch a piece of cotton across the hole and glue or tape both ends.

2. Do the same again several times at a different angles. Make sure all the threads cross at the centre of the hole.

3. Starting at the centre, glue a long piece of thread to one of the cross-pieces, then to the next cross-piece but slightly farther away from the centre, and so on. Work your way round in a growing spiral until you reach the edge. That's the way that real spiders make webs.

◄ The bolas spider makes a sticky ball and sticks it to a length of silk. It then whirls this rope around like a lasso and catches insects flying past.

Eight-legged hunters

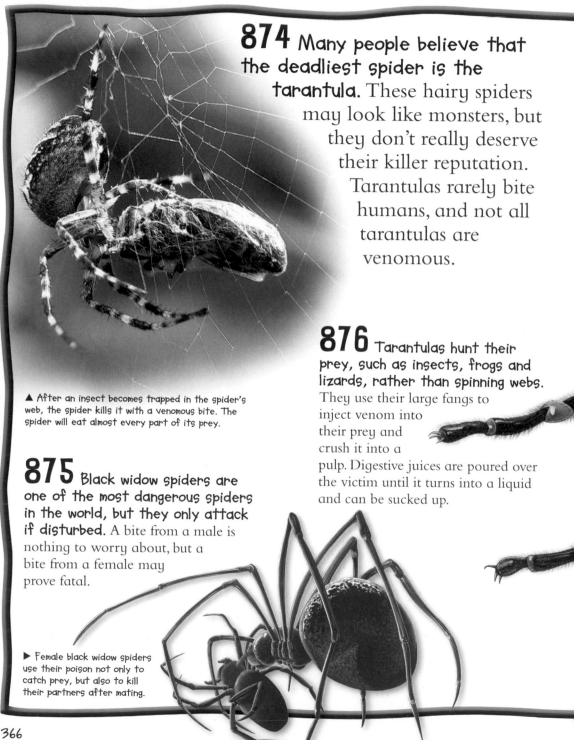

874 Many people believe that the deadliest spider is the tarantula. These hairy spiders may look like monsters, but they don't really deserve their killer reputation. Tarantulas rarely bite humans, and not all tarantulas are venomous.

▲ After an insect becomes trapped in the spider's web, the spider kills it with a venomous bite. The spider will eat almost every part of its prey.

875 Black widow spiders are one of the most dangerous spiders in the world, but they only attack if disturbed. A bite from a male is nothing to worry about, but a bite from a female may prove fatal.

876 Tarantulas hunt their prey, such as insects, frogs and lizards, rather than spinning webs. They use their large fangs to inject venom into their prey and crush it into a pulp. Digestive juices are poured over the victim until it turns into a liquid and can be sucked up.

► Female black widow spiders use their poison not only to catch prey, but also to kill their partners after mating.

877 Spiders belong to a group of animals called arachnids, along with scorpions and ticks. Some ticks can kill without using deadly poison. They attach themselves to the bodies of humans and other animals, and suck their blood. This can spread deadly diseases.

QUIZ

1. How do ticks kill animals?
2. Is the male or female black widow spider more dangerous?
3. Which spider stands on its hind legs when it feels threatened?

Answers:
1. They suck their blood and spread diseases 2. Female 3. Funnel web spider

878 There are many types of funnel web spider, and some of them are very venomous. When a funnel web spider is threatened, it stands on its hind legs and rears, showing its huge fangs. These killers bite their prey many times, injecting poison.

▲ The fangs of the funnel web spider are so strong that they can pierce human skin, even fingernails. Its bite can cause death in just 15 minutes.

A sting in the tail

879 A scorpion has eight legs. It is not an insect. Like a spider, it is an arachnid. Scorpions live in warm parts of the world. Some are at home in dripping rainforests while others like baking deserts. The scorpion has large, crablike pincers, called pedipalps, to grab its prey, and powerful jaws like scissors to chop it up.

880 The scorpion has a dangerous poison sting at the tip of its tail. It may use this to poison or paralyse a victim, so the victim cannot move. Or the scorpion may wave its tail at enemies to warn them that, unless they go away, it will sting them to death!

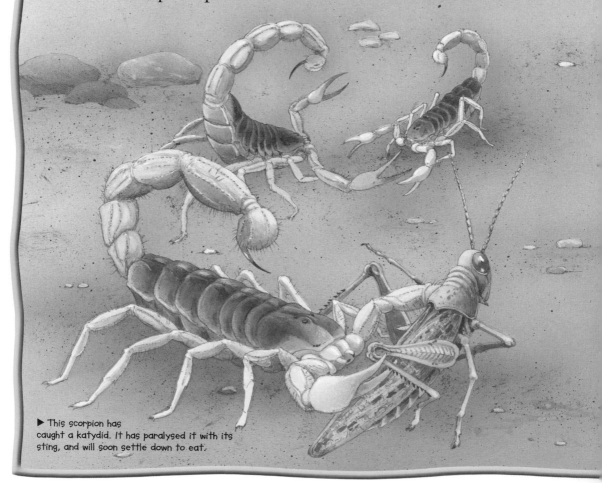

▶ This scorpion has caught a katydid. It has paralysed it with its sting, and will soon settle down to eat.

881 The sun spider or solifuge is another very fierce, eight-legged, spider-like hunter, with a poisonous bite. It lives in deserts and dry places, which is why it's sometimes called the camel spider. It can give a painful bite with its large mouthparts.

Sun spider

882 The false scorpion looks like a scorpion, with big pincers. But it does not have a poisonous sting in its tail. It doesn't even have a tail. And it's tiny – it could fit into this 'O'! It lives in the soil and hunts even smaller creatures.

False scorpion

King crab

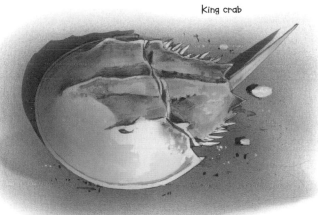

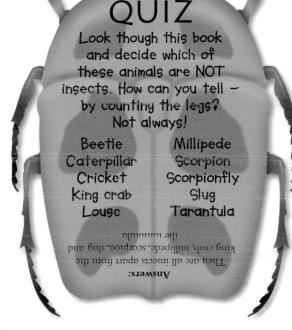

QUIZ

Look though this book and decide which of these animals are NOT insects. How can you tell – by counting the legs? Not always!

Beetle   Millipede
Caterpillar   Scorpion
Cricket   Scorpionfly
King crab   Slug
Louse   Tarantula

Answers:
They are all insects apart from the king crab, millipede, scorpion, slug and the tarantula

883 A crab may seem an odd cousin for a spider or scorpion. But the horseshoe or king crab is very unusual. It has eight legs – so it's an arachnid. It also has a large domed shell and strong spiky tail. There were horseshoe crabs in the seas well before dinosaurs roamed the land.

◄ Female horseshoe crabs can grow up to 60 centimetres in length, including the tail.

Too late to save

884 In the last few hundred years, many kinds of animals have become endangered, and dozens have died out. They include fish, frogs, snakes, birds and mammals. Studying why these extinctions happened can help to save today's endangered animals.

▶ Steller's sea cow was 8 metres long and almost as heavy as an elephant. However, size was no protection, as its herds were slaughtered by sailors for meat, blubber and hides.

885 Being very common is no safeguard against human threats. Five hundred years ago there were perhaps 5000 million passenger pigeons. They were shot and trapped by people for their meat, and their natural habitats were taken over by crops and farm animals. The last passenger pigeon, 'Martha', died in Cincinnati Zoo in 1914.

886 A creature that went from discovery to extinction in less than 30 years was Steller's sea cow. It was a huge, 3-tonne cousin of the manatee and dugong, and lived in the Arctic region. It was first described by scientists in 1741. So many were killed in a short space of time, that Steller's sea cow had died out by 1768.

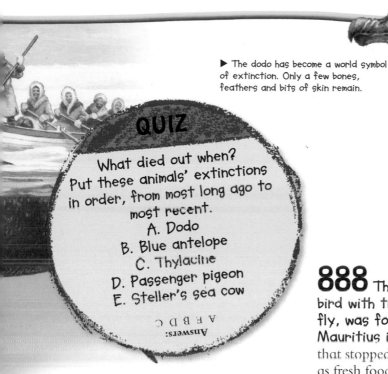

▶ The dodo has become a world symbol of extinction. Only a few bones, feathers and bits of skin remain.

QUIZ

What died out when?
Put these animals' extinctions
in order, from most long ago to
most recent.
A. Dodo
B. Blue antelope
C. Thylacine
D. Passenger pigeon
E. Steller's sea cow

Answers:
A E B D C

888 The dodo, a turkey-sized bird with tiny wings that could not fly, was found on the island of Mauritius in the Indian Ocean. Sailors that stopped at the island captured dodos as fresh food. So many were killed that all dodos were extinct by 1700. This has led to the saying 'as dead as a dodo'.

887 Many animals have become endangered, and died out forever. They include the blue antelope of Southern Africa (around 1800), the flightless seabird known as the great auk (1850s), the doglike marsupial (pouched mammal) known as the thylacine or Tasmanian tiger (1936), and the Caribbean monk seal (1950s). The list is very long, and very sad.

▶ Every 7 September, Australia holds National Threatened Species Day. The day is in memory of the last thylacine that died on this date in 1936 at Hobart Zoo, in the state of Tasmania.

How endangered?

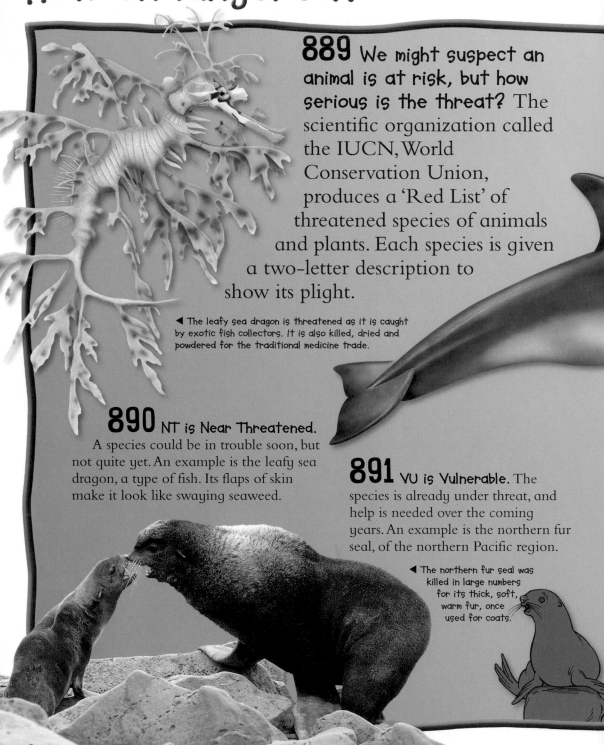

889 We might suspect an animal is at risk, but how serious is the threat? The scientific organization called the IUCN, World Conservation Union, produces a 'Red List' of threatened species of animals and plants. Each species is given a two-letter description to show its plight.

◄ The leafy sea dragon is threatened as it is caught by exotic fish collectors. It is also killed, dried and powdered for the traditional medicine trade.

890 NT is Near Threatened. A species could be in trouble soon, but not quite yet. An example is the leafy sea dragon, a type of fish. Its flaps of skin make it look like swaying seaweed.

891 VU is Vulnerable. The species is already under threat, and help is needed over the coming years. An example is the northern fur seal, of the northern Pacific region.

◄ The northern fur seal was killed in large numbers for its thick, soft, warm fur, once used for coats.

▶ Cheetahs once lived across most of Africa and the Middle East, and were even partly tamed and kept as pets by royalty. They may disappear before long.

892 EN is Endangered. The species faces big problems and the risk of extinction over the coming years is high. An example is the cheetah, the fastest runner on Earth.

893 CR. is Critically Endangered. This is the most serious group. Unless there is a huge conservation effort, extinction is just around the corner. An example is the vaquita, the smallest kind of porpoise, from the northern Gulf of California.

▲ Polluted water, drilling for oil and gas, and being caught in fishing nets are all deadly dangers for the 1.5-metre-long vaquita.

▼ Hawaiian crows are only found in captivity. Attempts to breed and release them have so far failed.

MATCH UP

Can you place these threatened creatures in their correct animal groups?

A. Whale shark   1. Bird
B. Spix macaw   2. Fish
C. Vaquita   3. Amphibian
D. Caiman   4. Mammal
E. Olm   5. Reptile

Answers:
A2 B1 C4 D5 E3

894 EW is Extinct in the Wild. The species has disappeared in nature, although there may be a few surviving in zoos and wildlife parks. An example is the Hawaiian crow. The last two wild birds disappeared in 2002, although some live in cages. EX is Extinct, or gone forever. Usually this means the animal has not been seen for 50 years.

On the critical list

895 **The most threatened animals in the world are CR, Critically Endangered.** One of the most famous CR mammals is the mountain gorilla. There are just a few hundred left in the high peaks of Central Africa. They suffer from loss of their natural habitat, being killed for meat and trophies, and from catching human diseases.

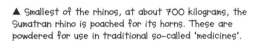

▲ Smallest of the rhinos, at about 700 kilograms, the Sumatran rhino is poached for its horns. These are powdered for use in traditional so-called 'medicines'.

896 **The most threatened group of big mammals is the rhinos.** Of the five species, three are CR – the Javan and Sumatran rhinos of Southeast Asia, and the black rhino of Africa. The Indian rhino is endangered, EN. They all suffer from loss of natural living areas and being killed for their horns.

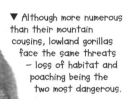

▼ Although more numerous than their mountain cousins, lowland gorillas face the same threats – loss of habitat and poaching being the two most dangerous.

MAKE A RHINO NOSE

You will need:
large sheet of card   sticky tape

A rhino's nose horn may be more than one metre long! Make your own by rolling some card into a cone shape and taping it firmly. Hold the 'horn' angled up from your own nose. How do rhinos see where they are going?

897 The kouprey or Cambodian forest ox is another critical mammal. It has big horns and weighs more than one tonne, but there are probably fewer than 250 left in Southeast Asia. Apart from losing its natural habitat, the kouprey is hunted by local people and it catches diseases from farm cattle. It is also killed for food by soldiers who fight for local warlords and hide in the forest.

▲ The kouprey grazes on grasses by night and hides in the thick forest during the day.

▼ Right whales are slow swimmers and stay near the surface, which made them easy targets for whalers.

898 The northern right whale has never recovered from being slaughtered during the mass killing of whales in the last century. There are now probably less than 600 left. These whales breed so slowly that they may never increase in numbers.

899 Apart from big, well-known mammals, many other smaller mammal species are on the critical list. They include the hispid hare (Assam rabbit) and dwarf blue sheep of the Himalaya Mountains, and the northern hairy-nosed wombat of northeast Australia.

375

All kinds under threat

900 Mammals such as pandas, whales and tigers are not the only endangered animals – there are many other threatened species from all animal groups. Among the birds is the Bermuda petrel, the national seabird of the island of Bermuda. Only about 250 survive and the islanders are making a huge conservation effort to help them.

▲ The young Bermuda petrel stays at sea for about five years before it comes back to land to breed.

901 A critical reptile is the Batagur baska (river turtle or terrapin) of India and Southeast Asia. One reason for its rarity was that people collected its eggs, especially in Cambodia, to give as presents to the king. King Norodom Sihamoni of Cambodia has now given orders to protect the baska.

▼ The batagur 'royal turtle' grows to more than one metre long and 30 kilograms in weight. It eats all kinds of foods, from plants to fish and crabs.

902 An endangered amphibian is Hamilton's frog of New Zealand. It is perhaps the rarest frog in the world. Hamilton's frog does not croak, does not have webbed feet, and hatches from its egg not as a tadpole, but as a fully formed froglet.

▶ Hamilton's frog is less than 5 centimetres long. There may be as few as 300 left in the wild.

▼ The Devil's Hole pupfish is one of several very rare fish, each found in one small pool.

904 A fish that is vulnerable (VU) is the Devil's Hole pupfish. It lives naturally in just one warm pool, Devil's Hole, in a limestone cave in the desert near Death Valley, USA. There are usually around 200–400 pupfish there, but after problems with floods and droughts, the number by 2006 was less than 50.

903 One of the rarest insects is the Queen Alexandra's birdwing butterfly. It lives in a small area on the island of Papua New Guinea. In 1950, a nearby volcano erupted and destroyed much of the butterfly's forest habitat, so it is now endangered (EN).

▶ Like many tropical butterflies, the female and male Queen Alexandra's birdwing look quite different from each other.

Male

Female

I DON'T BELIEVE IT!

The Bermuda petrel was thought to be extinct for over 300 years until a breeding group was discovered on some coastal rocks in 1951.

377

The greatest threat

905 Endangered animals face dozens of different threats, but the greatest problem for most of them is habitat loss. This means the wild places or natural habitats where they live are being changed or destroyed, so animals, plants and other wildlife can no longer survive there.

906 Today, habitat loss is happening at a terrifying rate, especially for tropical forests. These forests are 'hot spots' that have the richest range of wildlife, known as biodiversity. They occur mainly in Central and South America, West Africa and Southeast Asia – and this is where most endangered animals live.

907 Habitat loss is not a new threat – it has been happening for thousands of years. Across much of Europe, farmland for crops and livestock gradually replaced once-great woods and forests. This meant the disappearance from Britain of forest animals such as bears, wild boars, wolves and beavers.

908 The muriquis or woolly spider monkeys of Brazil are critically endangered. Trees in their tropical forests have been chopped down for logs and the timber trade. Then the land is cleared for farm animals and crops. The monkeys, along with thousands of other forest species, have fewer places to live.

909 In Borneo, animals are under threat as their forests are cleared for oil palm trees and other crops. Oil palm plantations are one of the main reasons for habitat loss across the tropics. The vegetable oil from the fleshy fruits is used for cooking, to make margarine and prepared meals, and for a vehicle fuel known as biodiesel.

▼ Tropical forests are chopped down for their valuable hardwoods such as teak and mahogany. What remains is burnt and the land cleared for crops.

HISTORY

910 History is the details of our past. People began to write things down from about 2500 BC. We know a lot of things that happened before 2500 BC, even though nothing was written down, because historians have found remains and artefacts. For example, historians know that the river Nile was important for the ancient Egyptians. The Nile provided water for drinking and for watering crops, and it was also a trade route for the Egyptians.

▼ The Nile supported many activities of ancient Egypt such as trade and farming, it was an important water source.

Ruling ancient Egypt

911 The rulers of ancient Egypt were called pharaohs. The word 'pharaoh' means great house. The pharaoh was the most important and powerful person in the country. Many people believed he was a god.

912 Ramses II ruled for over 60 years. He was the only pharaoh to carry the title 'the Great' after his name. Ramses was a great builder and a brave soldier. He was also the father of an incredibly large number of children – 96 boys and 60 girls.

Ramses II

▶ Here the pharaoh is holding the symbols of his rule, the hook and flail. Workers used these tools to separate grain from the stalks.

▼ These people are paying tribute to the pharaoh. This means that they have come from the surrounding countries to give him presents and tell him how great he is!

▲ On her wedding day, the bride wore a long linen dress or tunic.

915 Over 30 different dynasties ruled ancient Egypt. A dynasty is a line of rulers from the same family.

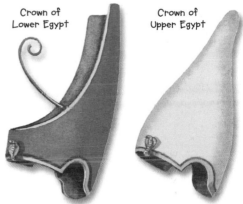

Crown of Lower Egypt

Crown of Upper Egypt

▲ The double crown of Egypt was made up of two crowns, the bucket-shaped red crown of Lower Egypt and the bottle-shaped white crown of Upper Egypt.

913 The pharaoh often married a close female relative, such as his sister or half-sister. In this way, the blood of the royal family remained pure. The title of 'pharaoh' was usually passed on to the eldest son of the pharaoh's most important wife.

914 Officials called viziers helped the pharaoh to govern Egypt. Each ruler appointed two viziers — one each for Upper and Lower Egypt. Viziers were powerful men. Each vizier was in charge of a number of royal overseers. Each overseer was responsible for a particular area of government, for example the army or granaries where the grain was stored. The pharaoh, though, was in charge of everyone.

▲ This vizier is checking the sacks of grain that have been brought in from the harvest while a criminal awaits his punishment. The viziers of ancient Egypt were among the most important people in the country.

Tutankhamun, the boy-king

916 **Tutankhamun is one of Egypt's most famous pharaohs.** He became king in 1334 BC when he was eight years old. Because he was too young to carry out the important work of ruling Egypt, two of his ministers took charge. They were Ay, chief minister, and Horemheb, head of the army. They made decisions on Tutankhamun's behalf.

◄ This model of Tutankhamun was buried with him in his tomb.

▼ Tutankhamun was buried in three separate coffins that fitted inside each other. This is the middle coffin, which is made of gold and decorated with a gem called lapis lazuli.

917 **Tutankhamun was pharaoh for about nine years.** He died when he was 17 years old. His body was mummified and buried in a tomb cut into the side of a valley. Many pharaohs were laid to rest in this valley, known as the Valley of the Kings. Tutankhamun was buried with valuables for use in the next life.

918 **The tombs in the Valley of the Kings were meant to be secret.** However robbers found them, and stole the precious items buried there. They found Tutankhamun's tomb, but were caught before they could do much damage. Years later, when the tomb of Rameses VI was being dug, rubble rolled down the valley and blocked the entrance to Tutankhamun's tomb. After that, it was forgotten about.

◄ Tutankhamun's throne. The back is decorated with a picture of the pharaoh, who is seated, and a princess.

919 In 1922, British archaeologist Howard Carter discovered the tomb of Tutankhamun. He had spent years searching for it. Other archaeologists thought he was wasting his time. They said all the tombs in the valley had already been found. Carter refused to give up, and in November 1922 he found a stairway that led to the door of a tomb.

920 Behind the door was a corridor. At the end of it was a second door, which Carter made a hole in. He peered through the hole, and said he could see 'wonderful things'. It took ten years to remove all the objects from the tomb – jewellery and a gold throne were among the treasures. A gold mask covered the king's head and shoulders. It was made of 10 kilograms of pure gold.

Egypt – land of pyramids

① Pit burial

Mound of sand over pit

Dead person with grave goods

922 **The ancient Egyptians didn't suddenly decide to start building pyramids.** Around 3100 BC there was a change in the way important people were buried. Instead of burying them in holes in the desert, they were buried in underground tombs carved into the rock. A low platform of mud-brick was built over the tomb, called a mastaba.

Mud-brick platform

② Mastaba

▲ ► At first, bodies were buried in pits (1). Later on, the pits were covered with mud-brick platforms, or mastabas (2). Finally, several platforms were put on top of each other to make the first pyramid – the Step Pyramid (3).

Graves below ground surface

921 **The word 'pyramid' was introduced to the English language by the ancient Greeks.** They saw that Egyptian loaves were a similar shape to Egypt's huge buildings. The Greeks called Egyptian loaves 'pyramides', meaning 'wheat cakes'. In time, this word changed into the English word 'pyramid'.

③ Step Pyramid

Underground passages and chambers

923 Pyramids developed from
mastabas. The first pyramid was built for Djoser, one of the first Egyptian pharaohs (kings). It began as a mastaba, but was built from stone instead of mud-brick. A second platform was added on top of the mastaba, followed by a smaller one on top of that. The mound grew until it had six platforms. It looked like an enormous staircase, which is why it is known as the Step Pyramid.

QUIZ

1. How many steps does the Step Pyramid have?
2. What type of tombs did pyramids grow out of?
3. Who was buried inside the Step Pyramid?
4. Who was the architect of the Step Pyramid?

Answers:
1. Six 2. Mastaba tombs 3. King Djoser 4. Imhotep

924 The architect
Imhotep built the Step Pyramid. He was Djoser's vizier, or chief minister, and was in charge of all building projects. It was his idea to build Djoser's tomb from stone, and to create a pyramid. Imhotep was also a poet, a priest, and a doctor. Many years after his death he was made into a god, responsible for wisdom, writing and medicine.

925 The Step Pyramid is at
Saqarra – an ancient Egyptian cemetery. The pyramid was built around 2650 BC. It is about 60 metres high and its sides are more than 100 metres in length. King Djoser was buried inside one of the chambers that were carved into the solid rock beneath the pyramid.

▶ The Step Pyramid was a series of platforms on top of each other. It was an experiment in building a tall structure, and it led the way to true pyramids with smooth sides.

The Giza Pyramids

926 **Egypt's most famous pyramids are at Giza.** In ancient Egyptian times a burial ground was known as 'kher neter', meaning 'the necropolis'. Giza was a necropolis and this was where three of ancient Egypt's most famous kings were buried in pyramids.

▼ The Giza pyramids. From left to right they are the pyramids of Menkaure, Khafre and Khufu.

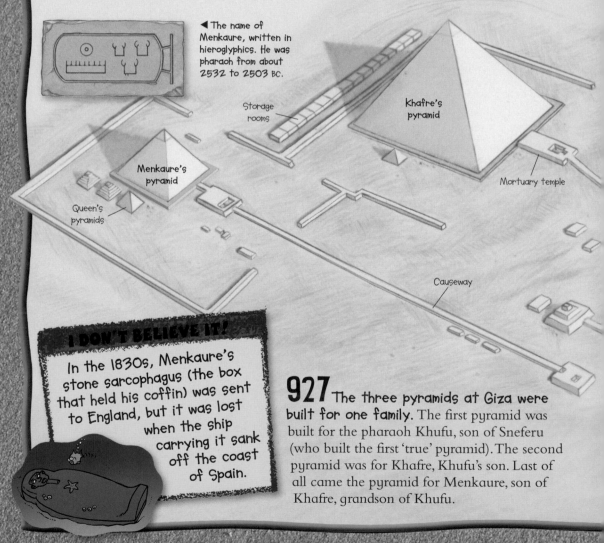

◄ The name of Menkaure, written in hieroglyphics. He was pharaoh from about 2532 to 2503 BC.

Storage rooms

Khafre's pyramid

Menkaure's pyramid

Queen's pyramids

Mortuary temple

Causeway

I DON'T BELIEVE IT!

In the 1830s, Menkaure's stone sarcophagus (the box that held his coffin) was sent to England, but it was lost when the ship carrying it sank off the coast of Spain.

927 **The three pyramids at Giza were built for one family.** The first pyramid was built for the pharaoh Khufu, son of Sneferu (who built the first 'true' pyramid). The second pyramid was for Khafre, Khufu's son. Last of all came the pyramid for Menkaure, son of Khafre, grandson of Khufu.

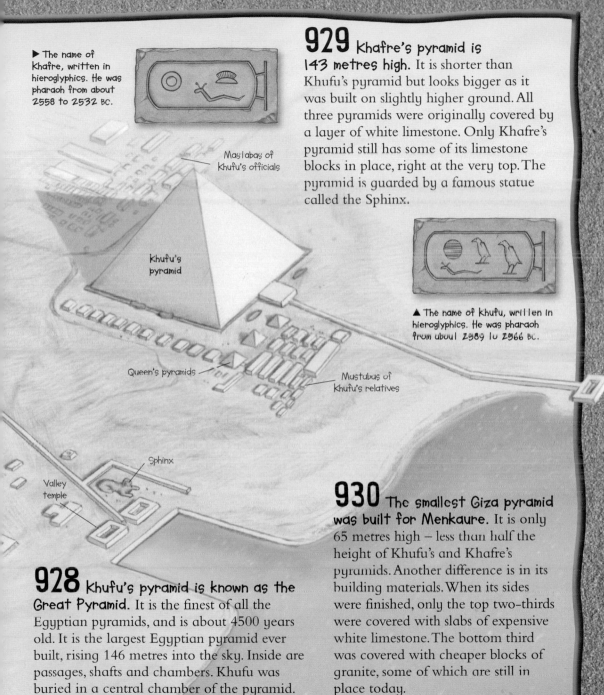

▶ The name of Khafre, written in hieroglyphics. He was pharaoh from about 2558 to 2532 BC.

Mastabas of Khufu's officials

Khufu's pyramid

Queen's pyramids

Mastabas of Khufu's relatives

Sphinx

Valley temple

929 Khafre's pyramid is 143 metres high. It is shorter than Khufu's pyramid but looks bigger as it was built on slightly higher ground. All three pyramids were originally covered by a layer of white limestone. Only Khafre's pyramid still has some of its limestone blocks in place, right at the very top. The pyramid is guarded by a famous statue called the Sphinx.

▲ The name of Khufu, written in hieroglyphics. He was pharaoh from about 2589 to 2566 BC.

930 The smallest Giza pyramid was built for Menkaure. It is only 65 metres high – less than half the height of Khufu's and Khafre's pyramids. Another difference is in its building materials. When its sides were finished, only the top two-thirds were covered with slabs of expensive white limestone. The bottom third was covered with cheaper blocks of granite, some of which are still in place today.

928 Khufu's pyramid is known as the Great Pyramid. It is the finest of all the Egyptian pyramids, and is about 4500 years old. It is the largest Egyptian pyramid ever built, rising 146 metres into the sky. Inside are passages, shafts and chambers. Khufu was buried in a central chamber of the pyramid.

The Great Pyramid

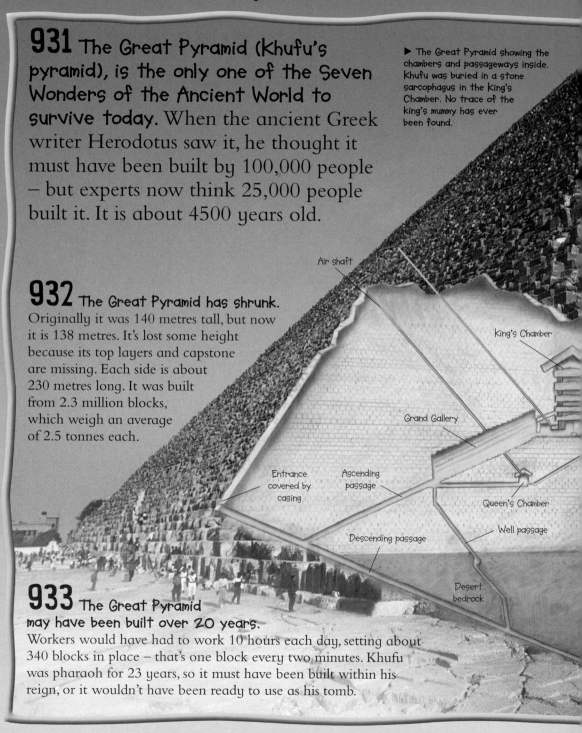

931 The Great Pyramid (Khufu's pyramid), is the only one of the Seven Wonders of the Ancient World to survive today. When the ancient Greek writer Herodotus saw it, he thought it must have been built by 100,000 people – but experts now think 25,000 people built it. It is about 4500 years old.

▶ The Great Pyramid showing the chambers and passageways inside. Khufu was buried in a stone sarcophagus in the King's Chamber. No trace of the king's mummy has ever been found.

Air shaft

King's Chamber

932 The Great Pyramid has shrunk. Originally it was 140 metres tall, but now it is 138 metres. It's lost some height because its top layers and capstone are missing. Each side is about 230 metres long. It was built from 2.3 million blocks, which weigh an average of 2.5 tonnes each.

Grand Gallery

Entrance covered by casing

Ascending passage

Queen's Chamber

Descending passage

Well passage

Desert bedrock

933 The Great Pyramid may have been built over 20 years. Workers would have had to work 10 hours each day, setting about 340 blocks in place – that's one block every two minutes. Khufu was pharaoh for 23 years, so it must have been built within his reign, or it wouldn't have been ready to use as his tomb.

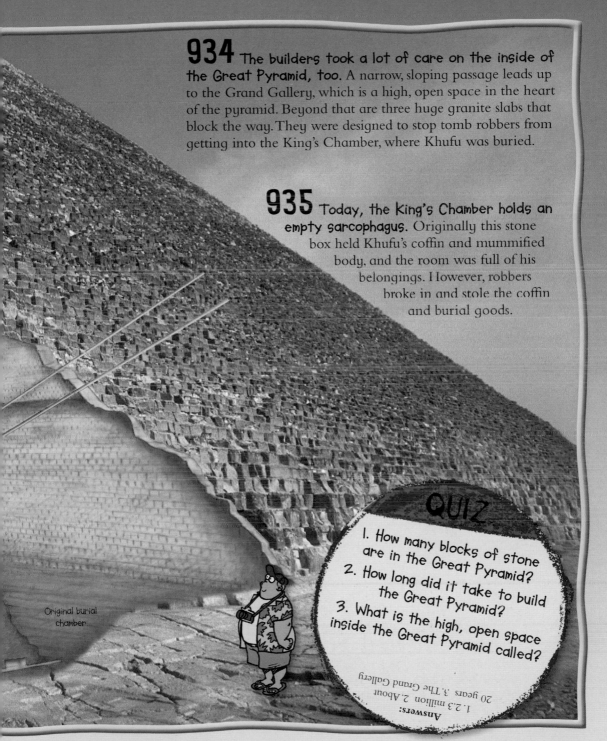

934 The builders took a lot of care on the inside of the Great Pyramid, too. A narrow, sloping passage leads up to the Grand Gallery, which is a high, open space in the heart of the pyramid. Beyond that are three huge granite slabs that block the way. They were designed to stop tomb robbers from getting into the King's Chamber, where Khufu was buried.

935 Today, the King's Chamber holds an empty sarcophagus. Originally this stone box held Khufu's coffin and mummified body, and the room was full of his belongings. However, robbers broke in and stole the coffin and burial goods.

Original burial chamber

QUIZ

1. How many blocks of stone are in the Great Pyramid?
2. How long did it take to build the Great Pyramid?
3. What is the high, open space inside the Great Pyramid called?

Answers:
1. 2.3 million 2. About 20 years 3. The Grand Gallery

391

Building a pyramid

936 The ancient Egyptians built their pyramids on the west bank of the river Nile. This was because the Egyptians linked the west with death, as this was where the sun set. The site had to be far enough away from the river to avoid flooding, but close enough for building materials to be transported to it.

QUIZ

1. Which kinds of rock were cut in the stone quarries?
2. Which side of the river Nile were pyramids built on?
3. What was a maul?
4. What was rubble carried in?

Answers:
1. Limestone and granite 2. The west side 3. A hammer made of stone 4. Woven reed baskets

▼ Builders made slots in the bedrock that were filled with water. The water was at the same level in every slot, showing the builders how much rock to remove in order to make the site flat.

937 After a site was chosen, the position of the pyramid was decided. Egyptian pyramids have sides that face north, south, east and west, but it is not clear how this was worked out. People may have used the stars to work out the position of north. Once they knew where north was, it was easy to work out the positions of south, east and west.

938 The site had to be flat, so the pyramid would rise straight up. One idea is that the builders flooded the site with water, and measured down from the surface. By keeping the measurement the same across the site, it showed them how much bedrock had to be cut away to make the site level.

▶ At the stone quarries, teams of men had specific jobs to do. Some split and levered rough blocks away from the bedrock. Others smoothed the sides of the blocks, and then they were ready to transport to the building site.

939 Pyramid workers used simple tools. Mattocks (digging tools) were used to clear the building site, and the rubble was carried away in woven reed baskets. In the stone quarries, stone was cut using mauls (stone hammers), copper chisels, and wedges. Woodworkers cut and shaped wood using copper saws and chisels, drills, hammers and planes.

940 Hundreds of men usually worked in the stone quarries. At busy times there may have been a few thousand. They worked in teams, cutting blocks of limestone and granite. The bedrock was marked with the outlines of blocks, and then the outlines were chiselled away to leave a grid of grooves. Copper wedges were knocked into the grooves to make the bedrock split. Last of all, wooden levers prised the blocks free.

Raising the blocks

941 **Moving the heavy blocks was a hard job.** Some quarries were close to the building site, but many were far away. The best limestone came from quarries on the east side of the river Nile, and granite came from the south. Barges (large ships), transported these blocks along the river to harbours built close to the pyramid sites.

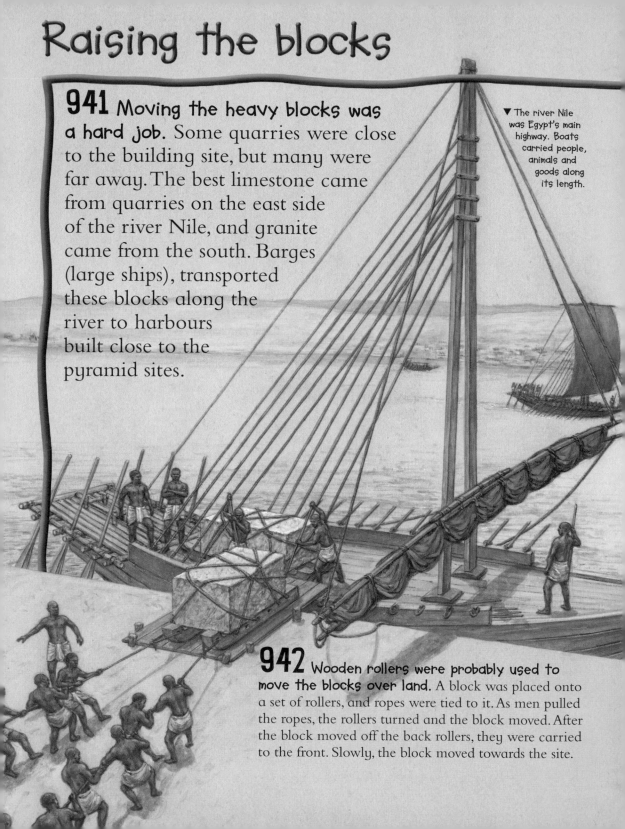

▼ The river Nile was Egypt's main highway. Boats carried people, animals and goods along its length.

942 Wooden rollers were probably used to move the blocks over land. A block was placed onto a set of rollers, and ropes were tied to it. As men pulled the ropes, the rollers turned and the block moved. After the block moved off the back rollers, they were carried to the front. Slowly, the block moved towards the site.

943 How the blocks reached their final destination is a puzzle. Historians agree that they were dragged up ramps made from hard soil and rubble – but there's disagreement about what shape the ramps were. One idea says there was one ramp that wrapped around the growing pyramid in a spiral shape. Another says there was a straight ramp against one side of the pyramid. A third idea is that there were four ramps, one on each side of the pyramid.

▶ Pharaohs probably inspected their pyramids as they were built. Their crowns showed which part of Egypt they ruled – the White Crown represented Upper Egypt, whereas the Red Crown represented Lower Egypt.

944 Once a block had been moved up the ramp, it was set in place. This was skilled work, and the stone setters had to make sure the blocks fitted neatly together. They used wooden levers to move the blocks around, and by the time one block was in place, another one had been brought up the ramp to be fitted. It was non-stop work.

945 Stonemasons built the chambers and passages inside the pyramid. Outside, the last block was put in place. This was the capstone, or pyramidion, a pyramid-shaped block that went at the top. It was covered in a thin layer of gold, which shone brightly in the sunlight.

946 Finally, the ramps were removed. As the ramps came down, workers set slabs of limestone in place. These gave the sides a smooth finish. Inside, painters decorated the burial chamber walls and ceilings with pictures and magical spells. The pyramid was finished, and was ready to be used as a pharaoh's tomb.

ANCIENT ART
Use books and the Internet to find pictures of the beautiful paintings that the Egyptians created on the walls of burial chambers. You could even try to paint some of your own!

Supreme beings

947 The ancient Egyptians worshipped more than 1000 different gods and goddesses. The most important god of all was Ra, the sun god. People believed that he was swallowed up each evening by the sky goddess Nut. During the night Ra travelled through the underworld and was born again each morning.

◀ The sun god Ra later became Amun–Ra. He was combined with another god to make a new king of the gods.

948 A god was often shown as an animal, or as half-human, half-animal. Sobek was a god of the river Nile. Crocodiles were kept in pools next to Sobek's temples. Bastet was the goddess of cats, musicians and dancers. The cat was a sacred animal in ancient Egypt. When a pet cat died, the body would be wrapped and laid in a cat-shaped coffin before burial in the city's cat cemetery. The moon god Thoth usually had the head of an ibis, but he was sometimes shown as a baboon. The ancient Egyptians believed that hieroglyphic writing came from Thoth.

▼ Some of the well known gods that were represented by animals.

Sobek

Bastet

Thoth

949 As god of the dead, Osiris was in charge of the underworld. Ancient Egyptians believed that dead people travelled to the kingdom of the underworld below the Earth. Osiris and his wife Isis were the parents of the god Horus, protector of the pharaoh.

Isis   Osiris   Horus

QUIZ

1. Who was buried inside the Great Pyramid?

2. Describe the crown of Upper Egypt.

3. What was a vizier?

4. Which pharaoh ruled for more than 90 years?

Answers:
1. King Khufu 2. A bottle-shaped white crown 3. An important governor 4. Pepi II

950 Anubis was in charge of preparing bodies to be mummified. This work was known as embalming. Because jackals were often found near cemeteries, Anubis, who watched over the dead, was given the form of a jackal. Egyptian priests often wore Anubis masks when preparing mummies.

951 A pharaoh called Amenhotep IV changed his name to Akhenaten, after the sun god Aten. During his reign Akhenaten made Aten the king of all the gods.

▼ Anubis preparing a body for mummification.

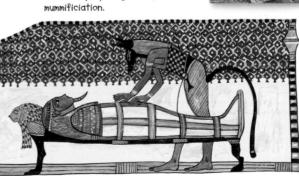

397

In tombs and temples

952 From about 2150 BC pharaohs were not buried in pyramids, but in tombs in the Valley of the Kings. At that time it was a fairly remote place, surrounded by steep cliffs lying on the west bank of the Nile opposite the city of Thebes. Some of the tombs were cut into the cliffside, others were built deep underground.

▲ Robbers looted everything from the royal tombs — gold, silver, precious stones, furniture, clothing, pots — sometimes they even stole the dead ruler's body!

▶ Carter, and his sponsor Lord Carnarvon, finally found Tutankhamun's tomb after five years of archaeological exploration in Egypt. Carnarvon died just four months after he first entered the tomb. Some people said he was the victim of Tutankhamun's 'curse' because he had disturbed the pharaoh's body. In fact Carnarvon died from an infected mosquito bite.

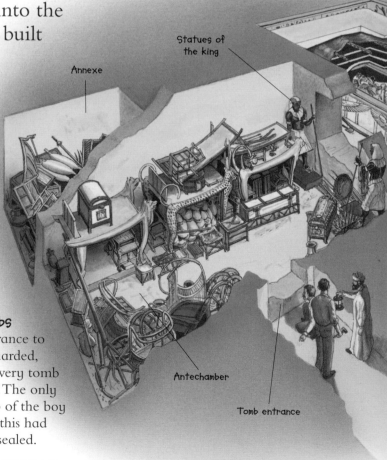

Annexe

Statues of the king

Antechamber

Tomb entrance

953 Like the pyramids, the riches in the royal tombs attracted robbers. The entrance to the Valley of the Kings was guarded, but robbers had broken into every tomb except one within 1000 years. The only one they missed was the tomb of the boy king Tutankhamun, and even this had been partially robbed and re-sealed.

954 The ancient Egyptians built fabulous temples to worship their gods. Powerful priests ruled over the temples, and the riches and lands attached to them. Many of the finest temples were dedicated to Amun-Ra, king of the gods.

I DON'T BELIEVE IT!

Temple visitors had to shave off their hair and eyebrows before they were allowed to enter the sacred buildings.

Decorated shrines, with the coffins and sarcophagus

Decorated walls of the burial chamber

Anubis, the jackal-headed god

955 The temple at Abu Simbel, in the south of Egypt, is carved out of sandstone rock. It was built on the orders of Ramses II. The temple was built in such a way that on two days each year (22 February and 22 October) the Sun's first rays shine on the back of the inner room, lighting up statues of the gods.

Golden shrine containing the canopic jars

Treasure room

▼ Four enormous statues of Ramses II, each more than 20 metres high, guard the temple entrance at Abu Simbel.

Mummies of ancient Egypt

956 The most famous mummies were made in ancient Egypt. The Egyptians were skilled embalmers (mummy-makers). Pharaohs and ordinary people were made into mummies, along with many kinds of animal.

▲ Even pet dogs were mummified in ancient Egypt.

▲ This man died 5200 years ago in Egypt. His body slowly dried out in the hot, desert conditions, and became a natural mummy.

▲ Two people walk through the Field of Reeds, which was the ancient Egyptian name for paradise.

957 Mummies were made because the Egyptians thought that the dead needed their bodies in a new life after death. They believed a person would live forever in paradise, but only if their body was saved. Every Egyptian wanted to travel to paradise after death. This is why they went to such trouble to preserve the bodies of the dead.

958 Ancient Egypt's first mummies were made by nature. When a person died, their body was buried in a pit in the desert sand. The person was buried with objects to use in the next life. Because the sand was hot and dry, the flesh did not rot. Instead, the flesh and skin dried and shrivelled until they were stretched over the bones. The body had been mummified. Egypt's natural mummies date from around 3500 BC.

960 The ancient Egyptians made their first artificial mummies around 3400 BC. The last mummies were made around AD 400. This means the Egyptians were making mummies for 4000 years! They stopped making them because as the Christian religion spread to Egypt, mummy-making came to be seen as a pagan (non Christian) practice.

▼ Many Egyptian coffins were shaped like a person and beautifully painted and decorated.

959 When an old grave was found, perhaps by robbers who wanted to steal the grave goods, they got a surprise. Instead of digging up a skeleton, they uncovered a dried-up body that still looked like a person! This might have started the ancient Egyptians thinking – could they find a way to preserve bodies themselves?

A very messy job

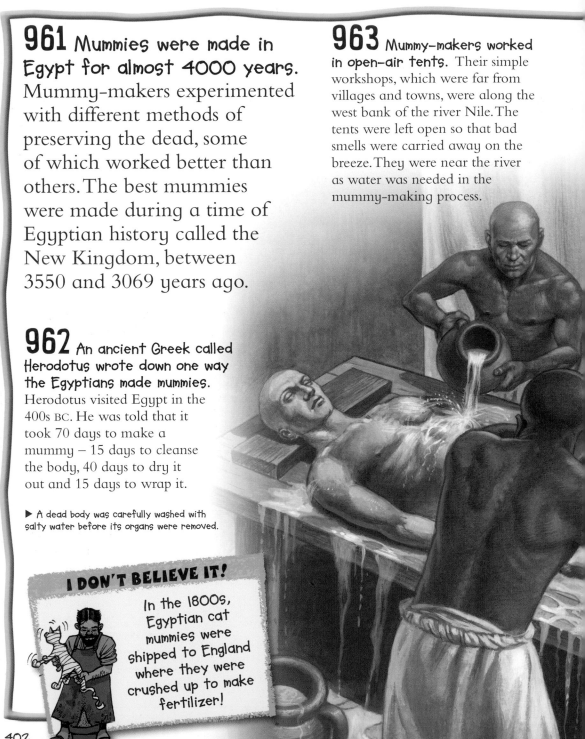

961 Mummies were made in Egypt for almost 4000 years. Mummy-makers experimented with different methods of preserving the dead, some of which worked better than others. The best mummies were made during a time of Egyptian history called the New Kingdom, between 3550 and 3069 years ago.

962 An ancient Greek called Herodotus wrote down one way the Egyptians made mummies. Herodotus visited Egypt in the 400s BC. He was told that it took 70 days to make a mummy – 15 days to cleanse the body, 40 days to dry it out and 15 days to wrap it.

▶ A dead body was carefully washed with salty water before its organs were removed.

963 Mummy-makers worked in open-air tents. Their simple workshops, which were far from villages and towns, were along the west bank of the river Nile. The tents were left open so that bad smells were carried away on the breeze. They were near the river as water was needed in the mummy-making process.

I DON'T BELIEVE IT!

In the 1800s, Egyptian cat mummies were shipped to England where they were crushed up to make fertilizer!

▶ To remove the brain, a metal hook was pushed up through the left nostril. It was then used to pull the brain out through the nose.

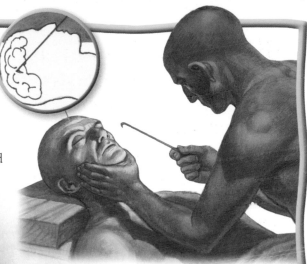

964 Mummy-making skills were handed down from one generation to the next. It was a job for men only, and it was a father's duty to train his son. A boy learned by watching his father at work. If his father worked as a slitter – the man who made the first cut in the body – his son also became a slitter.

965 The first 15 days of making a mummy involved cleaning the body. In the Place of Purification tent, the body was washed with salty water. It was then taken to the House of Beauty tent. Here, the brain was removed and thrown away. Then a slit was made in the left side of the body and the liver, lungs, intestines and stomach were taken out and kept.

966 The heart was left inside the body. The Egyptians thought the heart was the centre of intelligence. They believed it was needed to guide the person in the next life. If the heart was removed by mistake, it was put back inside. The kidneys were also left inside the body.

Drying the body

967 After the insides had been taken out, the body was dried. Mummy-makers used a special salt called natron to do the drying. The salt was a powdery-white mixture and was found along the edges of lakes in the north of Egypt. The natron was put into baskets, then taken to the mummy-makers.

970 The liver, lungs, intestines and stomach were also dried. Each of these organs was placed in a separate pottery bowl, and natron was piled on top. Just like the body, these organs were also left for 40 days, during which time the natron dried them out.

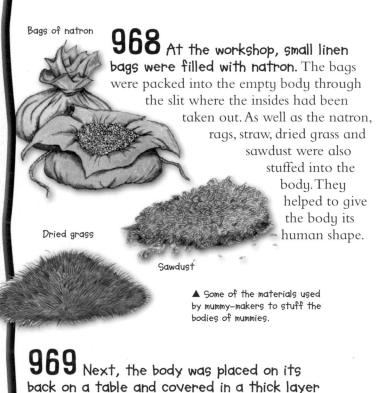

Bags of natron

Dried grass

Sawdust

968 At the workshop, small linen bags were filled with natron. The bags were packed into the empty body through the slit where the insides had been taken out. As well as the natron, rags, straw, dried grass and sawdust were also stuffed into the body. They helped to give the body its human shape.

▲ Some of the materials used by mummy-makers to stuff the bodies of mummies.

969 Next, the body was placed on its back on a table and covered in a thick layer of natron. No flesh was left exposed. The body was left to dry out under the natron for 40 days.

971 Fisherman first used natron to dry the fish they caught. They realized that natron's salty crystals sucked juices out of dead flesh, leaving it dry. Dried, or salted, fish did not rot. This was why the mummy-makers began to use natron to preserve the dead.

972 During the 40 days of drying, the natron absorbed the body's juices. At the end of this time, the mummy-makers scraped away the natron and removed the materials used to stuff the body. The dried body had lost about three-quarters of its original weight and was shrivelled, hard and blue-black in colour. It hardly looked like a body at all.

▲ The body was covered in natron, a kind of salt, to dry it out. Up to 225 kilograms were needed.

405

Wrapped from head to toe

973 The next job was to make the body appear lifelike. The body cavity was filled and the skin was rubbed with oil and spices to make it soft and sweet-smelling. Then it was given false eyes and a wig, and make-up was applied. Lastly, tree resin was poured over it. This set into a hard layer to stop mould growing.

974 The dried-out organs were wrapped in linen, then put into containers called canopic jars. The container with the baboon head (the god Hapi) held the lungs, and the stomach was put into the jackal-headed jar (the god Duamutef). The human-headed jar (the god Imseti) protected the liver, and the intestines were placed in the falcon-headed jar (the god Qebehsenuef).

975 The cut on the left side of the body was rarely stitched up. Instead, it was covered with a wax plaque. On the plaque was a design known as the Eye of Horus. The Egyptians believed it had the power to see evil and stop it from entering the body through the cut.

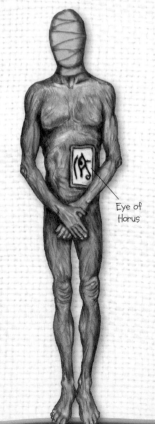

1. Head wrapped

Eye of Horus

Hapi

Imseti

◀ The four canopic jars represented the sons of the god Horus.

Duamutef

Qebehsenuef

976 **In the final part of the process, the body was wrapped.** It took 11 days to do this. The body was wrapped in strips of linen, 6 to 20 centimetres wide. There was a set way of wrapping the body, which always started with the head. Lastly, the body was covered with a sheet of linen, tied with linen bands.

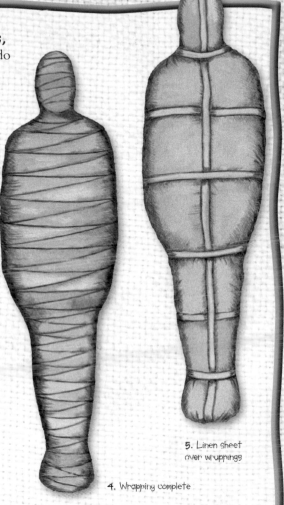

5. Linen sheet over wrappings

4. Wrapping complete

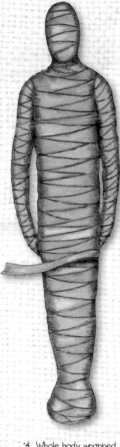

3. Whole body wrapped

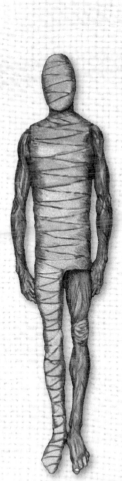

2. Limbs and torso wrapped

▲ There was a five-stage sequence for wrapping the body, which always started with the head.

977 **During the wrapping, amulets (lucky charms) were placed between the layers of linen.** These protected the person from harm on their journey to the afterlife. Magic spells written on the wrappings were another form of protection. After it was wrapped, resin was poured over the mummy to make it waterproof. Last of all, it was given a face mask.

Home sweet home

978 Egyptian houses were made from mud bricks dried in the sun. Mud was taken from the river Nile, and straw and pebbles were added to make it stronger. The trunks of palm trees supported the flat roofs. The inside walls of houses were covered with plaster, and often painted. Wealthy Egyptians lived in large houses with several storeys. A poorer family, though, might live in a crowded single room.

◀ A mixture of mud, straw and stones was poured into wooden frames or shaped into bricks and left to harden in the sun.

979 In most Egyptian homes there was a small shrine. Here, members of the family worshipped their household god.

◀ The dwarf god, Bes, was the ancient Egyptian god of children and the home.

980 Egyptians furnished their homes with wooden stools, chairs, tables, storage chests and carved beds. A low three- or four-legged footstool was one of the most popular items of furniture. Mats of woven reeds covered the floors.

981 Rich families lived in spacious villas in the countryside. A typical villa had a pond filled with fish, a walled garden and an orchard of fruit trees.

982 They cooked their food in a clay oven or over an open fire. Most kitchens were equipped with a cylinder-shaped oven made from bricks of baked clay. They burned either charcoal or wood as fuel. They cooked food in two-handled pottery saucepans.

▼ Family life in ancient Egypt with children playing board games.

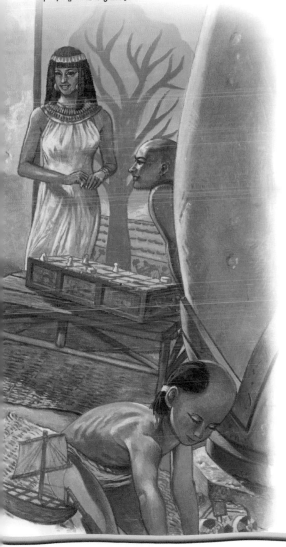

QUIZ

1. What were bricks made from?
2. How did Egyptians light their homes?
3. What was Bes the god of?
4. What were ovens made from?

Answers:
1. They were made from mud 2. They filled pottery lamps with oil and burned a wick 3. Children and the home 4. Ovens were made from clay

983 Pottery lamps provided the lighting in Egyptian homes. They filled the container with oil and burned a wick made of cotton or flax. Houses had very small windows, and sometimes none at all, so there was often very little natural light. Small windows kept out the strong sunlight, helping to keep houses cool.

984 In Egypt it was good to eat with your fingers! In rich households, servants would even bring jugs of water between courses so that people could rinse their hands.

Clever Egyptians

985 The insides of many Egyptian tombs were decorated with brightly coloured wall paintings. They often depicted scenes from the dead person's life, showing him or her as a healthy young person. The Egyptians believed that these scenes would come to life in the next world.

Sunken relief

▶ The Egyptians produced raised reliefs by cutting away the background, and sunken relief by cutting stone from inside the outline.

Raised relief

986 Egyptian sculptors carved enormous stone statues of their pharaohs and gods. These were often placed outside a tomb or temple to guard the entrance. Scenes, called reliefs, were carved into the walls of temples and tombs. These often showed the person as they were when they were young, enjoying scenes from daily life. This was so that when the god Osiris brought the dead person and the tomb paintings back to life, the tomb owners would have a good time in the afterlife.

987 The ancient Egyptians had three different calendars: an everyday farming one, an astronomical and a lunar (Moon) calendar. The 365-day farming calendar was made up of three seasons of four months. The astronomical calendar was based on observations of the star Sirius, which reappeared each year at the start of the flood season. Priests kept a calendar based on the movements of the Moon which told them when to perform ceremonies for to the moon god Khonsu.

▲ The days on this calendar are written in black and red. Black days are ordinary, but the red days are unlucky.

◄ Several artists worked on the tomb paintings. A junior artist drew the outlines of the scene, which were then checked and corrected by a more senior artist. Next, painters filled in the outlines in colour.

988 Astronomers recorded their observations of the night skies. The Egyptian calendar was based on the movement of Sirius, the brightest star in the sky. The Egyptians used their knowledge of astronomy to build temples that lined up with certain stars or with the movement of the Sun.

I DON'T BELIEVE IT!

Bulbs of garlic were used to ward off snakes and to get rid of tapeworms from people's bodies.

989 Egyptian doctors knew how to set broken bones and treat illnesses such as fevers. They used medicines made from plants such as garlic and juniper to treat sick people. The Egyptians had a good knowledge of the basic workings of the human body.

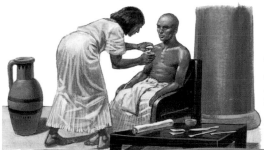

990 The Egyptians used a device called a nilometer to measure the depth of the river Nile. They inserted measuring posts into the riverbed at intervals along the bank so they could check the water levels at the start of each flood season.

411

From pictures to words

991 **The Egyptians had no paper – they wrote on papyrus.** It was made from the tall papyrus reeds that grew on the banks of the Nile. At first papyrus was sold as long strips, or scrolls, tied with string. Later the Egyptians put the papyrus sheets into books. Papyrus is very long lasting – sheets of papyrus have survived 3000 years to the present day.

992 **Ink was made by mixing water with soot, charcoal or coloured minerals.** Scribes wrote in ink on papyrus scrolls, using reed brushes with specially shaped ends.

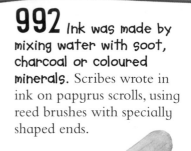

1. Papyrus was expensive because it took a long time to make. First people had to cut down the papyrus stems, and cut them up into lots of thin strips.

2. Then someone laid these strips in rows on a frame to form layers.

①

②

3. The papyrus strips were then pressed under weights. This squeezed out the water and squashed the layers together.

4. Finally, when the papyrus was dry, a man with a stone rubbed the surface smooth for writing.

③

④

993 The Rosetta Stone was found in 1799 by a French soldier in Egypt. It is a large slab of stone onto which three different kinds of writing have been carved – hieroglyphics, a simpler form of hieroglyphics called demotic and Greek. All three sets of writing give an account of the coronation of King Ptolemy V. By translating the Greek, scholars could understand the Egyptian writing for the first time.

994 The ancient Egyptians used a system of picture writing called hieroglyphics. Each hieroglyph represented an object or a sound. For example, the picture of a lion represented the sound 'l'; a basket represented the word 'lord'. Altogether there were about 700 different hieroglyphs. Scribes wrote them on papyrus scrolls or carved them into stone.

◄ A junior artist's work was checked by a senior artist, who then painted over the work in black paint.

995 In the 5th century BC a Greek historian called Herodotus wrote about life in ancient Egypt. As he travelled across the country he observed and wrote about people's daily lives, and their religion and customs such as embalming and mummification – he even wrote about cats!

WRITE YOUR NAME IN HIEROGLYPHICS

Below you will see the hieroglyphic alphabet. Can you write your name?

J A N E

A	B	C	D	E	F	G	H

I	J	K	L	M	N	O	P

Q	R	S	T	U	V	W	X	Y	Z

996 The hieroglyphs of a ruler's name were written inside an oval-shaped frame called a cartouche. The pharaoh's cartouche was carved on pillars and temple walls, painted on tomb walls and mummy cases and written on official documents.

Ancient Greece

997 The ancient Greeks were proud of their beautiful country. There were high snowy mountains, swift rushing streams, thick forests, flowery meadows and narrow, fertile plains beside the sea. Around the coast there were thousands of rocky islands, some small and poor, others large and prosperous.

◀ A carved stone figure of a woman found in the Cyclades Islands. The design is very simple but strong and graceful.

▼ This timeline shows some of the important events in the history of ancient Greece.

998 Greek civilization began on the islands. Some of the first evidence of farming in Greece comes from the Cyclades Islands. Around 6000 BC, people living there began to plant grain and build villages. They buried their dead in graves filled with treasures, such as carved marble figures, pottery painted with magic sun symbols and gold and silver jewellery.

TIMELINE OF GREECE

c. 40,000 BC
First people in Greece. They are hunters and gatherers

c. 2000–1450 BC
Minoan civilization on the island of Crete

c. 1250 BC
Traditional date of the Trojan War

c. 900–700 BC
Greek civilization grows strong again

c. 6000 BC
First farmers in Greece

c. 1600–1100 BC
Mycenean civilization on mainland Greece

c. 1100–900 BC
A time of decline – kingdoms weaken, writing stops

c. 776 BC
Traditional date of first Olympic Games

◄ This jar, made around 900 BC, is rather dull and plain. It suggests that times were troubled and Greek people had no money to spare for art.

999 Between 1100–900 BC, the history of Greece is a mystery. From 2000–1100 BC, powerful kings ruled Greece. They left splendid buildings and objects behind them, and used writing. But between around 1100–900 BC, there were no strong kingdoms, little art, few new buildings – and writing disappeared.

▶ Alexander the Great conquered an empire stretching from Greece to India.

1000 Migrants settled in distant lands. By around 700 BC, Greece was overcrowded. There were too many people, not enough farmland to grow food and some islands were short of water. Greek families left to set up colonies far away, from southern France to North Africa, Turkey and Bulgaria.

1001 When the neighbours invaded, Greek power collapsed. After 431 BC, Greek cities were at war and the fighting weakened them. In 338 BC, Philip II of Macedonia (a kingdom north of Greece) invaded with a large army. After Philip died, his son, Alexander the Great, made Greece part of his mighty empire.

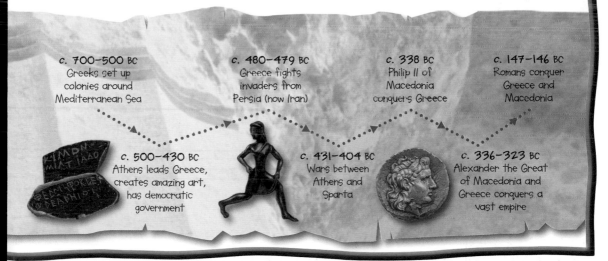

c. 700–500 BC
Greeks set up colonies around Mediterranean Sea

c. 480–479 BC
Greece fights invaders from Persia (now Iran)

c. 338 BC
Philip II of Macedonia conquers Greece

c. 147–146 BC
Romans conquer Greece and Macedonia

c. 500–430 BC
Athens leads Greece, creates amazing art, has democratic government

c. 431–404 BC
Wars between Athens and Sparta

c. 336–323 BC
Alexander the Great of Macedonia and Greece conquers a vast empire

415

Kings and warriors

1002 **King Minos ruled an amazing palace city.** The first great Greek civilization grew up at Knossos on the island of Crete. Historians call it 'Minoan' after its legendary king, Minos. Around 2000 BC, Minoan kings built an amazing palace-city, with rooms for 10,000 people. It was decorated with wonderful frescoes (wall paintings), statues and pottery.

▲ A section of the palace at Knossos on the island of Crete. A succession of powerful kings ruled a rich kingdom here.

1003 Minoan Greeks honoured a monster. Greek myths describe how a fearsome monster was kept in a labyrinth (underground maze) below the palace. It was called the Minotaur, and it was half-man, half-bull.

▲ Greek legends told how the young hero Theseus bravely entered the labyrinth and killed the Minotaur.

QUIZ

1. What was the Minotaur?
2. What was the labyrinth?
3. Where was Knossos?

Answers:
1. A monster – half-man, half-bull 2. A maze underneath the Minoan royal palace 3. On the Greek island of Crete

Oule = Hello

Khaire = Goodbye

▶ This golden mask was found in one of the royal tombs at Mycenae. It covered the face of a king who died around 1500 BC.

1004 Invaders brought the Greek language. Between around 2100–1700 BC, warriors from the north arrived in mainland Greece. They brought new words with them and their language was copied by everyone else living in Greece.

▼ Works of art found at Knossos include many images of huge, fierce bulls with athletes leaping between their horns in a deadly religious ritual.

1005 Mycenae was ruled by warrior kings. Around 1600 BC new kings took control of Minoan lands from forts on the Greek mainland. The greatest fort was at Mycenae, in the far south of Greece. Mycenaean kings sent traders to Egypt and the Near East to exchange Greek pottery and olive oil for gold, tin and amber. They used their wealth to pay for huge tombs in which they were buried.

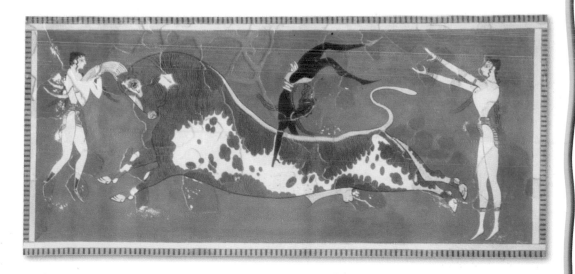

City-states

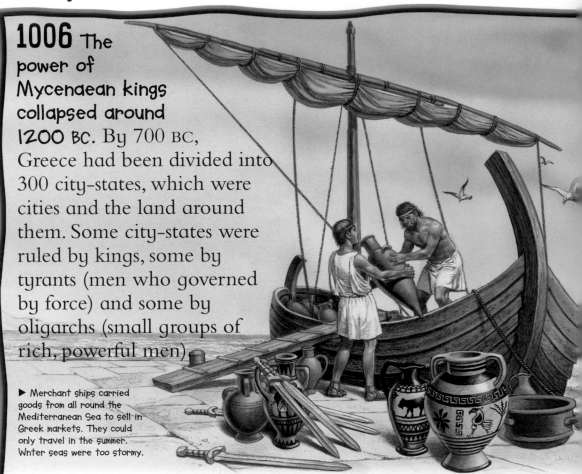

1006 The power of Mycenaean kings collapsed around 1200 BC. By 700 BC, Greece had been divided into 300 city-states, which were cities and the land around them. Some city-states were ruled by kings, some by tyrants (men who governed by force) and some by oligarchs (small groups of rich, powerful men).

▶ Merchant ships carried goods from all round the Mediterranean Sea to sell in Greek markets. They could only travel in the summer. Winter seas were too stormy.

1007 Most city-states grew rich by buying and selling. The agora (market-place) was the centre of many cities. Goods on sale included farm produce such as grain, wine and olive oil, salt from the sea, pottery, woollen blankets, sheepskin cloaks, leather sandals and slaves.

1008 Top craftsmen made fine goods for sale. Cities were home to many expert craftsmen. They ran small workshops next to their homes, or worked as slaves in factories owned by rich businessmen. Greek craftworkers were famous for producing fine pottery, stone-carvings, weapons, armour and jewellery.

1009 Coins displayed city wealth and pride.

They were invented in the Near East around 600 BC. Their use soon spread to Greece, and each city state issued its own designs, stamped out of real silver. Coins were often decorated with images of gods and goddesses, heroes, monsters and favourite local animals.

▶ The design on the top coin shows the head of Alexander the Great. The other is decorated with an owl, the symbol of Athens' guardian goddess, Athena.

1011 Cities were defended by strong stone walls.

City-states were proud, independent and quarrelsome. They were often at war with their rivals. They were also in constant danger of attack from neighbouring nations, especially Persia (now Iran). To protect their homes, temples, workshops, market-places and harbours, citizens built strong wooden gates and high stone walls.

◀▲ The walls and gates guarding the city of Mycenae were made of huge stone slabs. The gate had a huge sculpture of two lions above it.

1010 Within most city-states, there were different classes of people.

Citizens were men who had been born in the city-state, together with their wives and children. Foreigners were traders, sailors or travelling artists and scholars. Slaves belonged to their owners.

▶ Many Greek ships were wrecked together with their cargoes. Some have survived on the seabed for over 2000 years and are studied by divers today.

419

Mighty Athens

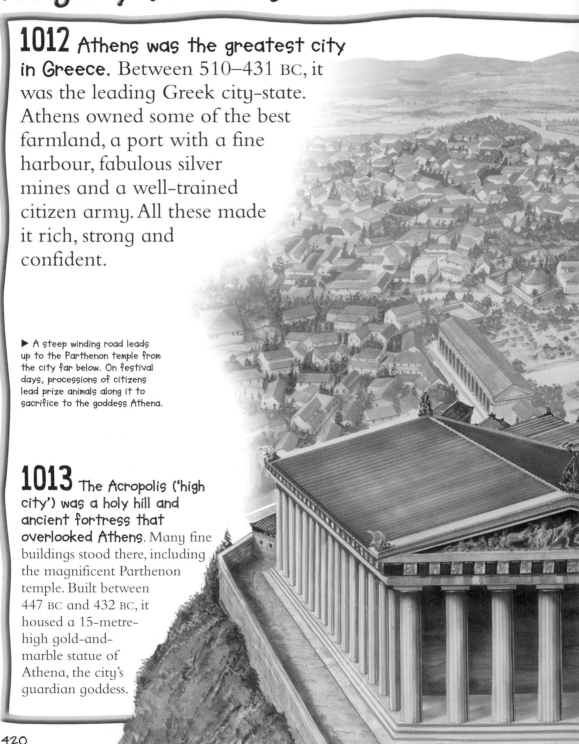

1012 Athens was the greatest city in Greece. Between 510–431 BC, it was the leading Greek city-state. Athens owned some of the best farmland, a port with a fine harbour, fabulous silver mines and a well-trained citizen army. All these made it rich, strong and confident.

▶ A steep winding road leads up to the Parthenon temple from the city far below. On festival days, processions of citizens lead prize animals along it to sacrifice to the goddess Athena.

1013 The Acropolis ('high city') was a holy hill and ancient fortress that overlooked Athens. Many fine buildings stood there, including the magnificent Parthenon temple. Built between 447 BC and 432 BC, it housed a 15-metre-high gold-and-marble statue of Athena, the city's guardian goddess.

1014 In 490 and 480 BC, armies from Persia (now Iran) invaded Greece. They were defeated, but Greek city-states felt threatened. They joined together in a League against the Persians. Athens took charge of the League, built a splendid navy and sent soldiers and government officials to 'advise' other city-states. By around 454 BC, Athens had taken control of most of Greece.

1015 Athenian city leaders paid for fine works of art. They invited the best artists, architects, sculptors, scientists and scholars to live and work in their city, and gave money to build temples, monuments and public buildings. They vowed to make their city 'an education to Greece'.

1016 Athenians are famous today – after more than 2000 years! Pericles was a great general and political leader. Socrates and Plato were philosophers and teachers who taught how to think and question. Aristotle was a scientist who pioneered a new way of studying by carefully observing and recording evidence.

Family life

1017 **Families were very important.** A person's wealth, rank and occupation all depended on their family circumstances, as did the part they played in community life. Some families were very active in politics and had powerful friends – and enemies.

1019 **Fathers were the heads of families.** They had power over everyone in their households – wives, children and slaves. However, families also worked as a team to find food, make a safe, comfortable home and train their children in all the skills they would need in adult life.

Bedrooms were upstairs

Pottery tiles

Mud-brick walls covered with plaster

Slaves cooked in the kitchen

Prayers were said around the altar each morning

1018 **All Greek parents longed for a son.** Boys passed on the family name to the next generation and they could protect family property and run businesses or farms. However, girls had to be fed and housed at the family's expense, then they left to get married.

▲ Greek houses were designed to provide security and privacy. They had high, windowless outer walls and a hidden inner courtyard, which only the inhabitants and trusted visitors could see.

1020 Most girls married very young, aged around 13 years. Their husbands, who were several years older, were chosen by their fathers for political or business reasons. A marriage linked two familes together. Romantic love was not important in marriage.

▼ Weddings took place at dusk. The bride was driven to the bridegroom's family home, accompanied by guests carrying flaming wooden torches.

1021 Women did not have the same rights as men. Many women had strong opinions about city and community life. However, according to the law, women could not vote, make a public speech or take any part in politics.

1022 Funerals were important family occasions. Wives and daughters spent most of their lives at home. However, they were allowed to attend family funerals. All family members said prayers together and made offerings to the gods in memory of the dead person.

Clothes and fashion

1023 **Greek clothes were just draped around the body.** They were loose and flowing, for comfort in the hot summer months. For extra warmth in winter, both men and women draped a thick woolly himation (cloak) over their shoulders.

1024 Each piece of cloth used to make a garment was specially made. It had to be the right length and width to fit the wearer. All cloth was handwoven, usually by women in their homes. Cool, smooth linen was the favourite cloth for summer. In winter, Greeks preferred cosy wool. Very rich people wore fine clothes of silk imported from India.

▶ Men's clothing was designed for action. Young men wore short tunics so they could work – and fight – easily. Older men's robes were longer.

◀ Women's clothing was modest and draped the body from top to toe. Respectable women covered their heads and faces with a veil when they went outside the house.

MAKE A GREEK CHITON

You will need:
Length of cloth twice as wide as your outstretched arms and half your height
safety pins   belt or length of cord

1. Fold the cloth in half.

2. Fasten two edges of the cloth together with safety pins, leaving a gap of about 30 cm in the middle.

3. Pull the cloth over your head so that the safety pins sit on your shoulders.

4. Fasten the belt or cord around your waist. Pull some of the cloth over the belt so that the cloth is level with your knees.

1025 Women – and men – took care of their skin. To keep their skin smooth and supple, men and women rubbed themselves all over with olive oil. Rich women also used sunshades or face powder to achieve a fashionably pale complexion. They did not want to look sun-tanned – that was for farm workers, slaves – and men!

Before 500 BC

500–300 BC

After 300 BC

1026 Curls were very fashionable. Women grew their hair long and tied it up with ribbons or headbands, leaving long curls trailing over their shoulders. Men, except for Spartan warriors, had short curly hair. Male and female slaves had their hair cropped very short – this was a shameful sign.

▲ Before 500 BC, long, natural hairstyles were popular. Between 500–300 BC, women tied their hair up and held it in place with ribbons or scarves. After 300 BC, curled styles and jewelled hair ornaments were popular and men shaved off their beards.

1027 The Greeks liked to look good and admired fit, slim, healthy bodies. Women were praised for their grace and beauty. Young men were admired for their strong figures, and often went without clothes when training for war or taking part in sports competitions. Top athletes became celebrities, and were asked by artists to pose for them as models.

1028 Sponges, showers and swimming helped the Greeks keep clean. Most houses did not have piped water. So people washed themselves by standing under waterfalls, swimming in streams or squeezing a big sponge full of water over their heads, like a shower.

◄ Athletes and their trainer (left) pictured on a Greek vase.

Gods and goddesses

1029 To the Greeks, the world was full of dangers and disasters that they could not understand or control. There were also many good things, such as love, joy, music and beauty, that were wonderful but mysterious. The Greeks thought of all these unknown forces as gods and goddesses who shaped human life and ruled the world.

▶ This statue of the goddess Aphrodite was carved from white marble – a very smooth, delicate stone. It was designed to portray the goddess' perfect beauty. Sadly, it has been badly damaged over the centuries.

▶ Poseidon was god of the sea and storms. He also sent terrifying earthquakes to punish people – or cities – that offended him.

1030 Gods and goddesses were pictured as superhuman creatures. They were strong and very beautiful. However, like humans, gods and goddesses also had weaknesses. Aphrodite was thoughtless, Hera was jealous, Apollo and his sister Artemis were cruel, and Ares was bad-tempered.

1033 The Greeks believed in magic spirits and monsters. These included Gorgons who turned men to stone, and Sirens – bird-women whose song lured sailors to their doom. They also believed in witchcraft and curses and tried to fight against them. People painted magic eyes on the prows of their ships to keep a look-out for evil.

▲ Odysseus and his shipmates were surrounded by the Sirens – beautiful half-women, half-bird monsters. They sang sweet songs, calling sailors towards dangerous rocks where their ships were wrecked.

1031 Individuals were often anxious to see what the future would bring. They believed that oracles (holy messengers) could see the future. The most famous oracles were at Delphi, where a drugged priestess answered questions, and at Dodona, where the leaves of sacred trees whispered words from the gods.

1032 Poets and dramatists retold myths and legends about the gods. Some stories were explanations of natural events – thunder was the god Zeus shaking his fist in anger. Others explored bad thoughts and feelings shared by gods and humans, such as greed and disloyalty.

▶ Herakles was a hero – a man who became a god. He performed amazing feats of strength and fought against many monsters. This statue shows him killing a centaur, half-man, half-horse.

War on land and sea

1034 As teenagers, all Greek male citizens were trained to fight. They had to be ready to defend their city whenever danger threatened. City-states also employed men as bodyguards and mercenary troops with special skills.

▼▶ Soldiers had different duties. Cavalrymen were messengers and spies. Peltasts had to move fast and were armed with javelins. Mercenaries fought for anyone who would pay them.

Peltast

Cavalry

Hoplite

Mercenary

1035 Each soldier paid for his own weapons and armour. Most soldiers were hoplites (soldiers who fought on foot). Their most important weapons were swords and spears. Poor men could not afford swords or armour. Their only weapons were slings for shooting stones and simple wooden spears.

1036 Soldiers rarely fought on horseback. At the start of a battle, hoplites lined up side by side with their shields overlapping, like a wall. Then they marched towards the enemy while the peltasts threw their javelins. When they were close enough, the hoplites used their spears to fight the enemy.

◀ A Corinthian-style helmet. Soldiers tried to protect themselves from injury with bronze helmets, breastplates, greaves (shin guards) and round wooden shields.

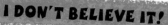

I DON'T BELIEVE IT!

Ancient Greek soldiers rarely rode horses — because stirrups had not yet been invented. Without stirrups to support him, a soldier on horseback who hurled a spear or stabbed with a sword was likely to fall off backwards!

1037 City-states paid for fleets of fast, fearsome wooden warships, called triremes. Each ship had a crew of about 170 oarsmen who sat in three sets of seats, one above the other. They rowed the ship as fast as they could towards enemy vessels, hoping that the sharp, pointed ram at its prow would smash or sink them. The most famous naval battle in Greece was fought at Salamis, near Athens, in 480 BC, when the Greeks defeated the Persians.

▼ Greek ships were made of wood. If they were holed below the waterline they sank very quickly.

Hoplites and phalanxes

1038 Hoplites were equipped with a shield, helmet, spear and sword. A Greek who lost his shield was a coward. The shield carried by hoplites was over one metre across and made of wood and bronze. It was very heavy, and anyone trying to run away from an enemy would throw it away, so men who lost their shields in battle were often accused of cowardice.

I DON'T BELIEVE IT!

Spartan hoplites were so tough that they reckoned they could easily win any battle, even if they were outnumbered by as many as five to one!

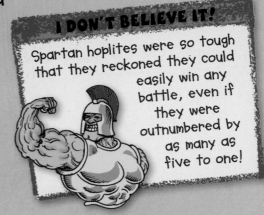

▶ The success of Greek soldiers in battle depended on them keeping tightly in formation so that enemy soldiers could not get past the line of shields.

1039 Hoplites fought in formations called phalanxes. When going into battle, hoplites stood shoulder to shoulder so that their shields overlapped, and pointed their spears forwards over the shields. A phalanx was made up of six or more ranks of hoplites, one behind the other.

1040 Greek spears had a 'lizard stabber'. Hoplite spears had a bronze spike at the bottom end. This was used to stick the spear upright into the ground and was called a 'sauroter', meaning 'lizard stabber'.

1041 The best helmets were made from a single sheet of metal. Skilled metalworkers in the Greek city of Corinth invented a way to make a helmet by beating a single sheet of bronze into shape. This produced a helmet that was much stronger than one made of several pieces of metal. The helmets were called 'Corinthian'.

Temples and festivals

1042 In Greece and the lands where the Greeks settled, we can still see the remains of huge, beautiful temples. They were built as holy homes for gods and goddesses. Each city-state had its own guardian god and many temples housed a huge, lifelike statue of him or her. People hoped that the god's spirit might visit them and live in the statue for a while.

▶ This gigantic statue of the goddess Athena was 15 metres high and was made of gold and ivory. It stood inside her finest temple, the Parthenon in Athens. In her right hand, Athena holds Nike, the goddess of victory.

QUIZ

1. What were temples?
2. Where did all the gods meet?
3. What did people offer to their gods and goddesses?
4. What happened at shrines?

Answers:
1. Holy homes for gods and goddesses 2. Mount Olympus 3. Prayers and sacrifices (gifts) 4. Secret rituals

1043 As well as visiting a temple, people hoped – or feared – that they might meet a god or goddess in a forest or on a mountain top. It was thought that all the gods met at Mount Olympus to feast, love, quarrel and make plans. Another high peak, Mount Parnassus, was sacred to the Muses – nine graceful goddesses who guided the arts, such as music and drama.

▲ The summit of the tallest mountain in Greece, Mount Olympus (1951 metres), was often hidden in clouds. It was remote, dangerous and mysterious – a suitable home for the mighty gods.

▼ The first temples were made of wood and shaped like ordinary houses. By around AD 600, temples were built of stone.

c. 800 BC tree trunks hold up the roof. Small inner room.

1044 People offered prayers and sacrifices (gifts) to their gods and goddesses. Gifts might be just a few drops of wine or a valuable live animal. The meat of the sacrifice was cooked and shared among the worshippers and the bones and skin were burned on the altar. People thought that smoke carried their prayers up to the gods.

c. 600 BC tree trunks replaced by stone columns. More rooms inside.

1045 City-states held festivals to honour their guardian gods. There would be a procession towards the city's main temple or to a shrine (holy place). At temples, crowds watched priests and priestesses making special sacrifices. At shrines, citizens might take part in secret rituals. Afterwards there could be music and drama or sports contests.

c. 440 BC temples are huge, with rows of columns and carved decorations.

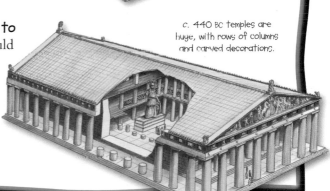

Olympic Games

1046 **The Olympic Games began as a festival to honour Zeus.** Over the centuries, it grew into the greatest sports event in the Greek world. A huge festival complex was built at Olympia with a temple, sports tracks, seats for 40,000 spectators, a campsite and rooms for visitors and a field full of stalls selling food and drink.

▶ Victory! The Greeks believed that winners were chosen by the gods. The first known Olympic Games was held in 776 BC, though the festival may have begun years earlier.

1047 **Every four years athletes travelled from all over Greece to take part in the Olympic Games.** They had to obey strict rules – respect for Zeus, no fights among competitors and no weapons anywhere near the sports tracks. In return they claimed protection – the holy Olympic Peace. Anyone who attacked them on their journeys was severely punished.

QUIZ

1. When was the first Olympic Games held?
2. Could women go to the Olympic Games?
3. What did winning athletes wear on their heads?

Answers:
1. 776 BC, though the festival may have begun years earlier 2. No. There was a separate women's games held 3. Crowns of holy laurel leaves

1048 The most popular events were running, long jump, wrestling and boxing. Spectators might also watch chariot races, athletes throwing the discus and javelin or weightlifting contests. The most prestigious event was the 200-metre sprint. There was also a dangerous fighting contest called pankration (total power).

▲ Boxers did not wear gloves. Instead they wrapped their hands in bandages.

1049 Many events featured weapons or skills that were needed in war. One of the most gruelling competitions was a race wearing heavy battle armour. The main Olympic Games were for men only – women could not take part. There was a separate women's games held at Olympia on different years from the men's competitions.

▲ Throwing the discus was a test of strength and balance. It was also useful training for war.

▲ Swimmer Michael Phelps sets a new world record at the Beijing Olympics, 2008. The modern Olympics is modelled on the ancient games and since 1896 has remained the world's greatest sports festival.

1050 Athletes who won Olympic contests were honoured as heroes. They were crowned with wreaths of holy laurel leaves and given valuable prizes of olive oil, fine clothes and pottery. Poets composed songs in their praise and their home city-states often rewarded them with free food and lodgings for life!

► A crown of laurel leaves was given to winning athletes as a sign of their godlike strength and speed.

435

Plays and poems

1051 Greek drama originated at religious festivals. In the earliest rituals, priests and priestesses sometimes played the part of gods or goddesses. They acted out stories told about them or famous local heroes. Over the years, these ancient rituals changed into a new art form – drama.

I DON'T BELIEVE IT!

Music for poetry was played on a lyre. This was rather like a small harp, but had a real (dead) hollow tortoise shell as a sounding-box!

1052 Drama became so popular that many city-states built splendid new open-air theatres. Greek theatres were built in a half-circle shape with tiers (raised rows) of seats looking down over an open space for performers. Most seats were filled by men – women were banned from many plays.

▶ The theatre at Epidaurus, in southern Greece, is one of the largest built by the ancient Greeks. It had seats for over 10,000 spectators.

1053 **All the parts in a play were performed by men.** They wore masks, wigs and elaborate costumes to look like women or magic spirits and monsters. Some theatres had ladders and cranes so that actors playing gods could appear to fly or sit among the clouds.

1054 **In some city-states, especially Athens, drama remained an important part of several religious festivals.** Writers competed for prizes for the best new plays. They wrote serious plays called tragedies and lively comedies. Some plays lasted all day long. Others had extra 'satyr plays' added on. These were short, funny pieces.

1055 **Plays were written like poetry.** The main actors were always accompanied by singers and dancers. Poems were also recited to music. Tunes were sad for tragic poems or rousing for those about war. Poets performed at men's dinner parties and in rich families' homes. Public storytellers entertained crowds by singing poems in the streets.

Barbarian – or monster – with wild, shaggy hair

Angry young man

▶ Actors wore masks to show which character they were playing. Bright-coloured masks were for cheerful characters and dark-coloured masks were more gloomy. Some masks were double-sided so that the actors could change parts quickly.

Huge, funnel-shaped mouths helped the actors' words reach the audience

Masks with beards and bald heads were for actors playing old men

Capital city

1056 More than a million people lived in Rome. By around AD 300, Rome was the largest city in the world. There were citizens who could vote and serve in the army, and there were non-citizens who did not have these rights. The government was run by nobles and knights who were usually very rich. Plebeians, or ordinary people, were usually fairly poor but were citizens of Rome. Slaves were not citizens. They were not free to leave their owners and had no rights.

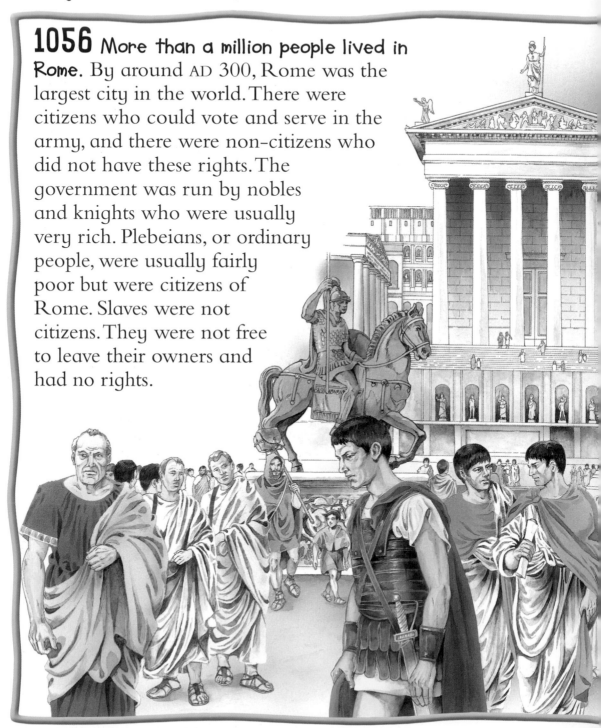

1057 The Forum was the government district in the centre of Rome. People went there to meet their friends and business colleagues, discuss politics, and to listen to famous orators who made speeches in the open air. The Forum was mainly a marketplace, surrounded by government buildings such as offices and law-courts.

1059 The Romans were great water engineers. They designed aqueducts, raised channels to carry water from streams in faraway hills and mountains to the city. The richest Roman homes were supplied with constant running water carried in lead pipes. Ordinary people had to drink from public fountains.

1060 Rome relied on its drains. Rome was so crowded that good drains were essential. Otherwise, the citizens could have caught diseases from sewage and died. The largest sewer, called the 'cloaca maxima', was so high and so wide that a horse and cart could drive through it.

1058 Rome was a well-protected city. It was surrounded by 50 kilometres of strong stone walls, to keep out attackers. All visitors had to enter the city through one of its 37 gates, which were guarded by soldiers and watchmen.

I DON'T BELIEVE IT!

Roman engineers also designed public lavatories. These lavatories were convenient, but not private. Users sat on rows of seats, side by side!

City life

1061 **The Romans built the world's first high-rise apartments.** Most of the people who lived in Ostia, a busy port close to Rome, had jobs connected with trade, such as shipbuilders and money-changers. They lived in blocks of flats known as 'insulae'. A typical block was three or four storeys high, with up to a hundred small, dirty, crowded rooms.

1062 **Rich Romans had more than one home.** Rome was stuffy, dirty and smelly, especially in summer time. Wealthy Roman families liked to get away from the city to cleaner, more peaceful surroundings. They purchased a house (a 'villa urbana') just outside the city, or a big house surrounded by farmland (a 'villa rustica') in the countryside far away from Rome.

1063 **Many Roman homes had a pool, but it was not used for swimming!** Pools were built for decoration, in the central courtyards of large Roman homes. They were surrounded by plants and statues. Some pools had a fountain; others had mosaics – pictures made of tiny coloured stones or squares of glass – covering the floor.

MAKE A PAPER MOSAIC

You will need:

large sheet of paper   scissors
pencil   glue
scraps of coloured and textured paper

1. Draw the outlines of your design on a large sheet of paper. Plan which colours to use for different parts of the mosaic.

2. Cut the paper scraps into small squares, all roughly the same size. The simplest way to do this is to cut strips, then snip the strips into squares.

3. Stick the paper squares onto the large sheet of paper following the outlines of your design.

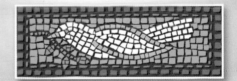

1064 Fortunate families had hot feet.

Homes belonging to wealthy families had underfloor central heating. Blasts of hot air, warmed by a wood-burning furnace, circulated in channels built beneath the floor. The furnace was kept burning by slaves who chopped wood and stoked the fire.

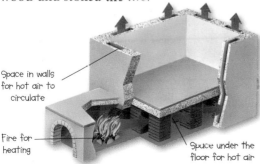

Space in walls for hot air to circulate

Fire for heating

Space under the floor for hot air

1065 Rome had its own fire brigade.

The 7000 firemen were all specially trained freed slaves. Ordinary families could not afford central heating, so they warmed their rooms with fires in big clay pots which often set the house alight.

Roman style

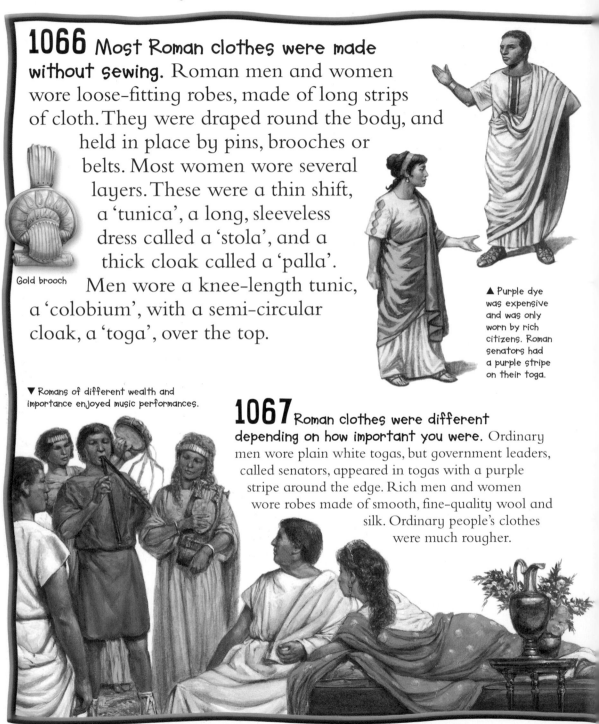

1066 **Most Roman clothes were made without sewing.** Roman men and women wore loose-fitting robes, made of long strips of cloth. They were draped round the body, and held in place by pins, brooches or belts. Most women wore several layers. These were a thin shift, a 'tunica', a long, sleeveless dress called a 'stola', and a thick cloak called a 'palla'. Men wore a knee-length tunic, a 'colobium', with a semi-circular cloak, a 'toga', over the top.

Gold brooch

▲ Purple dye was expensive and was only worn by rich citizens. Roman senators had a purple stripe on their toga.

▼ Romans of different wealth and importance enjoyed music performances.

1067 **Roman clothes were different depending on how important you were.** Ordinary men wore plain white togas, but government leaders, called senators, appeared in togas with a purple stripe around the edge. Rich men and women wore robes made of smooth, fine-quality wool and silk. Ordinary people's clothes were much rougher.

1068 **Clothes told the world who you were.** People from many different cultures and races lived in lands ruled by the Romans. They wore many different styles of clothes. For example, men from Egypt wore wigs and short linen kilts. Celtic women from northern Europe wore long woollen shawls, woven in brightly coloured checks. Celtic men wore trousers.

▼ These Roman sandals have metal studs in the soles to make sure that they don't wear down too quickly!

DRESS LIKE A ROMAN!

You can wear your very own toga! Ask an adult for a blanket or a sheet, then follow the instructions below!

 1. First ask an adult to find you a blanket or sheet. White is best, like the Romans.

2. Drape your sheet over your left shoulder. Now pass the rest behind your back.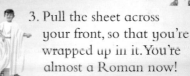

3. Pull the sheet across your front, so that you're wrapped up in it. You're almost a Roman now!

4. Finally, drape the last end over your right hand and there you have it, a Roman toga!

1069 **Roman boots were made for walking!** Roman soldiers and travellers wore lace-up boots with thick leather soles studded with iron nails. Other Roman footwear included 'socci', loose-fitting slippers to wear indoors. Farmers wore shoes made of a single piece of ox-hide wrapped round the foot, called 'carbatinae'. There were also 'crepidae', comfortable lace-up sandals with open toes.

Bath time

1070 The Romans went to the public baths in order to relax. These huge buildings were more than a place to get clean. They were also fitness centres and places to meet friends.

1071 Visitors could take part in sports, such as wrestling, do exercises, have a massage or a haircut. They could buy scented oils and perfumes, read a book, eat a snack or admire works of art in the baths own sculpture gallery!

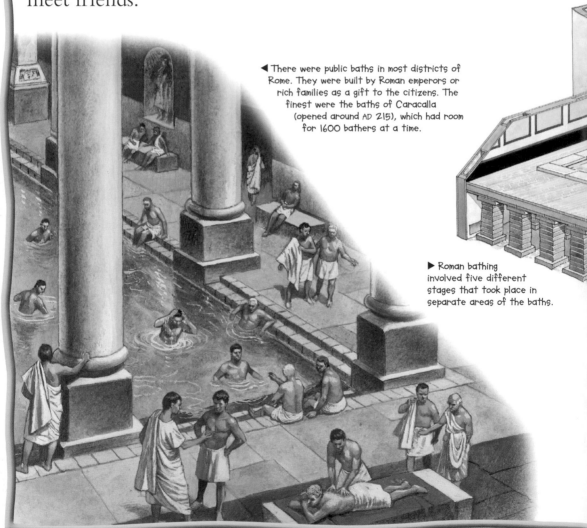

◄ There were public baths in most districts of Rome. They were built by Roman emperors or rich families as a gift to the citizens. The finest were the baths of Caracalla (opened around AD 215), which had room for 1600 bathers at a time.

► Roman bathing involved five different stages that took place in separate areas of the baths.

1072 Men and women could not bathe together. Women usually went to the baths in the mornings, while most men were at work. Men went to the baths in the afternoons.

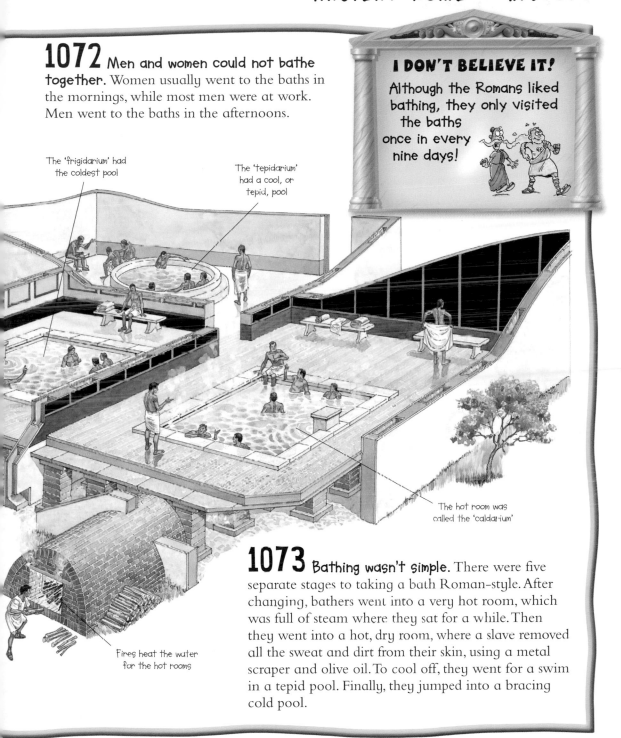

I DON'T BELIEVE IT!

Although the Romans liked bathing, they only visited the baths once in every nine days!

The 'frigidarium' had the coldest pool

The 'tepidarium' had a cool, or tepid, pool

The hot room was called the 'caldarium'

Fires heat the water for the hot rooms

1073 Bathing wasn't simple. There were five separate stages to taking a bath Roman-style. After changing, bathers went into a very hot room, which was full of steam where they sat for a while. Then they went into a hot, dry room, where a slave removed all the sweat and dirt from their skin, using a metal scraper and olive oil. To cool off, they went for a swim in a tepid pool. Finally, they jumped into a bracing cold pool.

Ruling Rome

1074 Rome used to be ruled by kings.

According to legend, the first king was Romulus, who came to power in 753 BC. Six more kings ruled after him, but they were unjust and cruel. The last king, Tarquin the Proud, was overthrown in 509 BC. After that, Rome became a republic, a state without a king. Every year the people chose two senior lawyers called consuls to head the government. Many other officials were elected, or chosen by the people, too. The republic lasted for over 400 years.

▲ Roman coin showing the emperor Constantine.

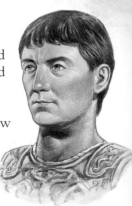
▼ Senators were men from leading citizen families who had served the Roman republic as judges or state officials. They made new laws and discussed government plans.

1075 In 47 BC a successful general called Julius Caesar declared himself dictator.

This meant that he wanted to rule on his own for life. Many people feared that he was trying to end the republic, and rule like the old kings. Caesar was murdered in 44 BC by a group of his political enemies. After this, there were many years of civil war.

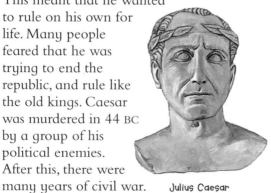
Julius Caesar

1076 In 27 BC an army general called Octavian seized power in Rome.

He declared himself 'First Citizen', and said he would bring back peace and good government to Rome. He ended the civil war, and introduced many strong new laws. But he also changed the Roman government for ever. He took a new name, 'Augustus' and became the first emperor of Rome.

Octavian

◀ Roman courts were busy places. There was a public gallery where people could watch cases that interested them. People who were accused of crime and refused to go to court could be made to attend by force. Lawyers called advocatus spoke on their behalf.

1077 The Romans were proud of their laws.

Everyone in Rome, from the emperor to the poorest beggar, was expected to obey the law. The first rules of the Roman legal system were recorded in 450 BC in a document called the Twelve Tables. Roman laws were strict but fair. Everyone was considered innocent until they had been proved guilty in an open trial. The Roman system forms the basis of many legal systems today.

I DON'T BELIEVE IT!

Some Roman emperors were mad and dangerous. The Emperor Nero was said to have laughed and played music while watching a terrible fire that destroyed a large part of Rome.

In the army

1078 Being a soldier was a good career, if you did not get killed! Roman soldiers were well paid and well cared for. The empire needed troops to defend its land against enemy attack. A man who fought in the Roman army received a thorough training in battle skills. If he showed promise, he might be promoted and receive extra pay. When he retired after 20 or 25 years of service, he was given money or land to help him start a business.

▲ Roman troops defended the empire from attack, they were well paid but it was a dangerous job.

I DON'T BELIEVE IT!

Roman soldiers guarding the cold northern frontiers of Britain kept warm by wearing short woollen trousers, such as underpants, beneath their tunics!

1079 The Roman army contained citizens and 'helpers'. Roman citizens joined the regular army, which was organized into legions of around 5000 men. Men who were not citizens could also fight for Rome. They were known as auxiliaries, or helpers, and were organized in special legions of their own.

1081 The army advanced 30 kilometres every day. When they were hurrying to put down a rebellion, or moving from fort to fort, Roman soldiers travelled quickly, on foot. Troops marched along straight, well-made army roads. On the march, each soldier had to carry a heavy pack. It contained weapons, armour, tools for building a camp, cooking pots, dried food and spare clothes.

1080 Soldiers needed many skills. In enemy territory, soldiers had to find or make everything they needed to survive. When they first arrived they built camps of tents, but soon afterwards they built permanent forts defended by strong walls. Each legion contained men with a wide range of skills, such as cooks, builders, carpenters, doctors, blacksmiths and engineers — but they all had to fight!

1082 Soldiers worshipped their own special god. At forts and army camps, Roman soldiers built temples where they honoured Mithras, their own god. They believed he protected them, and gave them life after death.

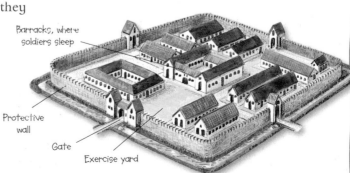

Barracks, where soldiers sleep

Protective wall

Gate

Exercise yard

Roman legions

▲ A Roman legion marches out of a border fortress supervised by the legate, who commands the legion.

1083 The legions were equipped with body armour, a helmet, a large rectangular shield, a sword and a throwing spear. Roman armour was made of metal strips. At the height of the Roman Empire, around ad 50 to ad 250, legionaries wore armour called lorica segmentata. It was made up of strips of metal that were bent to fit the body, and held together by straps and buckles.

◀ The armour of a legionary was made up of several pieces, each of which could be replaced if it was damaged.

1084 **Roman auxiliaries wore cheaper armour.** Every Roman legion included soldiers called auxiliaries (soldiers from places other than Rome). These units had to provide their own armour, often wearing tunics covered with mail or scale armour, which was made up of lots of small metal plates.

1085 **Roman swords were copied from the Spanish.** After 200 BC, Roman soldiers carried swords with straight blades and sharp points. They were copied from swords used by Spanish soldiers who defeated the Romans in battle.

1086 **Roman shields could form a 'tortoise'.** One tactic used by the Romans was called the 'testudo', or 'tortoise'. Soldiers formed short lines close together, holding their shields so they interlocked on all sides and overhead, just like the shell of a tortoise. In this formation they could advance on an enemy, safe from spears or arrows.

▼ An auxiliary soldier wearing a short mail tunic and helmet, and carrying an oval shield. He has a gladius and javelin as weapons.

The fall of Rome

1087 Later Roman infantry abandoned armour. By around AD 350, Roman legions preferred to fight by moving quickly around the battlefield. They stopped wearing heavy armour and relied upon large shields and metal helmets for protection.

1088 Later Roman armies used mercenary archers. Roman commanders found that archers were useful for attacking barbarian tribesmen. Few Romans were skilled at archery, so the Romans hired soldiers (mercenaries) from other countries to fight as archers in the Roman army.

1089 Roman shields were brightly coloured. Each unit in the late Roman army had its own design of shield. Some were decorated with pictures of eagles, scorpions or dolphins, while others had lightning bolts or spirals.

◄ Late Roman shields were brightly decorated. Each unit in the army had its own design.

1091 The eagle was a sacred standard. Each Roman legion had an eagle standard, the *aquila* – a bronze eagle covered in gold leaf mounted on top of a pole about 3 metres long. The *aquila* was thought to be sacred to the gods and it was a great humiliation if it was captured by the enemy.

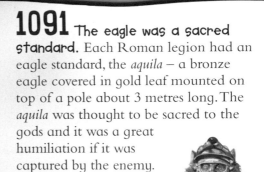

◄ By about AD 350, Roman armies had large numbers of cavalry that were used to fight fast-moving campaigns.

► A Roman *aquilifer* (standard bearer) carrying an eagle standard. Each legion had an eagle standard that was sacred to the gods. Units of cavalry and auxiliaries carried standards of other animals instead of an eagle.

1090 Later Roman cavalry had enormous shields. One later group of Roman mounted soldiers was the *scutati*. These men wore coats of mail, and carried enormous shields with which they were expected to defend themselves and their horses. They would gallop towards the enemy army, throw javelins and then ride away before the enemy could strike back.

I DON'T BELIEVE IT!

Alaric the Goth and his men looted Rome in AD 410. Alaric was famously known to carry a sword with a handle made of solid gold.

The first gladiators

1092 **The first gladiators were not from Rome.** The Romans did not invent the idea of gladiators. They believed the idea of men fighting in an arena probably came to Rome from the region of Etruria. But the first proper gladiators probably came from Campania, an area of Italy south of Rome.

▲ The city of Rome began as a small town between Etruria and Campania in central Italy.

QUIZ

1. What were the gladiators named after?
2. Did the Romans invent the idea of gladiators?
3. What word did the Romans use to describe a gladiator show?

Answers:
1. Gladiators were named after the gladius, a type of short sword. 2. No. The idea came from the people of Campania, an area to the south of Rome. 3. The Romans called a gladiator show a munus.

1093 **The first Roman gladiators fought in 264** BC. Six slaves were set to fight each other with swords, but they were not allowed to wear any armour. The fights did not last long before one of the slaves in each pair was killed.

► The gladius was the standard weapon used by early gladiators.

454

1094 The first gladiatorial fights were always part of a funeral. The name for a gladiatorial show, a munus, means a duty owed to the dead. The first fights were held at the funerals of politicians and noblemen, who ordered the games in their wills.

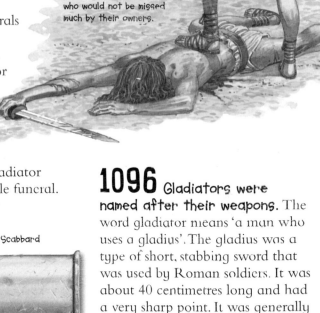

▶ The first gladiators were usually elderly slaves or troublemakers, who would not be missed much by their owners.

1095 In early funeral games, food was more important than gladiators. The Romans used funerals to show off how wealthy and important they were. Free food and drink were laid out at the funeral for any Roman citizen who wanted to come along. Gifts of money, jewellery and clothing were also handed out. The family of the person being buried would wear their finest clothes. The first gladiator fights were just one part of the whole funeral.

Scabbard

Gladius

1096 Gladiators were named after their weapons. The word gladiator means 'a man who uses a gladius'. The gladius was a type of short, stabbing sword that was used by Roman soldiers. It was about 40 centimetres long and had a very sharp point. It was generally used for slashing, not for cutting.

Not all gladiators used the gladius, but the name was used for all fighters in the arena.

Caesar's games

1097 **Julius Caesar borrowed money to buy his gladiators.** Julius Caesar rose to become the ruler of the Roman Empire. Early in his career he staged spectacular games to win votes in elections. But Caesar was too poor to afford to pay the bills, so he borrowed money from richer men. When he won the elections, Caesar repaid the men with favours and titles.

▲ Julius Caesar (102–44 BC) was a politician who won several elections after staging magnificent games to entertain the voters.

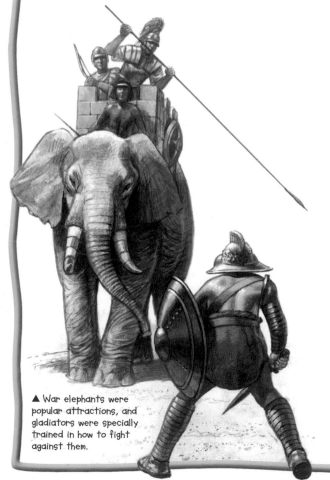

▲ War elephants were popular attractions, and gladiators were specially trained in how to fight against them.

1098 **Caesar's gladiators fought in silver armour.** In 65 BC, Julius Caesar staged the funeral games for his father, who had died 20 years earlier. Caesar was standing for election to be chief priest of Rome. To make his games even more special, Caesar dressed his 640 gladiators in armour made of solid silver.

1099 **Caesar brought war elephants to Rome.** In 46 BC Julius Caesar celebrated a victory in North Africa by staging gladiatorial games in Rome. Among the prisoners of war forced to fight in the arena were 40 war elephants, together with the men trained to fight them.

1100 Caesar turned senators (governors of Rome) into gladiators. On one occasion Caesar forced two rich noblemen to fight in the arena. They had been sentenced to death by a court, but Caesar ordered that the man who killed the other in the arena could go free.

1101 Caesar's final show was too big for the arena. The games staged by Julius Caesar when he wanted to become dictator of Rome were the grandest ever held. After weeks of shows and feasts, the final day saw a fight between two armies of 500 infantry (foot soldiers) and 30 cavalry. The battle was so large it had to be held in the enormous chariot race course, Circus Maximus.

QUIZ
1. Did Caesar's gladiators wear armour made of silver, gold or bronze?
2. Was Caesar's final show a big or small show?
3. Where did Caesar get the money to buy gladiators?

Answers:
1. Silver. 2. It was a big show.
3. He borrowed money from richer men.

▼ Chariot racing was a hugely popular sport that thrilled the crowds in ancient Rome.

The mighty Colosseum

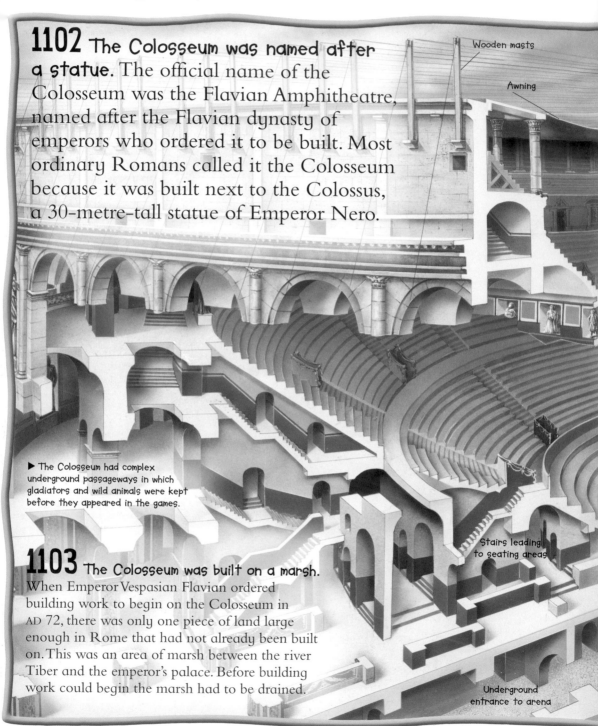

1102 **The Colosseum was named after a statue.** The official name of the Colosseum was the Flavian Amphitheatre, named after the Flavian dynasty of emperors who ordered it to be built. Most ordinary Romans called it the Colosseum because it was built next to the Colossus, a 30-metre-tall statue of Emperor Nero.

Wooden masts

Awning

▶ The Colosseum had complex underground passageways in which gladiators and wild animals were kept before they appeared in the games.

1103 **The Colosseum was built on a marsh.** When Emperor Vespasian Flavian ordered building work to begin on the Colosseum in AD 72, there was only one piece of land large enough in Rome that had not already been built on. This was an area of marsh between the river Tiber and the emperor's palace. Before building work could begin the marsh had to be drained.

Stairs leading to seating areas

Underground entrance to arena

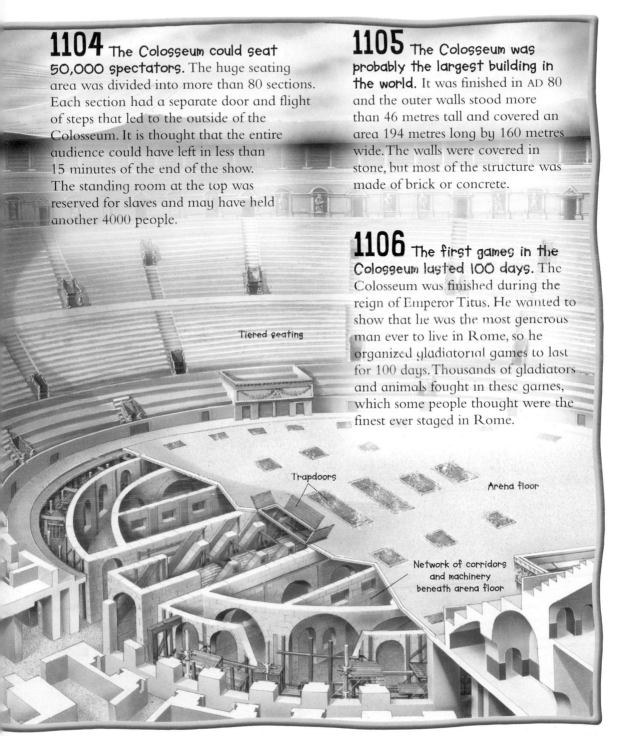

1104 The Colosseum could seat 50,000 spectators. The huge seating area was divided into more than 80 sections. Each section had a separate door and flight of steps that led to the outside of the Colosseum. It is thought that the entire audience could have left in less than 15 minutes of the end of the show. The standing room at the top was reserved for slaves and may have held another 4000 people.

1105 The Colosseum was probably the largest building in the world. It was finished in AD 80 and the outer walls stood more than 46 metres tall and covered an area 194 metres long by 160 metres wide. The walls were covered in stone, but most of the structure was made of brick or concrete.

1106 The first games in the Colosseum lasted 100 days. The Colosseum was finished during the reign of Emperor Titus. He wanted to show that he was the most generous man ever to live in Rome, so he organized gladiatorial games to last for 100 days. Thousands of gladiators and animals fought in these games, which some people thought were the finest ever staged in Rome.

Tiered seating

Trapdoors

Arena floor

Network of corridors and machinery beneath arena floor

Who were the gladiators?

1107 **Gladiators were divided into types based on their weapons.** Not all gladiators used the same weapons or fought in the same way. Some gladiators fought with weapons that had been popular in other countries or were used by different types of soldiers. Others used weapons and armour that were made especially for the arena.

Murmillo

1108 **Murmillo gladiators used army weapons and military armour.** These gladiators used shields and swords similar to those used by infantry in the Roman army. The shield was one metre long and 65 centimetres wide. The sword was used for stabbing, not cutting.

1109 **Thracian gladiators used lightweight armour.** The weapons of the Thracians were based on those used by soldiers from the kingdom of Thrace. The shield was small and square and the leg armour had long metal guards. The sword had a curved blade and the helmets were decorated with a griffin's head (a griffin was an imaginary bird).

Thracian

◄ ▲ ► Thracian, Murmillo and Provocator gladiators were all equipped with armour and heavy weapons. They usually fought each other, sometimes in teams. The lightly equipped Retiarius only had a net and trident.

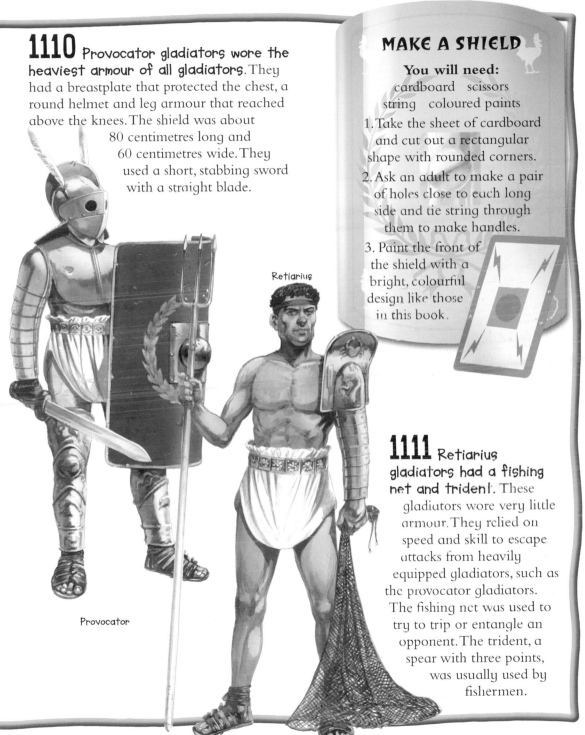

1110 Provocator gladiators wore the heaviest armour of all gladiators. They had a breastplate that protected the chest, a round helmet and leg armour that reached above the knees. The shield was about 80 centimetres long and 60 centimetres wide. They used a short, stabbing sword with a straight blade.

Retiarius

MAKE A SHIELD

You will need:
cardboard   scissors
string   coloured paints

1. Take the sheet of cardboard and cut out a rectangular shape with rounded corners.
2. Ask an adult to make a pair of holes close to each long side and tie string through them to make handles.
3. Paint the front of the shield with a bright, colourful design like those in this book.

1111 Retiarius gladiators had a fishing net and trident. These gladiators wore very little armour. They relied on speed and skill to escape attacks from heavily equipped gladiators, such as the provocator gladiators. The fishing net was used to try to trip or entangle an opponent. The trident, a spear with three points, was usually used by fishermen.

Provocator

461

Armour, shields and helmets

1112 Gladiator helmets were decorated with colourful plumes and crests. These were made from coloured feathers or dyed horsehair and made the gladiators look taller and bigger. Sometimes gladiators fought in teams and wore colours to show which team they belonged to.

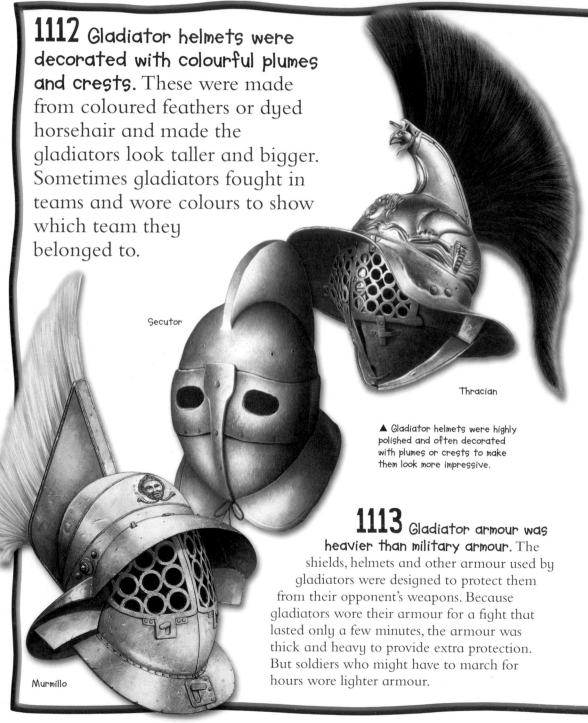

Secutor

Thracian

▲ Gladiator helmets were highly polished and often decorated with plumes or crests to make them look more impressive.

Murmillo

1113 Gladiator armour was heavier than military armour. The shields, helmets and other armour used by gladiators were designed to protect them from their opponent's weapons. Because gladiators wore their armour for a fight that lasted only a few minutes, the armour was thick and heavy to provide extra protection. But soldiers who might have to march for hours wore lighter armour.

1114 Some armour was covered with gold. Most gladiator armour was decorated with carvings and reliefs of gods such as Mars, god of war, or Victory, goddess of success. These decorations were often coated with thin sheets of pure gold.

1115 Padded armour was worn on the arms and legs. Thick layers of cloth and padding gave protection from glancing blows from the weapons or from being hit by the shield of the opponent.

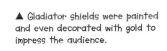

Leather binding

Cloth padding

▲ Gladiator shields were painted and even decorated with gold to impress the audience.

▲ Arms and legs were often covered with layers of woollen cloth tied on with leather bindings.

1116 The body was usually left without any armour at all. This meant that a single blow could kill them, or injure them so seriously that they had to ask for mercy. Gladiators needed to be skilful with both weapons and shields to survive.

I DON'T BELIEVE IT!

Gladiator helmets were very heavy — they weighed about 7 kilograms, twice as much as an army helmet!

Ancient explorers

1117 The ancient Greeks and Egyptians were great explorers, building boats to sail the oceans. Their kings and queens had enough money to pay for big exploring trips. They sent explorers to look for new lands, collect treasure and meet peoples from other parts of the world.

1118 Harkhuf of Egypt went exploring more than 4000 years ago. His king, Pharaoh Merenre, sent him to explore the land of Yam (now part of Sudan in Africa). Harkhuf brought back gifts of precious ivory, spices and wild animals such as leopards.

◄ An ancient Egyptian carving of Harkhuf.

1119 Egyptian Queen Hatshepsut sent explorers to look for a magical land she had heard about. The land, called Punt, was said to be full of treasure and beautiful animals. It was probably part of present-day Somalia, in Africa. Hatshepsut's sailors set off to find Punt. They brought back gold, ivory, monkeys, perfumes, special oils and resins, from which the Egyptians made make-up for their faces.

1120 In ancient times, the best sailors of all were the Phoenicians (say 'fuh-nee-shuns'). They came from what is now Syria and Lebanon and sailed all over the Mediterranean Sea. In 600 BC, an Egyptian king, Pharaoh Necho II, asked a crew of Phoenicians to see if they could sail all the way around Africa. The trip took them three years. It was 2000 years before anyone sailed around Africa again. The Phoenicians used the stars to help them to navigate (find their way).

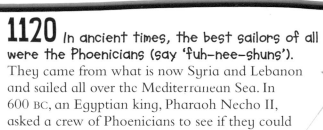

▼ For long-distance journeys, the Phoenicians used ships with both sails and oars.

1121 Pytheas was an ancient Greek who explored the icy north between 380 and 310 BC. He sailed out of the Mediterranean Sea, past Spain and Britain, and discovered a cold land he named Thule. This might have been Iceland, or part of Norway. Pytheas was the first Greek to see icebergs, the northern lights, and the Sun shining at midnight. However, when he returned to Greece, few people believed his stories.

◀ Hatshepsut stayed at home attending to her duties as queen, while her sailors set off to look for Punt.

I DON'T BELIEVE IT!

When Pytheas sailed past Scotland, he was amazed to see fish the size of boats. In fact they weren't fish at all — they were whales!

Marco Polo

1122 Marco Polo is one of the most famous explorers of all time. Marco lived in Venice in Italy in the 1200s and travelled to Asia at a time when most people in Europe never ventured far from their home village. Altogether, Marco travelled more than 40,000 kilometres.

◀ When Marco Polo visited Far Eastern lands such as China, hardly anyone in Europe had ever been there.

◀ This map shows Marco Polo's route across Asia. The journey home took three years.

Venice

CHINA

INDIA

INDIAN OCEAN

1123 Marco Polo started exploring when he was just 17 years old. His father and uncle were merchants who went to the Far East on business. When Marco was old enough, they took him with them. In 1271, they all set off for China – a journey that took them three years.

1124 In China, the Polos stayed with a mighty emperor called Kublai Khan. He had enormous palaces, rooms full of treasure, and many wives and servants. Kublai Khan gave Marco the job of travelling around his lands to bring him news. Marco went all over China and Southeast Asia.

◄ Coal, fireworks, eyeglasses, ice cream, pasta and paper money were some of the things Marco saw for the first time on his travels.

1126 **After 20 years away, the Polos were ready to go home.** They sailed most of the way in a junk — a Chinese sailing ship. More than 600 passengers and crew died of diseases on the way, but the Polos got home to Venice safely in 1295.

1127 **Later, there was a war in Italy and Marco Polo was captured.** He ended up sharing a prison cell with a writer, and told him his life story. The writer wrote down Marco's travel tales to make a book called *The Travels of Marco Polo*. It became a bestseller!

1125 **On his travels through Asia, Marco Polo discovered all kinds of amazing inventions.** He saw fireworks, coal, paper money, pasta, ice cream and eyeglasses for the first time. He was also impressed to find that the Chinese had a postage system and could post each other letters.

TRUE OR FALSE?

1. A junk is a type of carriage.
2. Marco discovered pizza in China.
3. The Polos sailed in a yacht.
4. Marco travelled more than 40,000 kilometres.

Answers:
1. False. It is a type of ship. 2. False. He discovered pasta, not pizza. 3. False. They sailed in a junk, a Chinese sailing ship. 4. True

Chinese explorers

▲ The Silk Road reached across Asia, from Europe to China.

1128 Some of the greatest ever explorers came from China. The first was a soldier, Zhang Qian, who lived around 114 BC. The Chinese emporer sent him to find a tribe called the Yueh-Chih, who they hoped would help them fight their enemies, the Huns. On their journey, the Huns captured Zhang Qian and put him in prison for ten years. When he finally escaped and found the Yueh-Chih, they said they didn't want to help!

1129 The explorer Xuan Zang was banned from going exploring, but he went anyway. The Chinese emperor wanted him to work in a temple but Xuan Zang wanted to go to India to learn about his religion, Buddhism. In the year 629, he sneaked out of China and followed the Silk Road to Afghanistan. Then he went south to India. Xuan Zang returned 16 years later, with a collection of Buddhist holy books and statues. The emperor was so pleased, he forgave Xuan Zang and gave him a royal welcome.

QUIZ

1. Which road did Xuan Zang take to Afghanistan?
2. What did Zheng He give the Chinese emperor?
3. Who was the first Chinese explorer?

Answers:
1. He took the Silk Road. 2. He gave the emperor a giraffe. 3. Zhang Qian, who was a soldier.

1130 **By the 1400s, the Chinese were exploring the world.** Their best explorer was a sailor named Zheng He. Zheng He used huge Chinese junks to sail right across the Indian Ocean as far as Africa. Wherever he went, Zheng He collected all kinds of precious stones, plants and animals to take back to China to show the emperor. The present that the emperor liked most was a giraffe from East Africa.

◀ The Chinese emperor was thrilled when Zheng He presented him with a live giraffe.

◀ A junk was a giant Chinese sailing ship, bigger than any other ships built at the time.

1131 **Zheng He's junks were the largest sailing ships on Earth.** The biggest was 130 metres long and 60 metres wide. On a typical expedition, Zheng He would take 300 ships and more than 1000 crew members, as well as doctors, map-makers, writers, blacksmiths and gardeners. The gardeners grew fruit and vegetables in pots on the decks, so that there would be plenty of food for everyone.

Discovering America

1132 **Lots of people think Christopher Columbus discovered America, but he didn't.** The Vikings were the first to sail there, in around the year 1000. They found a land with lots of trees, fish and berries, and called it Vinland. They didn't stay long – they went home after getting into fights with the native Americans. After that, many people forgot that Vinland existed.

▶ The *Santa Maria* was the leader of Columbus' fleet of ships. She was about 23 metres long and had three masts and five sails.

1133 Almost 500 years later, Christopher Columbus found America – by mistake! Columbus set sail from Spain in 1492, with three ships called the *Santa Maria*, the *Nina* and the *Pinta*. Columbus wasn't looking for a new land. Instead, he wanted to sail right around the Earth to find a new route to Asia, where he planned to buy spices. Although he was Italian, it was Queen Isabella of Spain who gave Columbus money for his trip.

1134 When Columbus found land, he was sure he'd sailed to Japan. In fact, Columbus had found the Bahamas, which are close to American mainland.

1135 Back in Spain, no one believed Columbus' story. They knew he couldn't have reached China in such a short time. Instead, they realized he must have found a brand new country. People called the new country the New World, and many more explorers set off at once to see it for themselves.

▲ Columbus and two of his men stepping ashore on the Bahamas, to be greeted by the local people.

1136 America wasn't named after Columbus. Instead, it was named after another famous explorer, Amerigo Vespucci. In 1507, a map-maker put Amerigo's name on a map of the New World, and changed it from Amerigo to America. The name stuck.

1137 It's thanks to Columbus that Native Americans were known as Indians. Since he thought he was in Asia, Columbus called the lands he found the West Indies, and the people he met Indians. They are still called this today – even though America is nowhere near India.

Around the world

▲ Ferdinand Magellan was a clever man who was very good at maths and science. These skills helped him on his exploration.

NORTH AMERICA

Portugal

ATLANTIC OCEAN

PACIFIC OCEAN

SOUTH AMERICA

1138 At the start of the 1500s, no one had ever sailed around the world. Portuguese explorer Ferdinand Magellan wanted to sail past South America, and across the Pacific Ocean. It is possible that, like Columbus before him, Magellan thought he could get to Asia that way, where he could buy spices. Then he could sail home past India and Africa – a round-the-world trip.

1139 Magellan fell out with the king of Portugal, but the king of Spain agreed to help him. The king paid for five ships and Magellan set off in 1519. Magellan sailed down the coast of South America until he found a way through to the Pacific Ocean. Sailing across the Pacific, many of the crew died from a disease called scurvy. It was caused by not eating enough fresh fruit and vegetables.

ASIA

EUROPE

INDIAN OCEAN

OCEANIA

▲ Magellan set off from Spain on his round-the-world trip. X marks the spot where Magellan died, on the island of Mactan.

1141 In the end, just one of Magellan's ships made it back to Spain. It picked up a cargo of spices in Indonesia and sailed home. Magellan had taken over 200 crew with him, but less than 20 of them returned. They were the first people to have sailed all the way around the world.

1142 Another 55 years went by before anyone sailed around the world again. Queen Elizabeth I asked an English privateer (a kind of pirate) named Francis Drake to try a round-the-world trip in 1577. He made money on the way by robbing Spanish ships (the Queen said he could!). After his three-year voyage, Drake returned to England. Queen Elizabeth gave him a huge reward of £10,000.

1140 Magellan made it across the Pacific – but then disaster struck. After landing in the Philippines in 1521, Magellan made friends with the king of the island of Cebu. The king was fighting a war and he wanted Magellan to help him. Magellan and some of his crew went into battle, and Magellan was killed. The rest of the crew took two of the ships and escaped.

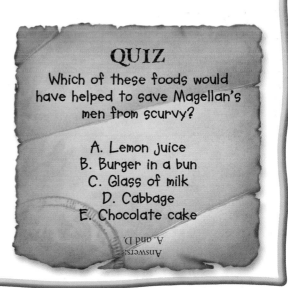

QUIZ
Which of these foods would have helped to save Magellan's men from scurvy?

A. Lemon juice
B. Burger in a bun
C. Glass of milk
D. Cabbage
E. Chocolate cake

Answers:
A. and D.

Captain Cook

1143 Captain James Cook spent just 11 years exploring, from 1768 to 1779. But he was still one of the greatest explorers. Cook sailed all over the Pacific Ocean and made maps that have helped sailors ever since. He also sailed around the world, north to the Arctic, and south to the Antarctic.

▼ As well as studying the planets, Cook took wildlife experts with him on his explorations. They collected plants that weren't known in Europe, and drew sketches and made notes about them.

Dividers

Pen holder

1144 In 1768 the British navy asked Cook to go on an important mission. He was to go to the Pacific island of Tahiti, to make measurements and observations of the planet Venus passing in front of the Sun. After that, Cook went to look for a new continent in the far south – but he didn't find one. Instead, he explored Australia, New Zealand and the Pacific Islands and made new maps.

Parallel ruler

Sector

◄ Cook needed high-quality drawing instruments to help him make his measurements for maps.

1145 Many people still believed there was an unknown continent in the south. So they sent Cook back to look for it again in 1772. He sailed further south than anyone had been before, until he found the sea was frozen solid. Cook sailed all the way around Antarctica, but he was never close enough to land to see it. It wasn't explored until 1820, nearly 50 years later.

1146 For Cook's third voyage, he headed **north.** He wanted to see if he could find a sea route between the Pacific Ocean and the Atlantic Ocean, across the top of Canada. After searching for it in 1778, he went to spend the winter in Hawaii. At first, the Hawaiians thought Cook was a god named Lono!

I DON'T BELIEVE IT!

Captain Cook was the first European to discover Hawaii, in 1778. He called it the Sandwich Islands.

1147 Cook found his way around better than any sailor before him. An inventor named John Harrison had created a new clock (called the chronometer) that could measure the time precisely, even at sea. Before that, clocks had pendulums, so they didn't work on ships. From the time that the sun went down, Cook could work out exactly how far east or west he was.

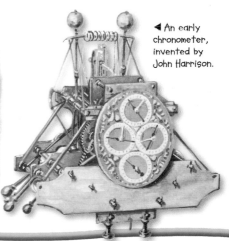

◀ An early chronometer, invented by John Harrison.

475

Arctic adventures

1148 **The Arctic is the land and sea around the North Pole.** Explorers first went there to search for the Northwest Passage – the sea-route leading from the Atlantic Ocean to the Pacific Ocean. They spent 400 years trying to find it, and many explorers died of cold or drowned in the Arctic Ocean.

1149 **Norwegian explorer Roald Amundsen was the first to sail through the Northwest Passage.** Amundsen used a small fishing boat that made it easier to sail along shallow channels and between chunks of floating ice. But the journey still took him three years – from 1903 to 1906. Amundsen learned a lot about surviving in the cold from local peoples he met on the way.

1150 **There was still part of the Arctic where no one had been – the North Pole.** Another Norwegian explorer, Fridtjof Nansen, built a ship called the *Fram*, which was designed to get stuck in the ice without being damaged. As the ice moved, it carried the *Fram* nearer to the Pole. Nansen almost reached the Pole in 1895 – but not quite.

1151 Next, an American named Robert Peary and his assistant Matthew Henson, set off for the North Pole. Peary had always wanted to be the first to get there. After two failed attempts, Peary used dogsleds and Inuit guides to help him reach the pole in the year 1909.

1152 When Peary announced that he had been to the Pole, he was in for a shock. Another explorer, Frederick Cook, who had been Peary's friend, said he had got there first! The two men had an argument. Then it was revealed that Cook had lied about another expedition. After that, nobody believed he had been to the North Pole either.

▲ Peary and Henson used traditional sealskin clothes for their journey, and paid local Inuit people to make their clothes and equipment.

◀ Fridtjof Nansen's boat, the *Fram*, was specially shaped so that when it was squeezed by ice, it lifted up instead of getting crushed. This allowed the ship to move safely with the ice towards the North Pole.

I DON'T BELIEVE IT!

Some experts think Peary didn't actually reach the North Pole. If this is true then the first person at the North Pole was Wally Herbert, who walked there in 1969.

477

Antarctic adventures

1153 Antarctica was explored less than 200 years ago. This large and mountainous continent is at the southern tip of the Earth. It is even colder than the Arctic and very dangerous. In the early 1900s, explorers such as Robert Scott and Ernest Shackleton tried to reach the South Pole and failed. In 1909, Shackleton came within 155 kilometres of the South Pole, but had to turn back.

▶ Amundsen's team used lightweight dogsleds. If a dog died or became too weak to go on, it was fed to the other dogs. This reduced the amount of food the men had to carry.

1154 In 1910, British explorer Robert Scott decided to set off for the South Pole again. He took motor sleds and ponies to carry all his supplies. He decided that when his men got near the Pole, they would pull their own sleds. In Antarctica, he also wanted to collect rock samples to study.

1155 Meanwhile, Roald Amundsen was on his way to try to reach the North Pole. But when he heard that Robert Peary had already got there, he decided to race Scott to the South Pole instead. Amundsen used different methods from Scott – sleds pulled by husky dogs carried supplies.

1156 In 1911, both Scott and Amundsen reached Antarctica, and set off for the South Pole. Amundsen left first and got there quickly with his dogs. Scott's motor sleds broke down and his ponies died. His team trudged to the Pole, only to find Amundsen had been there first. On the way back, Scott's men got stuck in a blizzard. They ran out of food, and died of cold and hunger.

▲ When Scott's team reached the South Pole, they took photos of each other, but their faces showed how upset they were not to be there first.

1157 Shackleton never got to the South Pole — but he had a very exciting Antarctic adventure. He wanted to trek across Antarctica in 1914. But before he could start, his ship, the *Endurance*, was crushed by the ice. The crew were left on the frozen ocean with just three lifeboats. Shackleton left his men on an island while he took one tiny boat to get help. He had to cross a stormy ocean and climb over icy mountains before he found a village. All his men were rescued and came home safely.

The first castles

1158 In the beginning, castles were mostly built from wood on top of a hill. Sometimes castle builders piled up soil to make the hill artificially. On top of the hill, called a motte, stood a wooden tower, or keep. This was the central part of the castle and the easiest part to defend.

▶ This is a motte and bailey castle. The Normans from France introduced this kind of castle in the 1000s, and it soon became popular across Europe.

◀ Castles and forts have been built all over the world since the earliest times. This is the fortified town of Great Zimbabwe, in modern day Zimbabwe. The oldest part dates from the 700s.

▶ By the 1500s the Japanese were building strong, permanent castles of their own. Castles were often built with different layers to fire on the enemy from different heights.

1159 At the bottom of the motte was a courtyard called a bailey. It was usually surrounded by a wooden fence. Castle builders dug a deep ditch, called a moat, all around the outside of the motte and bailey. They often filled the moat with water. Moats were designed to stop attackers reaching the castle walls.

◀ For extra protection, a wooden fence was often built around the top of the motte. The top of each wooden plank was shaped into a point to make it harder for the enemy to climb over.

I DON'T BELIEVE IT!

The builders of the early wooden castles covered the walls with wet leather – to stop them from burning down.

1160 Wooden castles were not very strong – and they caught fire easily. From around 1100 onwards, people began to build castles in stone. A stone castle gave better protection against attack, fire and cold rainy weather.

Gatehouse

Inner defensive wall

Outer defensive wall

Keep

▶ Sometimes an extra wall was built on the inside of the strong outer wall. Archers could stand on the inner wall and fire down onto the outer wall if it was captured.

Turret

Building a castle

1161 **The best place to build a castle was on top of a hill.** A hilltop position gave good views over the surrounding countryside, and made it harder for an enemy to launch a surprise attack. Sometimes a castle was built on the banks of a river or lake, and its waters were used to create a moat.

▼ Building a castle took a lot of time and work. It could be a dangerous task.

1162 The lord of the castle and his family lived in the safest part of the castle — the keep. The walls of the keep were built to be very strong, and at least 3.5 metres thick in some castles. Inside the keep were large rooms for receiving visitors and holding banquets, as well as smaller storerooms and guardrooms. The family's bedrooms were on the top floor of the keep. All these rooms and defences made building a castle very slow and expensive.

DESIGN YOUR OWN CASTLE

Imagine you have been asked to design a castle for your local lord. It is important that he can defend his castle and his family against attacks by his enemies.

Draw a plan of your ideal castle, making sure it has plenty of defences. And don't forget the drawbridge to let the lord and his family in and out of their castle.

Who's who in the castle

1163 A castle was the home of an important and powerful person, such as a king, a lord or a knight. The lord of the castle controlled the castle itself, as well as the lands and people around it. The lady of the castle was in charge of the day-to-day running of the castle. She controlled the kitchens and gave the servants their orders for feasts and banquets.

▼ The lord and lady were the most important people in the castle.

1164 The constable was in charge of defending the castle. He was usually a fierce and ruthless man. He trained his soldiers to guard the castle properly and organized the rota of guards and watchmen. The constable was in charge of the whole castle when the lord was away.

1165 Many servants lived and worked inside the castle, looking after the lord and his family. They cooked, cleaned, served at table, worked as maids and servants and ran errands.

▼ A man called the steward was in charge of all the servants.

Servant

Steward

Cooks

1166 Inside the castle walls were many workshops where goods were made and repaired. The castle blacksmith was kept busy making shoes for all the horses. The armourer made weapons and armour.

Armourer

Blacksmith

▶ The master of the horse had to look after the lord's horses.

I DON'T BELIEVE IT!

There was no bathroom for the castle's servants. They had to take a dip in the local river to wash – and get rid of any fleas and lice!

1167 Local villagers would shelter in the castle when their lands were under attack. They were not allowed to shelter inside the keep itself, so they stayed inside the bailey with their families and all their animals.

How to be a good knight

1168 **It took about 14 years of training to become a knight.** The son of a noble joined a lord's household aged seven. He learned how to ride, to shoot a bow and arrow and how to behave in front of nobles. He then became a squire, where he learned how to fight with a sword, and he looked after his master's armour and weapons. If he was successful, he became a knight at 21.

▶ Sons of noblemen practised how to fight against one another, before becoming knights.

1169 **The ceremony of making a new knight was known as dubbing.** A knight had to spend a whole night in church before his dubbing ceremony took place. First, he had a cold bath and dressed in a plain white tunic. After this he went on to his vigil.

◀ Before dubbing a knight held an all-night watch called a vigil. He spent the night on his knees praying and confessing his sins.

1170 The dubbing ceremony changed over time. In the beginning a knight was struck on the back of the neck. Later, dubbing involved a tap on the knight's shoulder with a sword.

I DON'T BELIEVE IT!
A French knight called Jaufré Rudel sent love poems to the Countess of Tripoli even though he had never met her. When he finally saw her beautiful face he fell into her arms and died.

1171 Knights had to behave according to a set of rules, known as the 'code of chivalry'. The code involved being brave and honourable on the battlefield, and treating the enemy politely and fairly. It also instructed knights how to behave towards women.

1172 A knight who behaved badly was disgraced and punished. A knight in disgrace had either behaved in a cowardly way on the battlefield, cheated in a tournament or treated another knight badly.

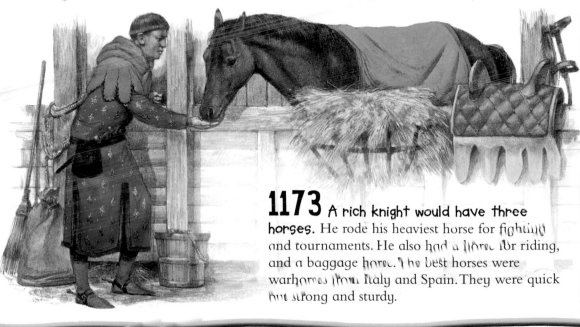

1173 A rich knight would have three horses. He rode his heaviest horse for fighting and tournaments. He also had a horse for riding, and a baggage horse. The best horses were warhorses from Italy and Spain. They were quick but strong and sturdy.

Early knights

1174 **The first knights wore mail armour.** Around the year 1000, most body armour in Europe was made of mail. This was flexible to wear and could stop a sword blow with ease. Such armour was expensive to make so only richer men could afford to wear it.

1. Iron ring

2. Holes pierced in ends

3. Ends joined with a rivet

▲ Mail armour was made by linking together hundreds of small iron rings. The rings could be linked in a number of different ways, just like knitting a sweater.

1175 **Shields were decorated to identify their owners.** From about 1150, knights wore helmets that covered their faces for extra protection. Around the same time, they began to paint heraldic designs (coats of arms) on their shields so that they could recognize each other in battle.

1176 **Early knights sometimes used leather armour.** Mail armour was effective, but heavy and expensive, so some knights wore armour made of boiled, hardened leather. This was lighter and easier to wear, and was still some defence against attack.

◀ A knight in about 1100. He wears a shirt and trousers made of mail and a helmet shaped from a sheet of steel. His shield is made of wood.

1177 **Plate armour gave better protection than mail.** By about 1300, new types of arrow and swords had developed to pierce mail armour. This led to the development of plate armour, made of sheets of steel shaped to fit the body, which arrows and swords could not easily penetrate.

1178 **The mace could smash armour to pieces.** The most effective of the crushing weapons developed to destroy plate armour, the mace had a big metal head on a long shaft. A blow from a mace crushed plate armour, breaking the bones of the person wearing it.

The armour around the stomach and groin had to be flexible enough to allow bending and twisting movements

The most complicated section of plate armour was the gauntlet that covered the hands. It might contain 30 pieces of metal

The legs and feet were protected by armour that covered the limbs entirely

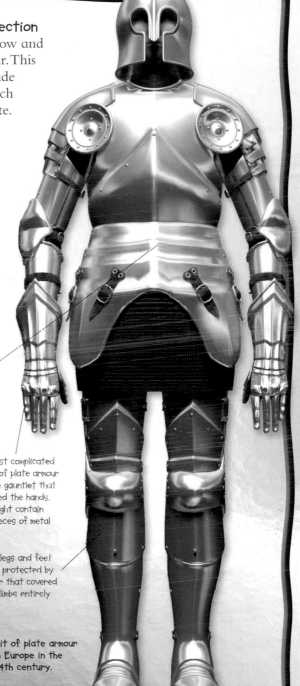

▶ A suit of plate armour made in Europe in the early 14th century.

QUIZ

1. Why did knights paint coats of arms on their shields?
2. How was leather armour treated to make it tough?
3. Which was the most effective crushing weapon?

Answers:
1. So that they could recognize each other in battle 2. It was boiled 3. The mace

Later knights

1179 Armoured knights were the most important troops. Knights had the best arms and armour and were the most experienced men in any army, so they were often put in command.

1180 Knights sometimes fought on foot, instead of on horseback. English knights fought on foot after about 1300. This enabled them to hold a position more securely and co-operate more effectively with other soldiers.

▶ The bascinet helmet had a visor that could be lifted so the wearer could see and breathe.

I DON'T BELIEVE IT!

At the Battle of Agincourt in France in 1415, the English killed 10,000 Frenchmen, but only about 100 Englishmen lost their lives.

1181 Horse armour made of metal and leather was introduced to protect horses. By about 1300, knights began to dress their horses in various sorts of armour. Horses without armour could be killed or injured by enemy arrows or spears, leaving the knight open to attack. Men with armoured horses were put in the front rank during battle.

▶ Horse armour was shaped to fit the horse's head and neck, then was left loose to dangle down over the legs.

1182 The flail was a difficult weapon to use. It consisted of a big metal ball studded with spikes and attached to a chain on a wooden handle. It could inflict terrible injuries, but also swing back unexpectedly, so only men who practised with it for hours each day could use it properly.

◀ A knight uses a flail in foot combat.

1183 Each man had his place in battle. Before each battle, the commander would position his men to ensure that the abilities of each were put to best use. The men with the best armour were placed where the enemy was expected to attack, while archers were positioned on the flank (left or right side) where they could shoot across the battlefield. Lightly armoured men were held in the rear, ready to chase enemy soldiers if they began to retreat.

Colours and coats of arms

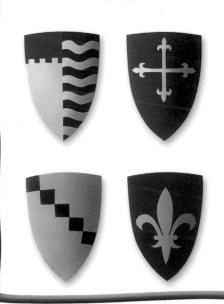

1184 When a knight went into battle in full armour wearing a helmet with a visor, no one could recognize him. This problem was solved by putting a different set of coloured symbols on each knight's shield. These sets of symbols became known as coats of arms, and each family had its own personal design. No other family was allowed to use that design.

◄ ▲ ► Coats of arms were displayed on a knight's shield. This system became known as heraldry. Many different symbols and signs were used, but only in a few colours.

1185 Only certain colours and styles of design could be used to create a coat of arms. The colours allowed were red, blue, black, green, purple, silver and gold. The arms also indicated the wearer's position in his family. So, a second son showed a crescent symbol, and a seventh son displayed a rose.

1186 On the battlefield, each nobleman had his own banner around which his knights and other soldiers could meet. The nobleman's colours and coat of arms were displayed on the banner. Banners decorated with coats of arms also made a colourful display at tournaments and parades.

◄ The banner of a nobleman was a very important symbol during battle. If the person holding the banner was killed in battle, someone had to pick the banner up and raise it straight away.

1187 Messengers called heralds carried messages between knights during battle. They had to be able to recognize each individual knight quickly. After coats of arms were introduced, the heralds became experts at identifying them.

◄ After a battle, it was the sad job of a herald to walk around the battlefield and identify the dead by their coats of arms.

DESIGN YOUR OWN COAT OF ARMS

Would you like your own personal coat of arms? You can design one by following the basic rules of heraldry explained on these pages. You will need the seven paint colours listed opposite, a paintbrush, a fine-tipped black felt pen, a ruler and some thick white paper. Good luck!

Practise for battle

1188 In a tournament, knights divided into two sides and fought each other as if in a proper battle. Tournaments were good practise for the real thing – war. The idea for these mock battles, called tourneys, probably started in France in the 12th century.

▼ Jousting knights charged at each other at top speed. Each one tried to knock his opponent off his horse with a blow from a long wooden lance.

▲ Edward I of England was a keen supporter of tournaments and jousts. He banned spectators from carrying weapons themselves because this caused too much trouble among the watching crowds.

1189 Tournaments took place under strict rules. There were safe areas where knights could rest without being attacked by the other side. Knights were not meant to kill their opponents but they often did. Several kings became so angry at losing their best knights that all tournaments were banned unless the king had given his permission.

I DON'T BELIEVE IT!
Some knights cheated in jousts by wearing special armour that was fixed onto the horse's saddle!

1192 Sometimes the knights carried on fighting on the ground with their swords. The problem was that this was as dangerous as a tourney!

1193 Jousts were very social events watched by ladies of the court as well as ordinary people. Knights could show off their skills and bravery to impress the spectators.

1190 Jousting was introduced because so many knights were killed or wounded during tournaments. More than 60 knights were killed in a single tourney in Cologne, Germany. Jousting was a fight between two knights on horseback. Each knight tried to win by knocking the other off his horse. Knights were protected by armour, and their lances were not sharp.

1191 A knight's code of chivalry did not allow him to win a tournament by cheating. It was better to lose with honour than to win in disgrace.

▼ A joust gave a knight the chance to prove himself in front of the woman he loved.

Under attack

1194 An attacking enemy had to break through a castle's defences to get inside its walls. One method was to break down the castle gates with giant battering rams. Attackers and defenders also used siege engines to hurl boulders at each other.

1195 A siege is when an enemy surrounds a castle and stops all supplies from reaching the people inside. The idea is to starve the castle occupants until they surrender or die.

▼ Attackers used many different machines to invade the castle. Siege engines and wooden ladders were just some of these.

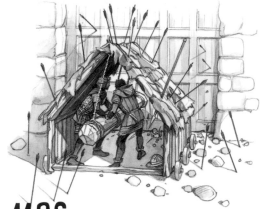

▼ Battering rams were used to bash down castles defences. A roof over the battering ram stopped attackers from being hit by arrows or spears.

1196 A riskier way of trying to get inside a castle was to climb over the walls. Attackers either used ladders or moved wooden towers with men hidden inside them into position beside the walls.

1197 Giant catapults were sometimes uses to fire stones or burning pieces of wood inside the castle. The Romans were some of the first people to use catapults in warfare.

▶ Attackers could also dig a tunnel under a wall or a tower. They would then light a fire that burnt away the tunnel's supports. The tunnel collapsed, and brought down the building above.

▲ This siege engine was called a trebuchet. It had a long wooden arm with a heavy weight at one end and a sling at the other. A heavy stone was placed inside the sling. As the weight dropped, the stone was hurled towards the castle walls, sometimes travelling as far as 300 metres.

1198 The enemy sometimes succeeded in tunnelling beneath the castle walls. They surprised the defenders when they appeared inside the castle itself.

▼ Cannons were first used to attack castles and fortified towns and cities in the 1300s. Early cannons, called bombards, were made of bronze or iron and they were not very accurate.

I DON'T BELIEVE IT!

The ropes used to wind up siege catapults were made from plaits of human hair!

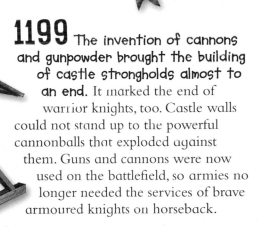

1199 The invention of cannons and gunpowder brought the building of castle strongholds almost to an end. It marked the end of warrior knights, too. Castle walls could not stand up to the powerful cannonballs that exploded against them. Guns and cannons were now used on the battlefield, so armies no longer needed the services of brave armoured knights on horseback.

Defending a castle

1200 When the enemy was first spotted approaching a castle, its defenders first pulled up the castle drawbridge. They also lowered an iron grate, called a portcullis, to form an extra barrier behind the drawbridge.

1201 The castle archers fired their arrows through narrow slits in the thick castle walls. They also fired through the gaps in the battlements.

▶ Crossbows were far slower to aim and fire than longbows.

1202 In the middle of the night, a raiding party might leave a besieged castle to surprise the enemy camped outside. The raiders would move along secret passages and climb out through hidden gates or doorways.

◀ Soldiers in the raiding party snuck out of the castle when the enemy was unprepared.

1203 Defenders poured boiling–hot water onto the heads of the enemy as they tried to climb the castle walls. Quicklime was also poured over the enemy soldiers, making their skin burn.

▶ Soldiers threw boulders and poured water onto the enemy's heads through holes in the stonework of the castle's battlements.

1204 Heavy stones and other missiles often rained down from the battlements onto the enemy below. Hidden from view by the high battlements, the defenders stood on wooden platforms to throw the missiles.

QUIZ

1. What is the name of the mock battles held between large numbers of knights?

2. Which weapon did jousting knights use when on horseback?

3. Which two countries fought a war that lasted 100 years?

4. Which machine was used to break down castle walls and gates?

Answers:
1. Tourneys 2. Lance
3. England and France
4. Battering ram

499

Index

Index

Index

Index

Index

Index

Acknowledgements

All artworks are from the Miles Kelly Artwork Bank

The publishers would like to thank the following sources for the use of their photographs:

(t = top, b = bottom, l = left, r = right, c = centre)

Page 44 QiangBa DanZhen/Fotolia.com; 51(t) Jean du Boisberranger/Hemis/Corbis, (bl) Ricardo De Mattos/iStockphoto.com; 52(t) koch valérie/iStockphoto.com; 54(bl) David Samuel Robbins/Corbis; 55 Lukáš Hejtman/iStockphoto.com; 58 Jim Sugar/Corbis; 62 nagelestock.com/Alamy; 63 Melissa Schalke/Fotolia.com; 65 Stephen Barnett/Photolibrary.com; 69 Maria Pavlova/iStockphoto.com; 70 Urbanhearts/Fotolia.com; 71(tl) Albo/Fotolia.com, (r) John Saxenian/Fotolia.com; 72 NASA; 73 JTB Photo/Photolibrary.com; 77(t) pkruger/iStockphoto.com; 82 George Burba/iStockphoto.com; 85(t) Paul A. Souders/Corbis, (b) Colin Monteath/Photolibrary; 89 Ecoview/Fotolia.com; 90 Phil Degginger/Photolibrary; 91(t) JTB Photo/Photolibrary, (b) Paul Chesley/Getty Images; 92 Jeremy Horner/Corbis; 93(l) NASA, (r) NASA; 98 MvH/iStockphoto.com; 99(l) Nick Hawkes/Ecoscene, (r) Peter Menzel/Science Photo Library; 100–101 Aurora/Getty Images, 100(c) Dan Brandenburg/iStockphoto.com, (t) flucas/Fotolia.com; 102 Warren Faidley/Corbis; 103(b) dswebb/iStockphoto.com; 104 Eric Nguyen/Corbis; 106(t) NASA, (b) Mike Goldwater/Getty Images; 107(t) Sipa Press/Rexfeatures; 109(t) Phill Hunt/iStockphoto.com, (b) NOAA/Science Photo Library; 111(b) micheldenijs/iStockphoto.com; 112 tomos3/iStockphoto.com; 113(t) Scott Latham/Fotolia.com, (b) schaltwerk/Fotolia.com; 114–115 Yann Arthus - Bertrand/Corbis; 114(t) egdigital/iStockphoto.com, (bl) Vivianne Moos/Corbis; 115(b) Ben Blankenburg/iStockphoto.com; 116 Per-Anders Pettersson/Getty; 117(t) Fotolia.com, (b) dejan750/iStockphoto.com; 130(l) Susan Stevenson/iStockphoto.com, (inset, second from bottom) Andres Rodriguez/Fotolia.com; 218 Layne Kennedy/Corbis; 219 DK Limited; 224 Martin B Withers/FLPA; 225 Sheila Terry/Science Photo Library; 226 Ted Soqui/Corbis; 227(t) Reuters/Corbis; 234 Jurgen & Christine Sohns/FLPA; 235(t) BIOS - Auters Watts Dave/Still Pictures, (b) Professor Jack Dermid/Oxford Scientific; 238(t) Eric Isselée/iStockphoto.com, (c) Animals Animals/Earth Scenes/Photolibrary; 243 Thomas Barnes/iStockphoto.com; 245 Natalie Becker/iStockphoto.com; 248 Cyril Ruoso/JH Editorial/Minden Pictures/FLPA; 249 Gary Wales/iStockphoto.com; 250 Photolibrary Group Ltd; 251 emin kuliyev/iStockphoto.com; 265 Bruce Davidson/naturepl.com; 270 Photolibrary Group Ltd; 274 Photolibrary Group Ltd; 286 Rob Reijnen/Foto Natura/FLPA; 287 William Dow/Corbis; 308 Grigory Kubatyan/Fotolia.com; 319 James Warren/Fotolia.com; 322 Marian Bacon/Photolibrary.com; 325 studio vision1/Fotolia.com; 327 Daniel Heuclin/NHPA; 329 Eric Gevaert/Fotolia.com; 331 Shane Kennedy/Fotolia.com; 344 milosluz/iStockphoto.com; 347 Cathy Keifer/iStockphoto.com; 362(bl) DavidHCoder/iStockphoto.com, (br) Audrey Eun/Fotolia.com; 366 beute/Fotolia.com; 374(t) Save the Rhino International; 378 Frans Lanting/Corbis; 384 TopFoto.co.uk; 385 Topham Picturepoint TopFoto.co.uk; 390 Richard T. Nowitz/Corbis; 400 (tr) The British Museum/HIP/TopFoto.co.uk; 419 Charles Stirling (Diving)/Alamy; 427 Danilo Ascione/iStockphoto.com; 428 Keith Binns/iStockphoto.com; 433(t) Richard Cummins/Corbis; 435 KPA/Zuma/Rex Features; 436–437 Jose Fuste Raga/Corbis

All other photographs are from:
Corel, digitalSTOCK, digitalvision, John Foxx, PhotoAlto, PhotoDisc, PhotoEssentials, PhotoPro, Stockbyte

Every effort has been made to acknowledge the source and copyright holder of each picture. Miles Kelly Publishing apologises for any unintentional errors or omissions.